IN EVERY PEW SITS A

BROKEN HEART

RUTH GRAHAM

Daughter of Ruth and Billy Graham
with Stacy Mattingly

IN EVERY PEW SITS A

BROKEN HEART

Hope for the Hurting

ZONDERVAN™

GRAND RAPIDS, MICHIGAN 49530 USA

ZONDERVAN™

In Every Pew Sits a Broken Heart
Copyright © 2004 by Ruth Graham

This title is also available as a Zondervan audio product.
Visit www.zondervan.com/audiopages for more information.

Requests for information should be addressed to:
Zondervan, *Grand Rapids, Michigan 49530*

Library of Congress Cataloging-in-Publication Data

Graham, Ruth, 1950–.
    In every pew sits a broken heart : hope for the hurting / Ruth Graham with Stacy
Mattingly.—1st ed.
      p. cm.
    ISBN 0-310-24339-4
    1. Suffering—Religious aspects—Christianity. 2. Graham, Ruth, 1950–.
3. Consolation. I. Mattingly, Stacy. II. Title.
BV4909.G73 2004
248.8'6—dc22
                                                    2004005090

Interior design by Beth Shagene

Printed in the United States of America

04 05 06 07 08 09 10 /❖ DC/ 10 9 8 7 6 5 4 3 2 1

For You

CONTENTS

FOREWORD

From earliest childhood, our daughter Ruth loved the Lord and wanted to please him. However, her life has taken many twists and turns, causing us many times of joy and thanksgiving, challenge and tears. As she recounts in this book, she has been through a number of difficult experiences, but in the end she has come out with a renewed dedication and a strong faith in the Lord. Her mother and I love her, support her, and thank God for her.

Ruth has told us that her one desire in giving up her privacy in order to honestly share her personal experience in this book is that it will help people who are going through traumatic times in their own lives, and give insight to those who are trying to help a friend or loved one who is going through deep waters. If in these pages you see your own life's experience mirrored in our daughter's, may you, too, find a personal relationship with the same heavenly Father who continues to be her strength, comfort, and joy.

Billy Graham

IN MY PEW SAT A BROKEN HEART
Seeing God in the Ruins

I wound my way up my parents' steep, mountain driveway in western North Carolina, unsure if I would be welcomed or rejected. I was broken by the choices I had made. Stubborn and willful, I had followed my own path, and now I would have to face the consequences. I had caused pain for my children and loved ones. I feared I had embarrassed my parents. It seemed I had wrecked my world. The shame was almost unbearable.

I had driven sixteen hours from South Florida, stopping to pick up my youngest daughter at boarding school, and now I was tired and anxious. The familiarity of my childhood environs did little to subdue my fears. The February mountain air was crisp and clean. The bare trees—maple, poplar, and oak—lining the drive up to my parents' house afforded a view this time of year, but I was too absorbed to notice.

What would my life be like now? I had gone against everyone's advice. My family had warned me. They had tried to stop me. But I had not listened. I needed to do what was best for *me*, I had told them. And now my life was a shambles. I was a failure in my own eyes and certainly would be in the eyes of others when they learned what "Billy Graham's daughter" had done. I feared I had humiliated those I held dearest. How would I be able to face them?

Driving up the mountain, my fears multiplied. Adrenaline kept my foot on the gas. I felt my hands grip the steering wheel. My mind was spinning. I tried to remember my mother's insistent tone from our phone conversation a few days earlier: "Come home," she had urged. I was desperate when I called her. I told her of my mistake and was trying to piece together a plan when she interjected with the voice of a loving, protective parent. But how would she and

11

my father respond when they saw me? What would they say to me? Would they say, "You've made your bed; now lie in it"? Would they condemn me? Would they reject me? Despise me? They had every right.

As I rounded the last bend in the driveway, Daddy came into view. He was standing in the paved area where visitors usually park. Rolling the car to a stop, I took a deep breath and prepared to greet my father. I turned off the ignition, opened the car door, and stepped onto the driveway. Then I looked up— Daddy was already at my side. Before I could say a word, he took me into his arms and said, "Welcome home."

Is There a Broken Heart in Your Pew?

I know what it's like to sit in the pew with a broken heart. For years I sat in church with my fears, doubts, and disappointments, thinking I was alone in my condition. Those around me seemed to have it all together. They looked so "spiritual." Did they not struggle as I did? Was I the only one whose dreams had fallen to pieces? Was I the only one who had blown it? Was I the only one depressed and feeling beyond hope? To protect myself and to fit in, I masked my shortcomings and dared not whisper my failures. I worked hard to create the impression that my life was neat and orderly. I knew the posture and language well—and I carried it off. Few knew or guessed the truth. But I was miserable.

Perhaps you too have walked this tightrope. You are hurting. Something in your life is causing you great distress and unspeakable pain. But you cover it over with a smile. Perhaps you are depressed or feel inadequate, unable to cope with life. Perhaps you have been rejected by someone close to you. Maybe your spouse has walked out. Maybe your child has run away from home. Maybe you are lonely or struggling with an addiction. Overwhelmed, you want to scream. You need to scream. But it is a silent scream. Because you are afraid to let anyone know the depth of your pain.

Have you experienced this kind of pressure? Are you experiencing it now? Are you broken and worried you have nowhere safe to open your heart? Do you fear you may never recover from the blows life has dealt you? Is it hard for you to imagine being normal again? Are you saddled with shame and guilt, or resentment and anger? Have you lost hope?

Let us walk together through these pages and find healing and comfort in the arms of a God who will never reject us. God will not abandon you. He is not like the people who have failed you. He never throws up his hands and walks away. He never quits loving. I would not compare my father with God, but on that February day in our driveway, my dad offered me exactly what God offers us. God stands with his arms wide open, waiting to renew us in his embrace. When we come to him broken, with our fears multiplied and more questions than answers, God wraps his arms around us and says, "Welcome home."

Do you know someone who is broken? Do you want to help? Perhaps you recognize that living among you right now are people hiding deep wounds. You may be sitting unaware in church week after week with suffering people, even as friends and acquaintances sat beside me while I smiled and behaved as though I didn't have a care in the world. If your desire is to help, then let us explore ways to create safe places in which our wounded neighbors, friends, and loved ones can express themselves. Like my father, you might become the welcoming arms of God to the broken person in your pew. Let us hope so— let us pray it may be so. For this is what we were made to be: God's arms of love, both as individuals and as the church. Scripture says, "Bear one another's burdens, and thus fulfill the law of Christ" (Galatians 6:2).

FAILURE IS NEVER FINAL

I am not qualified to write this book because I am Billy Graham's daughter. I am not qualified by position or vastness of expertise. I am qualified to write this book because I am flawed. Because I am a sinner saved by God's grace. Because I am headstrong and slow to learn. Because I have made mistakes. Many mistakes. And have failed often.

My own story is not tidy. Nor is it simple. My story is messy and complicated and still being written. I have known betrayal, divorce, depression, and the consequences of bad judgment. I have struggled to parent my children through crisis pregnancy, drug use, and an eating disorder. I have known heartbreak, desperation, fear, shame, and a profound sense of inadequacy. This is not the life I envisioned. Far from it.

Revisiting the dark chapters of our lives can be a painful experience. Some things we would rather not remember—costly mistakes, severed relationships, words misspoken, actions taken or not taken. Even glancing in the direction of some of our memories can open up a world of hurt. We prefer to trudge ahead, as the Bible says, "forgetting what lies behind" (Philippians 3:13).

Yet there are times in life when God gently draws us back to our places of pain and invites us to take another look. He does not call us back to aggravate our wounds or cause us emotional harm. When God calls, he calls with good purpose; and when he urges us back to a hard place, he does so in order to heal us. Only then can we truly move on.

We learn in Scripture that Abraham's wife, Sarah, treated her maid, Hagar, severely. Sarah, who was barren, had encouraged Abraham to become intimate with Hagar so he could produce children. Now Hagar was pregnant, and Sarah felt disrespected by her maid. In response, Sarah mistreated Hagar enough to drive the woman to flee to the wilderness. There the angel of God spoke to Hagar:

> Now the angel of the LORD found her by . . . the spring on the way to Shur.
>
> And he said, "Hagar, Sarai's maid, where have you come from and where are you going?" And she said, "I am fleeing from the presence of my mistress Sarai."
>
> Then the angel of the LORD said to her, "Return to your mistress, and submit yourself to her authority."
>
> GENESIS 16:7–9

No destination would have been more dreadful to Hagar at this point than Sarah's home. Yet God called the maid to go back. *Return to your mistress. Go back to where you have suffered.* While Hagar must have listened in bewilderment, God did not leave her with a confusing command. He drew her with a promise: "I will greatly multiply your descendants so that they shall be too many to count" (Genesis 16:10).

When the Lord prompts us, like Hagar, to return to our places or memories of suffering, we too carry a promise of restoration and hope for the future. The prophet Isaiah expressed the promise this way:

> The LORD will surely comfort Zion
> and will look with compassion on all her ruins;
> he will make her deserts like Eden,
> her wastelands like the garden of the LORD.
> Joy and gladness will be found in her,
> thanksgiving and the sound of singing.
>
> ISAIAH 51:3 NIV

Failure is never final. God specializes in restoration—it is his best work. He loves to create out of chaos. Consider where he started in Genesis, bringing order to an earth that was "formless and void" (Genesis 1:2). God likewise steps into our ruins, picks up the pieces, and reassembles our mistakes, hurts, faults, and failed plans in ways that are wonderful and surprising. He never wastes anything. *He will make her deserts like Eden.*

Isaiah tells us that God looks on our ruins "with compassion." Imagine God's look of compassion. Imagine his love, his tenderness. God does not condemn us for our mistakes. He sees hope where others see failure. He sees a future where others see wreckage. His desire is to bring us out of our devastation, healed and strengthened, with a song in our hearts. That is his promise. *Joy and gladness will be found in her.*

A View from the Ruins

It is difficult to perceive God's hand when we are living in the ruins, isn't it? We cannot understand what God is doing, what emotional patterns he is dismantling, whether God is even there, or where we will end up. But with distance and divine help, we can learn to see the past with new eyes. As I reexamined my own ruins in preparation for this book, I realized aspects of God's persistent involvement with me that I previously had missed. I recognized God moving in my life at times when I feared he had abandoned me. I saw the way he used my circumstances over a stretch of years to help me overcome hidden weaknesses. I became aware that certain events I had forgotten were, in fact, key turning points in my life.

Though I often felt dejected and alone while living through my difficult seasons, I now understand that God was at work in my life all along. In my pain, in my suffering, in my mistakes—even in the dark—God was always present, working out his good purpose. Jesus is called Emmanuel, "God with us" (Matthew 1:23 KJV). In taking another look at my life, I came to recognize as never before the reality of God's faithfulness. He *is* with us. Nothing can make him give us up. The depth of this realization is part of his restorative work in me.

Eventually, I discovered I was not the only one in church whose life had taken unwelcome turns. I was not the only one who had missed opportunities. I was not the only one who had sinned. In particular, I found that when others were honest with me about their faults and imperfections, I became more comfortable sharing my own mistakes. Once we take off our masks—once we expose our ruins—we give others permission to do the same. And that is when real ministry and healing take place.

In this same spirit, I now share my story with you. I will start with a dark moment of my own. As God leads you, consider your own difficult moments and test them against the message written here. Let us ask the Lord to help us reach for his "Welcome home."

HOW COULD THIS BE HAPPENING TO ME?
The Shock of Brokenness

My husband, Ted, turned forty-two on a balmy Saturday in May 1987. The day was unusually idyllic. Ted, our three children, and I entertained a potential business partner over lunch at a local restaurant and then spent the afternoon swimming in our pool. We made ice cream and later grilled hamburgers. The children—Noelle, 13; Graham, 11; and Windsor, 8—were especially cooperative. Ted and I were relaxed. Our 185-acre horse farm in Virginia's Shenandoah Valley afforded us privacy and peace. We lacked for nothing, and in many ways, it seemed our life as a family was beginning to resemble the life I had dreamed about for years. My relationship with my husband had deepened, and the kids truly seemed happy. We were enjoying one another.

That evening I fixed a fruit salad for the following day's Sunday lunch, which we had been invited to share with friends. I joined Ted in our room, and we talked leisurely about the events of the day. As we conversed, I decided to ask Ted the question that had been haunting me for the last several months. Actually, I had wanted to ask Ted this question for some time, but whenever I planned to go through with it, I ended up pulling back. Weeks earlier, while we were out of town on business together, I had intended to ask the question, only to realize when we got to our destination that I was unprepared for Ted's response. That I might hear my suspicions confirmed seemed a threatening prospect. Did I really want to know the answer?

Since returning from that trip, I had become more anxious under the weight of my unspoken question, and I concluded I would be better off simply knowing the truth. I was tired of suspecting. I needed some relief. I wanted the matter settled and decided I would ask Ted when the time seemed right.

With our marriage relationship seemingly stronger than ever, I supposed I could handle what he might say. Now, lying next to my husband on his birthday, with a good day behind us, I thought it would be safe for me to ask.

Turning to Ted in the dark, I gathered my courage and said, "I want to ask you something." The environment in our room felt intimate and nonthreatening. I gazed in my husband's direction, and then, as I had imagined on so many occasions, I spoke the words:

"Have you ever been unfaithful to me?"

Ted did not respond. I could not see his face, but his silence communicated everything. At once I knew the answer. I braced myself, both wishing he would say something and regretting I had ever asked. A moment later he told me what I dreaded to hear.

"Yes," he said soberly. "Yes."

I felt like a shotgun had blasted me in the stomach, or like a fullback had knocked the wind out of me. The shock was seismic—it took my breath away. I felt flattened. Completely leveled. Then, somehow, I managed to recoup and focus on Ted. On the guilt he must have been carrying. On the courage he must have mustered to answer honestly. I tried to comfort him as he haltingly told me the truth. I told him I forgave him. But I had a million questions. Was it more than once? Where did it happen? When? Ted answered these questions, though it would be months before I knew everything. The infidelities had occurred over a period of years while we were living in Texas. More than one woman was involved. The details devastated me. Too tired to talk any more, I finally drifted into a fitful sleep. I didn't want to think. I wanted to forget. I wanted to forget it all.

The next morning, reality asserted itself like an open wound. "Woke up about 6:30 to realize what had happened," I wrote in my journal. "Sickness. Heaviness. Tried to act normal.... On the outside I'm calm & cool—inside I'm dying. I'm not even sure I know how I feel. And I'm afraid I'll come apart if I start."

At church that morning, I sat in the pew in a daze, outwardly carrying on as normal, but inwardly disconnected from what was going on around me. I felt little but the knot in my stomach. After the worship service, Ted, the kids, and I went to lunch at our friends' house as planned. Driving home, Ted reached over and took my hand while I stared out the window and watched the Shenandoah Valley go by. In the distance, I saw storm clouds gathering over the mountain peaks of the Blue Ridge. The sky looked dark and foreboding, and I remember having the sense that storm clouds were similarly gathering over my life. I wondered what darkness threatened to overtake me. And I was afraid.

MARRIED LIFE

Marriage had not come easily for Ted and me. We shared good times. We made good memories. But we struggled from the beginning. We married very young. I was just eighteen, and Ted was five years my senior. I knew little about life. The middle of five children, I only knew I was ready to feel significant. Both of my sisters had married young. Now I wanted to feel special. I wanted to be needed and loved.

To my parents' chagrin, I dropped out of college to get married. Mother taught my sisters and me that a woman's highest calling was to be a wife and mother, and I looked forward to fulfilling that calling. My parents strongly advocated my completing my studies, however; and as a student at Gordon College, I had majored in Bible because Mother suggested the knowledge would serve me well when I began to rear children. Otherwise, I felt unmoored academically, and being part of a high-profile family, I also felt like something of an odd duck on campus.

Ted Dienert stepped into my world when I was a college sophomore. We had first met at one of my father's evangelistic meetings in London when I was sixteen, but now Ted came into my life in a significant way. He was blonde, handsome, and athletic. He was a man with a huge presence, and he seemed to know where he was going. More than simply drawn to him, I was bowled over by him. His parents were friends of my parents, and he seemed to fit into my world. He pursued me with determination, and I fell hard. I was in love with Ted—and I was in love with love.

Our marriage, however, got off to a shaky start and could not seem to right itself. We lived in the Philadelphia area, where Ted worked for his father, a founder of the advertising agency that handled the Billy Graham Evangelistic Association account. Ted made a good living, but we struggled to get along. He traveled a lot, and I developed my own interests. Following the lead of my older sister, Anne, I helped start a class for Bible Study Fellowship (BSF)—a rigorous, life-encompassing program of in-depth Bible study—and organized occasional women's ministry events.

As the years passed, Ted and I learned better how to relate to one another, and our marriage seemed to improve. We started having children—our daughter, Elizabeth Noelle, in 1974 and our son, Graham Pierce, in 1975—and a new depth of intimacy developed in our marriage. Still, our old dynamics always seemed to resurface. Conflict persisted. Strain and frustration were ever a part of our lives. We managed, but it wasn't easy.

By the time I was pregnant with our third child, Windsor Ruth, we were ready to leave Philadelphia, and Ted's father agreed to let Ted open a new office for the company in Dallas. The transition proved difficult. Ted wanted to buy land and set up a ranch. Knowing I would be caring for three young children, I preferred being in the city, closer to Ted's office, closer to stores and community, and closer to a favorite aunt and uncle. Still, as Ted felt strongly about purchasing land, I tried to follow my mother's example and support my husband's dream. In the end, we bought fifty acres outside of Dallas in Argyle, built a house and a barn, and acquired several Arabian horses.

The years in Texas were the most challenging for Ted and me. We lived largely separate lives. Ted made the commute into Dallas every day for work. I stayed out in Argyle with the children. Our daily lives rarely intersected. I was heavily involved in the kids' activities during the school year, and in the summers, I drove the kids to my parents' home in Montreat to spend time with my sister Anne and her children.

Eventually, I took a part-time position as an acquisitions editor with book publisher Harper & Row, working from home and traveling occasionally to meet with authors. My personal outlet was Bible Study Fellowship. I had helped start a BSF class in Philadelphia; now in Texas I served in leadership. I learned a great deal of Scripture during these years, putting in countless hours studying the Bible and preparing for class. The women in BSF leadership were my closest friends and most ardent supporters. They were like sisters, and they made me feel part of a vital community.

Meanwhile, Ted and I were miles apart—not only physically, as he worked such long hours in town, but also emotionally. Much later, after I learned of Ted's infidelities, this period in my marriage made more sense. Ted and I rarely went on dates, and day-to-day we hardly saw each other. Though we did take vacations together and do some things with the children, we basically coexisted. We did not share our hearts with one another. We were not good friends.

In 1985, a new opportunity prompted us to leave Texas for Virginia's Shenandoah Valley, and our lives took a turn for the better. The Valley was home to my mother's family, and my grandfather's cousins offered Ted and me the chance to buy some of the family land. We fell in love with the property. When we first went to see it, I knew almost immediately I was "home." I met people who had known my grandparents, Nelson and Virginia Bell, to whom I was very close as a child. I encountered Valley residents who remembered playing with my mother when she and her parents and siblings would return to America on furlough from their medical missionary post in China. Being among such people in the Valley, I felt like I was part of something bigger than myself. I felt I belonged somewhere, and I knew I wanted to relocate.

Ted also welcomed the idea of a move to Virginia and sought to create in the Valley an expanded version of our Texas ranch. In all we bought nearly two hundred acres, about half of which had belonged to my mother's family. We enlarged the colonial house on the property, built a sixteen-stall, state-of-the-art barn for the horses, and christened our home and lands "Windmere Farm."

Virginia was a good move for us as a family. We built the barn to include space for Ted's office, which meant he was always nearby. He would talk to me about his business, and I felt included in his life in a way I never had previously. We found a church and got involved, developing a close relationship with our pastor and his wife. The kids seemed to thrive in their new environment. Ted and I were happier than ever before.

During these years, Ted poured a great deal of effort into improving our marriage. I also experienced significant personal growth, which affected the marriage positively. I became closer to God and more aware of my emotional needs. Ted and I became better able to talk openly with one another about our feelings. We discussed our relationship with a new honesty. We probed difficult aspects of our marriage and tried to trace the issues back to their roots. These were not easy conversations, but they produced trust. We were laying a new foundation.

By the spring of 1987—about two years into our new life in Virginia—I began to suspect Ted might have been unfaithful to me at some point during our marriage. He and I were closer now. I could read him better, and my suspicion began to bother me. Because we had grown closer, I thought I felt safe enough to ask my husband whether the infidelity I suspected was real or merely a figment of my imagination. I longed to put it to rest either way, and I thought our marriage could survive my asking. I thought I could survive my asking. I thought I could handle the outcome.

In fact, I discovered the outcome was a great deal harder to bear than I had foreseen. Later I even wondered if perhaps Ted should have kept the truth from me. Would we have done better if he had carried it to the grave? Many times I asked myself why I had broached the subject. Had I really wanted to know the answer? Of course, by then the point was moot. I had asked the question. But I had not adequately imagined the impact of betrayal.

SUFFERING: THE MISSING CHAPTER

After learning the truth the night of Ted's birthday, my emotions awakened to my altered marital terrain in fits and starts. My journal reads: "I told [Ted] that just because my reaction has been calm, not to minimize my pain & hurt . . . once all the emotions come out, I may need to work thru forgiveness again." This turned out to be an understatement.

Day by day, new information about the infidelity surfaced. The extent of it was far greater than I had dared to consider. I was incredulous. Even though I had suspected Ted, at the same time I never dreamed he would violate our marriage vows. "He has put us in a whole different category," I wrote in my journal. "I now am [in] a marriage that has experienced adultery. . . . Want to rage at him . . . but don't want to do that. My heart hurts so badly but my mind is 'in control' and knows all the right things to say."

Depression set in during the months that followed, and I did not know how to address it. I lost weight. I couldn't sleep. A huge weariness settled over me. Daily tasks took all the energy I could muster. "Driving home . . . I was numb," I wrote one day, "but the heaviness was worse. I felt like a beaten dog. Nowhere to turn. No hope. Kicked again and again by this pain."

I tried to comfort and strengthen myself by reading Scripture, and I wrote out touchstone passages in my journal. One was Isaiah 51:3, the verse about God looking with compassion on our ruins. This verse from Deuteronomy was another: "The eternal God is thy refuge, and underneath are the everlasting arms" (Deuteronomy 33:27 KJV).

Yet while I wrote these truths down, they did not seem to help me. They were words on a page. They seemed lifeless. I could not *feel* God's everlasting arms. I could not hear his voice or feel his presence. "It would be easier if the Lord were more real to me," I recorded. "If He felt close." And later: "I go through soul-searching, Bible reading, confession, prayer, and it seems as if nothing changes."

I wanted to hold everything in and let it all out. I would comfort Ted and then become hostile toward him. If Ted was away, then I wanted him near. If he was near, then I wanted him to go. I was needy one minute and resentful the next. I would withdraw and then lash out. I was angry with God, angry with Ted. Vulnerable. Raw. Lonely. Exposed. Like an egg without a shell. Runny. Messy. I couldn't pull it together.

The psalmist perfectly expressed my desperation:

> Save me, O God,
> For the waters have threatened my life.
> I have sunk in deep mire, and there is no foothold;
> I have come into deep waters, and a flood overflows me.
> I am weary with my crying; my throat is parched;
> My eyes fail while I wait for my God.
>
> PSALM 69:1–3

Fleeting thoughts of suicide passed through my mind. "Just to go see Jesus," I wrote in my exhaustion. Then I would think of the children.

I am not certain when it dawned on me that what I was doing was suffering. Early on as I tried to process my new reality, I recorded in my journal key Scriptures about suffering, but my understanding of suffering was vague and limited. "Suffering" had such a spiritual ring to it. The great Christian saints suffered for their faith. Ted's affairs were sin. They were ugly. I was broken because of them, but was I "suffering"?

Though I lacked personal understanding about suffering, it was a concept I had considered from an early age. The woeful narratives detailed in John Foxe's *Book of Martyrs* and stories about the persecuted Scottish Covenanters often were recounted to my siblings and me, highlighting the courage of Christians who held true to their beliefs in the face of torture and death. Marching through our young subconscious minds were accounts of men and women who met gruesome ends for refusing to renounce their faith in Christ. Some of these saints were buried alive. Others had their fingernails pulled off. Still others were dismembered.

We tease Mother and Daddy now about feeding our minds such gory fare, but as a little girl, I was scared to death! And yet I did not really believe mine would be a fate as grim as those detailed by my parents. Those stories were so unreal. Terrible things happened to other people, not to us. We lived in a happy cocoon.

My childhood in Montreat, North Carolina, was simple and bucolic. A little cove not far from the city of Asheville, Montreat is home to a popular Presbyterian conference center usually thronged by visitors in the summer. Otherwise, when I was growing up, the village was a modest community largely inhabited by retired Presbyterian missionaries and by students who attended Montreat College.

From before I was born, my beloved grandparents, Nelson and Virginia Bell—having retired from their work as medical missionaries in China—resided in Montreat. We lived across the street from them for a while and then moved "up the mountain" to a log cabin house my mother designed. "Little Piney Cove," as our new home was called, afforded us privacy from tourists and an uncomplicated, rural life among a menagerie that included cats, dogs, goats, and even snakes—although the snakes were kept strictly out of doors!

With my father traveling so often, it was Mother who on a daily basis modeled for us an intimate relationship with God. She kept her worn, leather Bible open on her desk, and we often came across her on her knees in prayer. Late at night we might hear her playing her favorite hymns on the piano. She was not one to complain or express self-pity. She took her feelings, hurts, and desires to God. While she confronted her share of ugliness in the world, Mother chose to see life's brighter side. Hers was a cheerful outlook. She trusted God completely and experienced a life-giving friendship with him. We children were witness to this.

Watching our parents and living around other godly men and women in Montreat, my siblings and I learned to believe in God's goodness and love. We were taught we could be certain of God. He would not fail us. He would take care of us. We might not understand God, but we did not have cause to be angry with him. He was good and loving, and he knew best. No matter what, we were to love him and obey his Word. We could trust God. He would be with us. He would look after us to the end.

But what of the martyrs whose grisly stories we heard so often? Didn't God promise to look after those people too? For whatever reason, I never asked this question. Somehow I lived virtually unfazed by what later became for me a difficult paradox: that God loved and took care of his people but allowed these same people to suffer for their love of him.

I suppose since those I most admired seemed able to live with this dilemma of suffering, I remained oblivious to it while young. My grandparents were privy to some horrible crimes and activities as missionaries in a China overrun with bandits. Children were kidnapped and sometimes dismembered to extract ransom money. People were tortured by thieves. Dead babies were literally discarded, their bodies left outside for the dogs to devour. Life was full of hardships. But my grandparents loved and trusted God with their whole hearts. They themselves lost an infant son to dysentery and suffered great heartbreak, yet when my grandmother told me the story, I was left with an image of two parents standing at their child's graveside singing the Doxology. Theirs was a story of victorious faith in a good, faithful, and all-wise God who would not leave them in their distress.

I think I first began to grapple with the issue of suffering some time after Ted and I were married. We were living in Philadelphia, and Darlene Deibler Rose—a missionary to New Guinea and Australia whose autobiography, *Evidence Not Seen: A Woman's Miraculous Faith in the Jungles of World War II,* I later acquired for Harper & Row—came to our church to share her testimony. Mrs. Rose was interned in a Japanese prison camp in the South Pacific for roughly four strenuous years during the war. She barely escaped being killed, and her then-husband died in captivity.

Mrs. Rose's testimony included many sorrowful stories, and I remember feeling confused after she finished. I recorded my thoughts in my journal: "My reaction was 'Why, God?' Does He heap misery on His loved ones until they break? . . . To me He seemed an unlovely, unjust God. I kept asking why. [Mrs. Rose] did not; she sweetly looked up into Jesus' face and searched her own heart. She who had suffered so much could sing, praise, and search her own heart for something wrong before God. It seemed ludicrous."

I had never articulated uncertainty of God like this before. Immediately, my instinct was to go to Scripture and correct myself. My journal reads: "In Hosea it says, 'for the ways of the Lord are right . . .' And in the Psalms it says '. . . and uphold me with a willing spirit.' Ah that I too might have faith and a willing spirit."

I was trying to imitate the faith of my parents and grandparents—a faith that clung to the goodness of God in the face of evil and heartache. But I could feel something in me begin to give way. My faith was still so young; *I* was still so young. And I was coming face-to-face with what seemed to me a blinding discrepancy between a God who cares for us and a God who allows his servants to suffer. If I was going to love and serve this God, then I would have to confront the reality that suffering one day might happen to me.

I must have overlooked the most obvious example of this paradox of the Christian life: Christ hanging on a cross. God allowed his Son—his one and only beloved Son—to suffer abuse, torture, rejection, and death. Suffering was God's *plan* for Jesus. By Christ's suffering, God made a way for me, a sinful person, to fellowship with him, a holy God. My very relationship with God was made possible because Jesus took responsibility for my sins by suffering. Suffering was at the heart of the gospel message. How had I missed it?

I also knew the Bible taught that followers of Christ would follow him not just in his victory over death—his resurrection—but also in "the fellowship of His sufferings" (Philippians 3:10). If Jesus suffered, Scripture explained, then so would those who followed him. Yet somehow I had skipped or blocked out this essential aspect of my faith. Suffering was the missing chapter in my theology. Maybe I thought suffering was for the "real" Christians serving God in the trenches abroad. I wondered, Was I a failure in God's eyes because I preferred comfort to deprivation?

I did not know what to do with these questions in Philadelphia during my early twenties; and now, confronted with Ted's infidelity, I still did not know. I thought my questioning somehow reflected a deficiency of faith. If Darlene Deibler Rose had trusted God in the face of suffering, sorrow, and death, then why couldn't I do the same in my adversity? An unquestioning faith seemed to work for my parents and grandparents. Why wasn't it working for me? Something must be wrong with me.

I did not feel I could take my questions about God to my family, nor did I believe I could share them with anyone outside of the family. I was Billy Graham's daughter. I thought I was supposed to have a special relationship with the God of my father. I thought I had to uphold an image. At a loss for what to do, I continued to parrot others, assuming they knew best; and I struggled privately.

GOD IN THE RUINS

Why a loving God allows us to suffer is a question without an easy answer. But we do know suffering does come. Suffering is part of the human condition. All of us *have* suffered, *are* suffering, or *will* suffer. The Bible promises us we will suffer. Paul writes to the Thessalonians, "we have been destined for this [affliction]" (1 Thessalonians 3:3). Life involves joy *and* sorrow, comfort *and* hardship. There is a saying, "I been in sorrow's kitchen and licked out all the pots." Perhaps this is exactly how you feel.

Knowing we will suffer does not make our pain, when it comes, any less difficult to bear. Yet grappling with our suffering is not a useless activity. Though it may be impossible to solve the mystery of suffering in this life, we can benefit as we endeavor to gain clarity about the paths we travel. As we consider the dimensions of our pain, we begin to better understand ourselves. We learn to talk to God more specifically about our feelings, our hurts, and the fallout from our experience. Our relationship with God deepens as a result, and we open ourselves to an even greater understanding of his love and faithfulness.

Suffering comes to us in life for various reasons. We suffer, for instance, when we decide to follow God with an undivided heart. The cost of obedience often includes suffering. Darlene Deibler Rose answered God's call to become a missionary, and she ended up in a Japanese prison camp. She obeyed, and she suffered. We suffer too when forced to endure circumstances we do not ask for or cause, such as tragedy, illness, or betrayal. My grandparents had to survive the loss of their infant son. Nothing they did or failed to do brought about their son's death. In the face of every prayer and effort to the contrary, their son passed away, and they suffered greatly. Finally, we suffer the consequences of our own sin. One of the most wonderful yet terrible principles in all of Scripture is that we reap what we sow (Galatians 6:7). Often the consequences of our choices are very painful, and we suffer.

How does God view our suffering and its causes? Suffering bitterly in the aftermath of Ted's admission, I often wondered if my plight could qualify me as one of those whom Scripture calls "partakers of Christ's sufferings" (1 Peter 4:13 KJV). I wasn't being persecuted for Christ's sake, but I wondered if I nonetheless could identify my suffering with that of Jesus and claim the partaker's promises in Scripture. I wanted to know: Where did my suffering fit into God's thinking? How was I to understand God's heart toward me in my condition?

As I worked through my emotions, I came to understand that, for a Christian believer, heartbreak of any kind could qualify as suffering for Christ. We may not be suffering for our faith in Christ, but we can turn our suffering over *to* him. Scripture instructs us to come to God "Casting all your care upon him; for he careth for you" (1 Peter 5:7 KJV). Notice the verse puts no conditions on our cares—it says cast "all your care" on God. God accepts all of our suffering, whatever its origin. He takes ownership of the pain we entrust to his keeping.

By placing our suffering in the Lord's hands, we are saying, "God, I cannot fix this. I am helpless. I am totally dependent on you." This act of surrender releases God to do whatever he pleases in us, through us, and for us in our suffering. There is great freedom in letting go of our cares and letting God work. And if we allow him, God will make our suffering into something useful and life-giving—for others and for us. That is his way. He uses our ruins. Our pain and mistakes become valuable materials in the hands of the Lord. Remember the promise of Isaiah: "he will make her deserts like Eden, her wastelands like the garden of the LORD" (Isaiah 51:3 NIV).

Perhaps the most important truth we can learn in suffering of any kind is that, however we have arrived at our condition, God lives with us in our experience. He does not leave us alone to get by—even if we are suffering consequences we created for ourselves. Scripture reads, "He Himself has said, 'I WILL NEVER DESERT YOU, NOR WILL I EVER FORSAKE YOU'" (Hebrews 13:5). The psalmist wrote, "The LORD is near to the brokenhearted" (Psalm 34:18). It is sometimes hard to imagine God forgiving us for our sin, let alone sticking with us and helping us clean up our mess. But, again, let's go back to what Isaiah says of God: "The LORD will surely comfort Zion and will look with compassion on all her ruins" (Isaiah 51:3 NIV). God loves us in our ruins. He is with us in our ruins. He is working in our ruins. Our ruins become places of hope in the eyes of God, for he sees their potential.

GOD IN *YOUR* RUINS

Consider the suffering you have experienced or are experiencing, and try to identify its causes. Maybe you have chosen to put your faith in Christ and are being slighted by family members who do not understand or agree with your choice. You are suffering for following God with an undivided heart. Perhaps you have been diagnosed with a serious illness; or maybe a friend has lied to you or betrayed you in some way. You are suffering a circumstance you did not choose or make happen. Maybe you are the one who has lied, and a relationship has been permanently damaged as a result. You are suffering the consequences of your sin. Where does your experience fall? Perhaps it includes more than one of these kinds of scenarios.

I encourage you to talk to God about what you are going through. Be specific. Start by describing how you feel. Be honest about your emotions, fears, confusion, and questions. You might say, "Lord God, I have made a decision to obey you. Now people are belittling me, shunning me, and telling me I will never succeed. I am suffering for following you. I thought life would get easier, and I am confused." Or, "Jesus, I did not ask for this diagnosis. I don't want this illness to invade my body. I am enduring something I didn't ask for. I am in pain and losing hope. I don't understand." Or, "Lord, I blew it. I took matters into my own hands. I hurt this person. I'm miserable, and there doesn't seem to be any end in sight. I can't imagine ever being happy again."

These will be ongoing conversations with God because the depth of your pain is ongoing. God wants us to talk to him about everything. His ear is open. Don't miss your opportunity to share your heart. Healing is available even as we simply express ourselves to God. In doing so, we grow closer to him, and the closer we get to the Healer, the healthier we become.

It is one thing to talk to God, but how do we turn our pain over to him? If freedom comes in letting go, then how do we do it? First, make the decision in your heart to relinquish your anxiety, fear, grief, or despair—whatever you are going through. Then tell God you are entrusting your circumstances and feelings to him. You may find you have to make this decision daily, or multiple times each day. So often we make a decision to trust God and then fall back on what is familiar—worry, fear, despair. God understands. He will help us as we renew our decision to trust him. He will meet us in that decision and reinforce it for us by showing himself trustworthy day by day. But we have to make the decision. God will not make it for us.

Once you have given your pain and your circumstances to God, ask him to use your situation to produce healing in your life and in the lives of others. Tell God you are counting on him to change your heart and make it stronger. Let him know you are depending on him to give you wisdom, stamina, and direction as you wait. The psalmist wrote, "Wait on the LORD: be of good courage, *and he shall strengthen thine heart*" (Psalm 27:14 KJV, emphasis mine). Take hold of this promise of strength and make it your own. Expect God to bring good out of your suffering. Ask him for the courage to hold on while he works in your situation.

When we pray this way—expressing dependence on God, asserting our belief in his power—we are praying in faith; and that is not easy to do. The prayer of faith is a costly prayer. In times of pain, it can be extraordinarily challenging to imagine anything good coming into our lives again. We often have to wrestle with our thoughts and emotions to keep our perspective buoyed and our faith intact. But trusting God is worth the cost. When we commit ourselves to his keeping, he will not drop us. He loves us totally and with a pure heart. He will never let us go. If we can just stay with him—submit to him, love him, cling to him—we will live to see his faithfulness. For he is working in our ruins. And his purposes will not fail.

FOR THE ONE WHO CARES

Perhaps someone you know is hurting deeply right now. You have thought about the different kinds of suffering described above and have identified the pain your friend or loved one is experiencing. Now pray for your friend with greater understanding. Talk to God about your friend's situation. Tell God exactly what is going on and how you feel about it. Express your own emotions, questions, and concerns. Let God know you want to help your friend, but articulate your confidence in him, the Lord, as the ultimate Healer. There is much you can do to help, as we will see, but God is the Restorer. He must lead you. Ask him for guidance. Tell God that, as much as you want to fix the situation for your loved one, you realize your strength and ability come from him, the Lord.

If you find yourself trying to rescue your friend or loved one, then ask God to help you let go of the burden. Rescue is not ultimately your responsibility; it is God's. Read Scriptures like Psalm 25:15 as you pray for yourself and your friend: "My eyes are ever on the LORD, for *only he* will release my feet from the snare" (NIV, emphasis mine). Tell God you recognize that "only he" can deliver your friend out of his or her situation. Let God know you are relying on him to work in and through your loved one's pain, and then commit that loved one to God for complete healing. Even as the sufferer prays, asking God to do something beautiful in his or her ruins, you pray also that God will work in the life of your friend in ways more extraordinary than you can imagine.

SEEING GOD'S HAND

As we pray and wait for God to restore us, it helps our morale to see evidence of his work in our lives along the way. While I was suffering heartache over my marriage, I did a spontaneous but invaluable exercise during my prayer time with God one morning. I decided to list in my journal all of the positive aspects of my situation. I titled the list "Praise."

Among the points on my list were the following: My marriage seemingly had become strong enough to endure the pressure, now that Ted's infidelity had come to light. My own personal growth during the months leading up to my conversation with Ted on his birthday had prepared me to face the issue and deal with it. I had learned the truth from Ted himself—not from another person. I had years of in-depth Bible training behind me, giving me a firm grasp on the truth of God's Word, which would sustain me in the storm. The infidelities had occurred in another state, meaning that in my daily life I would not have to encounter anyone touched by or involved in Ted's extramarital relationships.

By the time I got to the end of my list, I was truly encouraged. Instead of getting stuck thinking about what God had not done, I now could see what he *had* done. God had prepared me for what I was going through. Knowing this season of suffering was coming, God had gotten me ready. He was involved in my life. He cared about me. I came away from the exercise eventually assured of three foundational truths: God loved me, he would lead me, and he, in fact, would bring good out of my circumstances. These truths sustained me as my world came apart. I wrote them out in my journal. I prayed them over my life. I told others about them. In the years ahead, my determination to hold on to these foundational truths would factor significantly in my ability to survive the emotional strain.

I encourage you to make a "Praise" list—and, if you have not done so already, to begin keeping a journal as a record of what God is doing and saying in your daily life. By focusing on what God has already done for us, we cultivate hope for the future. Think back for a moment and consider the ways God has prepared you to make it through your current situation. How did he work in your various relationships to build your support system? Did he do anything to prepare you financially for hardship? Did he make adjustments in your career? In your children's lives? Did he spearhead personal growth so the pain you now feel wouldn't do you in?

Further, now that you are going through a hard time, what has God done to ease the hurt? Think about this. Sometimes we have difficulty seeing beyond our pain, but we must try. God has done something to bless you. Ask him to show you what that is. No matter how small the blessings may seem in relation to the hardship, we need to be able to see the proof of God's participation in our lives. When we can see his work, our faith increases. We start to believe that he really is helping us and that we just might make it to the other side.

We will continue to have low moments. Though I was able to see God's hand at various junctures in my situation, I did struggle with doubt. I battled fear. I questioned God a thousand times. Did he really know what he was doing? Could he actually bring good out of my situation? Once I asked a pastor if he believed Christianity really "worked"—I was back to my old dilemma about the plight of Darlene Deibler Rose in the Japanese prison camp. But even in the face of my distrust, God remained faithful, constantly bringing the truth of his love to mind. My low moments did not win the day; they were just moments. Aside from one grim episode, I never lost hope.

Of course, as my suffering over Ted's infidelity continued with little relief, I often wondered *how long* I could continue to hope. I wanted instant healing, instant answers. I wanted to forgive Ted and be relieved of the strain. I wanted us to get on with our lives. There are occasions when God does his work in us quickly. He does heal some people instantly. He does deliver some from drug addiction on the spot. He can and does work in immediate ways. So many of us, however, must go through a process; and this process can be long and arduous. Healing is not subject to a predetermined time frame, nor is it a reflection of our spiritual maturity. Some people bounce back right away. Others progress little by little. The pace is God's business; our part is to cooperate. I would have loved to have rebounded and seen my marriage healed overnight, but that did not happen. I had to remind myself that God's timeline is eternal. He sees our end from our beginning. In his mercy he sticks with us for the long haul, for the length of the journey can be the hardest part.

Reminders for Painful Times

- Sometimes all we feel is pain. Try to identify the source of yours. Is your suffering
  - the result of choosing to follow God with an undivided heart,
  - something you did not cause or ask for but must endure, or
  - the consequence of your own sin?
- Talk to God honestly about what you are going through.
- Turn your situation over to God. Tell him you trust him to work it out for good. As often as necessary, renew your decision to trust him.
- Let God know you are depending on him to strengthen and guide you.
- Make a "Praise" list of some of the things God has done for you both in the past and in your present circumstance. Begin keeping a journal as a record of God's activity in your life.

Tips for Those Who Care

- Talk to God about your friend or loved one—share your emotions and concerns about his or her situation.
- Commit your friend or loved one to God for complete healing and restoration.
- Ask for God's guidance as you seek to help in an appropriate, practical way. Express your dependence on God, and acknowledge him as the ultimate Healer.

MEMORY VERSE

Isaiah 51:3 NIV

The LORD will surely comfort Zion
and will look with compassion on all her ruins;
he will make her deserts like Eden,
her wastelands like the garden of the LORD.
Joy and gladness will be found in her,
thanksgiving and the sound of singing.

Principles for Reflection

God loves me, he will lead me,
and he will bring good
out of my circumstances.
He is with me and actively at work
in my ruins to restore them.

IS GOD REALLY IN CONTROL?
Trusting God to Carry Us in Hard Times

A few weeks following our birthday conversation, Ted left town to attend a series of my father's evangelistic meetings in another state. I tried to distract myself by keeping busy, but inside I felt anxious, devastated, confused. On the one hand, I was relieved to have Ted gone, to be able to walk through my home without my stomach knotting up every time our paths crossed. On the other hand, I longed for closeness and intimacy with him, for the reassurance that I could put the painful truth behind me and once again learn to trust my husband. This internal conflict was difficult to endure, and by the afternoon of one particular day, I was exhausted. Then the phone rang. It was Ted, calling to check in. With the sound of his voice came the familiar rush of frustration. We made small talk, conversing about my father's meetings and briefly about my day. Finally, Ted asked me how I was feeling.

"Sick to my stomach," I answered.

I imagined Ted was hoping for a more encouraging response. He wanted us to make it through this ordeal as badly as I did. But I could not yet wrap my mind around what had happened. The affairs seemed so unreal. I desperately wanted someone to tell me they had never taken place. I did feel sick. All the time.

Now on the phone, I waited for Ted to say something. What did he think of my curt reply? There was a pause. Then he spoke. He said, "Still?"

⌒

Walking through the fallout from Ted's admission, as I have written, was a demanding, often grueling process that continued for much longer than I expected—about four years. During that time, I labored to forgive Ted, sort through my emotions, rebuild my life, and maintain hope; and I almost always felt overwhelmed. My constant refrain was, "Lord, you've picked the wrong person for this!" So often I did not feel I could handle the mounting challenges of my trial; perhaps I thought that declaring my inadequacy would somehow get me out of it. At times, I believed I would have done just about anything to get relief.

Over the course of these years, I took solace in teaching a Bible class at my church to a group of women. One fall I taught a portion of Scripture from the book of Jeremiah. I found I related to this Old Testament prophet—he too felt inadequate on his path, albeit a more exalted one than mine. "Alas, Lord GOD!" Jeremiah exclaimed when God called him to be a prophet. "Behold, I do not know how to speak" (Jeremiah 1:6). Like me, Jeremiah told God he had picked the wrong person!

God went on to assure Jeremiah that he, the Lord, would equip him for a prophet's calling. God also assured me over and over that he would give me what I needed to endure the immense emotional strain I was experiencing in my marriage. But sometimes it helped just to read Jeremiah's expression of self-doubt and realize I was not the only one who had ever felt incapable.

In fact, I grew in strength and learned a great deal about God and his promises by studying the life and character of Jeremiah. The prophet's account of his experiences reinforced the foundational truths God had shown me when I made my "Praise" list. I came away from my encounters with Jeremiah in Scripture more convinced that God loved me, he would lead me, and he would bring good out of my circumstances. It is one thing to pray these truths in the abstract; it is another to see them affirmed and born out in the stories of people as related in Scripture. Ultimately, the time I spent poring over the writings of Jeremiah encouraged me in my conviction that God could and would do something useful with my ruins, that he was in control and would not let me go.

Before we proceed with my own story, let's take a closer look at the life of this dynamic Old Testament prophet. In hard times we wonder, *Is God really in control?* We need to understand the depth of God's involvement in our lives so we can continue to hope. As I have learned, we can gain confidence in both the power of God and his concern for us by examining the experiences of Jeremiah. What we learn from the prophet's story will serve as a foundation for the principles we will consider later.

PERSEVERING PROPHET

Jeremiah was a man of great substance and dimension. He was godly, courageous, bold, and persevering; yet he was also sensitive and emotional. He is called "the weeping prophet." When Jeremiah was a young man, God commanded him to preach a message of impending doom to Judah for the nation's disobedience, especially its sin of idolatry. Judah was going to be judged, God told his prophet, and Babylon would be the instrument of that judgment. This message broke Jeremiah's heart. He wept for the people—for their sin and coming destruction. But he faithfully preached all God told him to say. And for his obedience, he paid a steep price.

Jeremiah experienced rejection in many distasteful and life-threatening forms throughout his life due to the dire message he relentlessly proclaimed. He was beaten and put in stocks at the order of the priest (20:2). His people publicly seized and sought to kill him, and priests and prophets were numbered among those calling for his death (26:8, 11). He was falsely accused of treachery (37:11–16). He was imprisoned, thrown into a well, and left for dead (32:1–5, 37:11–38:6). The king of Judah even burned up Jeremiah's written record of everything God had spoken to his prophet (36:20–23). Jeremiah had his scribe rewrite the record, but what pains Jeremiah endured! His life was not pleasant. It wasn't comfortable. He was suffering.

Not only did God give his prophet controversial words to speak, but he also gave him challenging symbolic gestures to perform and live out. God told Jeremiah, for example, that he could not marry; he was not to have any children, for God said the sons and daughters of the people would perish in the land by disease, sword, and famine (16:1–4). God also charged Jeremiah to buy himself an undergarment, wear it and refrain from washing it, and then leave it exposed to the elements near the Euphrates River. The subsequently ruined garment was to picture the fate of the people in their disobedience and idolatry—they also would become ruined, worthless, and good-for-nothing (13:1–10).

God later told Jeremiah to wear a wooden yoke around his neck in order to symbolize for the people their coming subjugation to the king of Babylon. Unimpressed, another prophet publicly broke the yoke off of Jeremiah's neck as a sign that God was going to deliver Judah from Babylon's rule in short order. Jeremiah came back with a word from God that accused the other prophet of lying to the people and declared Babylon's rule over Judah so sure it would be like an *iron* yoke—unbreakable (27:2–8; 28:10–15).

The prophet Jeremiah did not live an uncomfortable life for just a week, a month, or even a year; he preached his difficult message and absorbed the subsequent wrath of others for roughly forty years until the people of Judah were taken captive into Babylon. All along, Jeremiah pleaded with the people, whom he loved, calling on them to repent for their sins. He begged the king of Judah to surrender to the king of Babylon and thus spare Jerusalem (38:17–23). Jeremiah cried over his people's refusal to repent. He suffered profound humiliation but kept on preaching in the hope that someone eventually would listen. In fact, Jeremiah found he could not do otherwise. He persevered, even when he wanted to quit! He wrote:

> I have become a laughingstock all day long. . . .
> But if I say, "I will not remember [God]
> Or speak anymore in His name,"
> Then in my heart it becomes like a burning fire
> Shut up in my bones;
> And I am weary of holding it in,
> And I cannot endure it.
>
> JEREMIAH 20:7, 9

WHY, GOD?

One of the things I love about Jeremiah is his honesty. Jeremiah was not passive. He told God exactly what he thought, and he was not happy about his troubles. He had not asked for the role of prophet; he had pointed to his own inadequacy from the beginning. Yet here he was, having to suffer for the role. He was upset with God and said so. He even accused God of deception:

> O LORD, Thou hast deceived me. . . .
> Everyone mocks me.
> For each time I speak, . . .
> I proclaim violence and destruction,
> Because for me the word of the LORD has resulted
> In reproach and derision all day long.
>
> JEREMIAH 20:7–8

Jeremiah was so distraught he cursed the day he was born, asking:

Why did I ever come forth from the womb
To look on trouble and sorrow,
So that my days have been spent in shame?

JEREMIAH 20:18

When life becomes burdensome and all but impossible to bear, often the only question we have for God is, "Why?" I have heard people say, "You can't ask God why." Yes we can. We can ask God why. We're in good company when we ask. Jeremiah asked God why. Many heroes of the faith have asked God why. I certainly wanted to know why God had allowed a trial like the one I experienced with Ted to surface in my life.

Asking why does not mean we have lost our faith. As I came to understand, asking why can be, rather, a sign of faith. Going back to my confusion over the plight of Darlene Deibler Rose, I saw that asking God why he had allowed Mrs. Rose to suffer adversity for her obedience was a natural question and one that presupposed God's goodness. When we ask why, we are asserting our desire to dialogue with the God in whom we have put a measure of trust. We expect he is listening and believe he is the source of the answers. For me, asking why about both Mrs. Rose and my situation with Ted affirmed that I understood God to be full of grace and compassion—asking was my way of seeking to reconcile circumstances that appeared from my limited human perspective to be inconsistent with God's love.

But won't we offend God if we ask why? Won't we make him angry? God is not threatened by our emotions. He is not shaken by our "why?" He did not strike Jeremiah down for expressing frustration and despair. God works with honesty. He invites honesty. We cannot throw anything at God that he hasn't heard before. He is bigger than our feelings, thoughts, and perceptions. At the same time, as we express ourselves to God, we must keep our hearts soft and open to him. For all of his distress, Jeremiah remained determined to obey God, no matter what the cost. He fussed, argued, and wrestled with God, but his heart was submitted to God. He trusted God even as he was questioning God.

Ultimately, Jeremiah did not allow himself to become bitter. In fact, in the midst of his suffering Jeremiah was able to pen some of the most beautiful lines about God in all of Scripture. He wrote:

It is of the LORD's mercies that we are not consumed, because his compassions fail not.

They are new every morning: great is thy faithfulness.

The LORD is my portion, saith my soul; therefore will I hope in him.

LAMENTATIONS 3:22–24 KJV

Recall the context in which Jeremiah lived, and then imagine him praying these words. Did he learn God's faithfulness while trapped at the bottom of the well? Did he know God's loving-kindness while wearing the yoke around his neck? Was he looking out over the remains of his city, now burned to the ground, when he recognized—and could declare—the goodness of God? Whatever our range of emotions, whatever our view of the circumstances unfolding around us, may we, like Jeremiah, keep our hearts open to God's faithfulness.

GOD IS IN CONTROL

To make some sense out of our suffering, we need to understand two important principles about God. First, he is in control; second, he will provide. Let's look at the first chapter of Jeremiah.

God tells Jeremiah:

> "Before I formed you in the womb I knew you,
> And before you were born I consecrated you;
> I have appointed you a prophet to the nations."
> JEREMIAH 1:5

Notice where God begins: "Before I formed you in the womb." Right off the bat, God makes it clear he is speaking as the Creator. He is sovereign, all-powerful. He made Jeremiah. He placed Jeremiah in his mother's womb and ordained his birth. Then God says, "I knew you." He is speaking as an all-knowing, all-wise God. He knew his prophet long before Jeremiah's conception. God knew his personality, his makeup, and his character. Further, God says, "before you were born I consecrated you; I have appointed you a prophet." Not only did God know his prophet before he was born, but he also had a plan for Jeremiah's life and appointed him to it. Reviewing this conversation, we can better grasp the depth of Jeremiah's pain when he later cursed the day of his birth. That curse spoke right to the heart of God's original call on his life. God said, I formed you for a purpose; Jeremiah, in effect, said, You made a mistake. Have you ever felt that way toward God?

Jeremiah was in great despair when he cursed his own birth. Later, of course, he recovered and was able to write of his Creator: "great is thy faithfulness." Despite his emotional lapse, Jeremiah understood that a loving, compassionate God was in control—both of his own life and the lives of his beloved people. God is sovereign in your life too. Before you were born he knew you. He knew your tastes, strengths, and weaknesses. He knew your personality. He knew his plan for you and appointed you for his purpose. Certainly he sees what you are suffering now. Nothing takes God by surprise. There is no breakdown of authority with God, no arbitrariness. He does not look at your life and say, "Oops." He knows where you are. Often as I reflect, I am amazed that the God of the universe knows me, knows my address, and attends to even the smallest of my needs.

Right now, take some time to reflect on God's greatness in your own life. You may not feel like he is in control. Perhaps you think he has forgotten you. Tell him how you feel, and then, simply as an act of obedience, begin to praise him. Use Jeremiah's beautiful words from Lamentations to aid you if needed. You might pray, "Lord, it is because of your mercies that I am not consumed or overwhelmed by my situation. Because your compassions fail not—they are new in my life every morning, even today. Great is your faithfulness. You are my portion, all that I need. Because of your goodness, I will hope in you." As you make the decision to override your emotions and to praise God in difficulty, your capacity to praise God will be enlarged. Your faith will be strengthened. And eventually peace and confidence will return to you.

We also strengthen our assurance of God's involvement in our lives by continually reviewing what he has done for us in the past. As I have explained, some time after my husband's infidelities came to light, I took the time to write down all the ways God had prepared me ahead of time for what I was then facing. This activity reinforced the truth that God was, in fact, in control of my situation. He had known what was coming, and he was faithful to get me ready for it. I found I could use the items on my "Praise" list as a springboard for the exercise of praise. I could pray, "Lord, thank you for prompting me to pursue personal growth before this crisis arose, for now I can face the issues head-on and look at them honestly. Thank you for giving me those years of in-depth Bible study and knowledge of your truth to sustain me now that this struggle has come. You were so wise to prepare me in these ways! I am amazed by you!"

Take some time to review your "Praise" list from chapter 2. When you consider the items on your list and notice God's daily participation in your life, do you see reasons to be grateful? When David meditated on God's loving concern for him, he could not contain his praise. He wrote, "How precious also are Thy thoughts to me, O God! How vast is the sum of them! If I should count them, they would outnumber the sand" (Psalm 139:17–18).

Can you say to God as David did, "How precious are your thoughts toward me"? Find your own words to convey what you feel when you reflect again on the ways God has helped you in your suffering. Talk in specific terms—not generalities. You don't need to use religious language. Be yourself. You can say, "Wow, God. What you did at that time blows me away! I can't believe how you made that circumstance with that person work out—you are just incredible!"

FOR THE ONE WHO CARES

If you know someone who is suffering, then you can do a similar praise exercise with your friend or loved one in mind. Begin by thinking about the history of your loved one's struggle. Ask God to show you what he has done specifically to help your friend along the way. Once you see God's involvement in the situation, begin to praise him. Thank God for loving your friend and for caring about his or her hardship. Praise God for being in control—for being big enough to heal your friend.

Use Jeremiah's words from Lamentations if you need to and plug in your friend's name. Pray: "It is of your mercies, Lord, that _____ is not consumed, because your compassions toward _____ fail not. They are new every morning. Great is your faithfulness to _____."

In fact, you will notice that praying the Scriptures on a regular basis for your friend or loved one will have a wonderful effect on your own life. Not only will your prayers help your friend—because God hears and answers the prayers of his people—but your prayers also will help *you*. This is the amazing thing about prayer. Prayer builds our faith and changes us! Praying the Word of God consistently for a suffering friend will help you better understand how God thinks and feels about your friend's situation. And as you get a better grasp on God's thoughts for your friend, you will become more confident that God is at work.

Just as important, you will maintain your awareness that God, not you, is responsible for fixing your friend's circumstances. As helpers we must remind ourselves of this truth constantly! We are so prone to anxiety when we help others. We often second-guess ourselves. What if I had done it this way? Maybe I should go back and do this? Did I give her enough encouragement on this point? Should I have said that to him? Can't I do more?

Hear God's voice telling you to be still. Again, you are not responsible for your friend's healing. Return to Psalm 25:15 and pray the verse as a prayer for yourself, plugging in your friend's name. Say: "My eyes are ever on you, Lord, for only you will release _____'s feet from the snare" (NIV). In continuing to assert God's sovereign power to effect change in the life of your loved one, you are affirming the principle that affords us great freedom as we serve: God is in control.

God Is in Control of Our Mistakes

We may see God's involvement in our lives. We may be able to recount the occasions when he has steered us on life's road. But we still may find it hard to believe God can use our mistakes to accomplish his purpose in us. After all, Jeremiah was a prophet who suffered for following God with an undivided heart, but what if we have brought our suffering on ourselves? What if *we* messed things up? What can God do with us now? Haven't we blown our purpose? These are real questions we ask ourselves. The answers are complex and multifaceted. We may never understand them fully in this life. But we can go to the Scriptures and ask God to shed some light.

Consider, for example, the history of the children of Israel. One summer as I was transferring my Old Testament notes from an old Bible into a new one, I noticed that from the time Moses led them out of Egypt, the people—God's chosen people—did a great deal to mess things up for themselves. They complained against God, worshiped a golden calf, and rebelled against the very one who had chosen them for a great purpose.

But God's ultimate purpose was not thwarted. The people eventually made it to the Promised Land—albeit a generation later and a little worse for the wear. Redemption still came to the world through this people. Christ still was born in the fullness of time, and he will return in the fullness of time. Despite the people's mistakes, which multiplied greatly over the years, God stuck with his own; and he remained in control. We can take heart that he is going to stick with us too. He loves us. He will lead us. He will bring good out of our circumstances, even our mistakes.

In the first chapter of Jeremiah, God asks his prophet, "What do you see?" (1:11). Jeremiah tells God he sees an almond branch—the "rod of an almond tree." There are many interpretations of Jeremiah's vision. By my reading, the almond branch was bare, dead-looking, unimpressive. God goes on to say, "'You have seen well, for I am watching over My word to perform it'" (1:12). God gives life to what looks dead. His word is creative. His word restores. When God performs his word, he makes the wasted places in us come alive. Remember, he is working in your ruins, even if those ruins are of your own making.

However, while God promises to create good out of our mistakes, and even our willful disobedience, his goodness does not give us license to do whatever we please. God is gracious to us, but we are not to take advantage of him. In fact, our love for God gives us the desire to do the things that please him. When we love him, we do not want to abuse his goodness. We receive his grace with gratitude and humility—even with amazement that he is still willing to work with people like us!

Being human, of course, we will fail to please God at times, and when we do fall short, grace is available and free. We do not have to despair. We do not have to set up camp in defeat. God always offers the gift of forgiveness and the promise of restoration. Our job is to tell God what we have done wrong (it won't shock him), to tell him we want to change, and to ask for his forgiveness and help in doing so. This is the process of confession and repentance. When we come to God in this way—humble, earnestly repentant, and at the end of ourselves—he welcomes and renews us so we can begin again.

The psalmist wrote, "For He Himself knows our frame; He is mindful that we are but dust" (Psalm 103:14). God knows what we are made of—he made us, after all. He knows we are weak and inadequate without him. In the psalmist's colorful metaphor, we are only animated dirt balls in reality! God loves us just as we are. He does not dismiss us because we are dust; he does not condemn us and say, "You stupid little piece of dust—why did you do it that way?" Rather, God looks at us with complete understanding and says, "You precious little piece of dust—of course you couldn't have done it any better without me!"

Have you fallen short? Are you feeling defeated by your own sin? As you've been reading, has anything come to mind that you need to bring to God in prayer? If so, stop here and take time with God to sort it out. Tell God what is bothering you. Let him know you want to be free of the sin in your life, and then if need be, make the choice to set your issue right with whomever has been affected by your actions. Be sure you make the necessary amends _soon_. The Bible says, "lay aside . . . the sin which so easily entangles us" (Hebrews 12:1). Maybe you have sinned against someone in the midst of your suffering, or theirs. Maybe you have been carrying prejudices in your heart toward others for their failures. Straighten these issues out with God. Let him clear things up for you and show you what to do.

GOD MAKES PROVISIONS FOR US

As we suffer, God works tirelessly to take care of our needs. If only we could see all that he does for us! Among the many provisions God makes to sustain us in hard times are his presence, his Word, and his vindication. We can identify all three in the first chapter of Jeremiah.

His Presence

When Jeremiah expressed his sense of inadequacy to God at the time of his commissioning as a prophet, God reassured him and answered, "Do not be afraid . . . , For I am with you to deliver you" (Jeremiah 1:8).

I am with you. God made this promise to Jeremiah twice on the occasion of the prophet's call. The second time, the promise was more specific: "And they will fight against you," God said, foretelling Jeremiah's persecution, "but they will not overcome you, for I am with you to deliver you" (1:19). How many times during his life Jeremiah must have returned to that promise of God's presence and repeated it back to God! When the prophet was beaten, put in the stocks, and publicly humiliated, did he remind God of his promise to be with him? When Jeremiah was seized by the people and threatened by the priests and prophets with death, did he call on God, crying out in the hope of that promise?

God was faithful to keep his promise to Jeremiah. God stayed with his prophet and delivered him from danger, opposition, and threat time and again. Plots against Jeremiah failed. After being thrown down the well, Jeremiah was rescued. Though a defiant king of Judah burned his writings, Jeremiah was able to rewrite and preserve them. In the aftermath of Jerusalem's overthrow, Jeremiah was spared. Indeed, so great was the favor granted Jeremiah after the city's capture that the Babylonian king ordered the captain of his bodyguard, in essence, to *serve* Jeremiah: "Take him and look after him, and do nothing harmful to him; but rather deal with him just as he tells you" (Jeremiah 39:12).

If God faithfully and repeatedly came through for Jeremiah in life-threatening ordeals—if God was faithful to his prophet in the chaos and disorder of the war zone in which Jeremiah spent so much of his life—then surely God will be with us where we are. Go back to God's promise as restated by the writer of Hebrews: "He Himself has said, 'I WILL NEVER DESERT YOU, NOR WILL I EVER FORSAKE YOU'" (Hebrews 13:5). That promise is for us too—not just for those in biblical times. When you read this verse, read it as God's personal word to you. Let God reassure you through his Word—you need his reassurance. You need to know his presence is with you.

But what does God mean when he says, "I am with you"? How do we recognize his presence? How do we *know* he is with us? Mostly, we take it on faith. Jeremiah may not have *felt* God's presence in every dismal circumstance he endured. He had to believe what God told him without seeing it. That is faith. Faith, the Bible tells us, is the "assurance of things hoped for, the conviction of things not seen" (Hebrews 11:1).

During the dark period of my life following Ted's admission of infidelity, I did not always feel God near me. Rather, I chose to believe he was near. To build my faith, I recorded Scriptures in my journal that promised me God's presence. At one particularly difficult moment, I wrote out these words of Jesus: "I am with you always, even unto the end of the world" (Matthew 28:20 KJV). Next to the verse I wrote, "Is my world ending?" It sure looked that way, but I was choosing to trust God to keep his word.

There were some instances when I did feel God's presence. I did sense his nearness at times when I was praying or reading the Bible. Again, not always. In fact, for long stretches I would feel nothing but despair and would wonder if God had forgotten me. But now and then I would experience the quiet assurance, or a simple knowing, that he was near. I recognized this assurance as a sign of his presence. I might also feel joy, peace, or hope in situations that seemed geared to produce anything but joy, peace, or hope. In these moments, I believed God was helping me with my emotions, and I would acknowledge his nearness.

People can be signs of God's presence as well. When I was depressed about my marriage, certain friends and family members loved me in a way that gave me strength. They listened while I shared, or they just made me laugh. They did not preach—nor did they let me off the hook when I was wrong. They loved me like Jesus. Unconditionally. Their love reminded me of God's nearness, and that reminder gave me hope. For the Bible says, "the nearness of God is my good" (Psalm 73:28).

FOR THE ONE WHO CARES

Are you a sign of God's presence for your hurting friend, neighbor, or loved one? Are you a "safe place" for him or her? Sometimes our mere facial expressions can be a balm for another person. The gift of time also is precious. My pastor and his wife spent hours with me just listening. They demonstrated love and concern. They kept my confidences. They let me walk through a range of emotions. They encouraged me to stay in God's Word.

By contrast, others caused me a lot of anxiety, wanting to know if I had crossed all the spiritual t's and dotted all the spiritual i's. They seemed more concerned with their interpretation of doctrine than with my emotional condition. Still others probed me for information when they did not have the right—they were only bystanders on the sidelines of my life. They did not help. Then there were those who just wanted to be "in the know," and others who were always offering advice. I did not want to be around persistent advice givers, though they may have been well-meaning. What I needed was encouragement, and advice given lovingly at appropriate times.

If you feel you can be of help to a friend or loved one in crisis, first talk to God and ask him to give you a sympathetic heart. Then move slowly and sensitively. Do not worry about being perfect. We all fail in our efforts to give comfort and support to the hurting. None of us have it all together. Look to God. He will make up for your weaknesses and enable you to be a sign of his presence. If you continue to pray, you will sense his leading.

His Word

Another thing God provides us when we are broken is his Word. Three times in the first chapter of Jeremiah, the prophet writes, "the word of the LORD came to me." Remember, God's Word is personal. It comes to *us*. During my experience with Ted, I became acquainted with the Word of God as a gift given personally to me. I often recorded Bible verses in my journal and plugged in my name where appropriate to remind myself that God was speaking his Word to me.

I strongly encourage you to make this practice a habit in your life. Whether you are in a dark time or helping someone through a dark time, make the Scripture verse or passage your own. You can take ownership of God's promises by writing your name into the Scripture portion—in your Bible, on note cards, in a journal, or whatever works best for you. My mother loves to say that all the promises of God are on the believer's side. We can pray the promises into our lives. We can claim them for our children. We can take God at his word and remind him of what that Word says.

Of course, in order to claim the promises in God's Word, we have to know what those promises are. That knowledge comes by reading Scripture—and reading it regularly. Early on in life, I developed the habits of daily Bible reading and prayer. These disciplines were necessary for my spiritual growth; but when my life hit the skids, I found the disciplines critical for my survival. I searched the Scriptures daily. I memorized verses. I wrote them down. I found I had to read truths over and over or else I would have forgotten them. We are like that—our minds drift; we forget what God believes about us. This is true when we are strong; it is especially true when we are struggling. I armed myself daily with Bible verses, not out of a sense of religious duty or obligation, but because my life depended on it.

Do you have a regular time set aside in the day for God? Do you take time to talk to God and listen to him? Are you in the Scriptures daily? I cannot overstress the importance of building this discipline into your life. I am talking about something other than the few quiet minutes with God you may grab during the day—I mean a regular "date" with God, daily. Because I had developed the habit of spending time with God daily *before* the darkness came, when it did come, I did not have to flounder; and for that I was so grateful. I simply proceeded as usual and let God use my habit as a channel through which he could send help.

You may ask, what if I'm suffering already, and I don't have a habit of talking to God daily? It is never too late to begin. Start today. Ask God to help you find the time in your schedule. Ask him to give you the ability each day to stick with your "date." Choose a time that works for you. No one is standing over your shoulder with a pointer. Some folks are morning people; others are night owls. Maybe a lunch hour would work best for you. There is no prescription. Get a Bible you can understand, and each day just read a few verses—maybe even a few phrases. Read until something speaks to you. Then mull the passage over throughout the day. As God brings his Word to mind, apply it to what you are going through. In this manner you allow the Scriptures to become relevant in your life.

As I suffered in my marriage, I particularly loved to read the psalms. They often expressed my own emotions and invariably pointed me to God, leading me with words of praise. You might also begin with the gospel of John. The Bible is a fascinating book full of comfort, grace, instruction, and illustration from the lives of real men and women whom God loved.

His Vindication

God asked Jeremiah a second time in that first chapter, "What do you see?" (Jeremiah 1:13). Jeremiah looked around and saw a boiling pot. The pot signified judgment. The Lord was going to send judgment to Judah in the form of war. To me the pot also signifies vindication. Judgment has to do with justice, with making things fair. So does vindication. God is a just God, a vindicator. He promises to make everything fair one day, whatever that means in our own personal circumstances.

Vindication is not vengeance. I had to remind myself of this distinction when I was experiencing fallout in my marriage to Ted. I was human, of course. I did want revenge for all the hurt my husband caused me. I did have a chip on my shoulder. I was angry. I did wish the earth would open up and swallow Ted. Those feelings were normal. But such scenarios were not what God had in mind when he promised to provide me vindication.

Ultimately, I understood I would be vindicated in heaven—everything would be set right there, and all pain would be gone. In the meantime, God would vindicate me by giving my life meaning in the ruins. I knew God loved me. I knew he would continue to work on my behalf. One day I believed I would see him bring good out of my circumstances. That was vindication.

Vindication comes through the cross of Christ. My vindication was secured when Jesus shed his blood for me. He took to the cross all of my feelings of revenge, anger, bitterness, malice, and spite; and he died in my place so God could do a new thing in my life. I needed him to do that new thing, and he did it. Gradually, I began to see that Ted was not my enemy. Fear, jealousy, pride, and self-condemnation—these were my enemies. These were the enemies fighting me from within, and God promised to defeat them on my behalf.

Further, I came to realize I was no better than Ted. God loved Ted as much as he did me; we were equal in God's eyes. Jesus died for everyone. No one is more sinful than anyone else. None of us can stand before God. We are all flawed. We all need redemption. Moreover, perhaps my invisible sin of self-righteousness was worse than any visible sin Ted had committed. I could hide my sin and dress it up, but in the end, God hates self-righteousness. Jesus had a lot to say about it when he was on earth. As long as I clung to my own view of what fairness and vindication should look like, I was blocking the healing work of God in my life. I had to let go of my ideas in this area and let God do his work in Ted. This was not easy. It was a daily battle. But it was very important.

Have you been wronged by someone? Do you find yourself wishing harm on him or her, or thinking about the kind of payback this person "deserves"? Consider for a moment what you deserve. Scripture teaches that we all deserve condemnation because of sin (Romans 6:23). Only because Jesus died on the cross do we have a chance for a new heart and a personal, intimate relationship with God. We are all in the same boat. Recognize that while God will vindicate your suffering, he also loves the person or people who caused it. This can be a hard truth to swallow. We want God to take our side when we are wronged. And he is on the side of the oppressed. But he loves the oppressor and has plans to bring a uniquely suited vindication to his or her life as well.

Start to see in a new light those who have wronged you. Ask God to change your mind about these offenders. Jesus said, "love your enemies, do good to those who hate you, bless those who curse you, pray for those who mistreat you" (Luke 6:27–28). We may not want to love those who hurt us. Blessing our enemies goes against everything we feel. But with God's help, we can do our part. Freedom will come this way, and freedom is part of our own vindication.

It took me a long time to battle through this understanding of God's provisions, and for much of that time, due to my own choices, I had little outside guidance. For eighteen months I kept silent about Ted's affairs, behaving with even my closest friends and family members as if all were well. Ted and I told only our pastor and his wife about our situation. No one else.

With Ted traveling so often to follow my father's ministry, the loneliness and the sense of helplessness I experienced during this period were often agonizing. But this was not the first time I had covered up problems in my marriage. By the time I learned of Ted's infidelity, I was very familiar with the art of masking; and now in my hour of deepest need, I fooled many who knew me best. I suppose I shouldn't have been surprised. In many respects, I had had a lifetime of practice.

Reminders for Painful Times

- Recognize that God is in control of your life. He promises he will bring good out of your circumstances and mistakes. Use Scripture to praise God and to pray for yourself.
- Review your "Praise" list and use it as a springboard for praise.
- Talk to God about any sin in your life. Ask God to forgive you, and tell him you want to make things right. Plan to address any wrongs you have done to others.
- Find time daily to be with God and to read his Word.
- Ask God to help you see in a new light those who have hurt you.

Tips for Those Who Care

- Reflect on what God has already done in the life of your hurting friend or loved one, and praise God for being in control of your friend's situation. Use the Scriptures as you pray.
- Remind yourself that only God has the power ultimately to heal your friend or loved one.
- Ask God to help you become a "safe place" for your friend, a channel of God's wisdom, grace, and love.
- Encourage your friend to spend time in prayer and Bible reading each day.

MEMORY VERSES

Lamentations 3:22–24 KJV

It is of the LORD's mercies that we are not consumed, because his compassions fail not.

They are new every morning: great is thy faithfulness.

The LORD is my portion, saith my soul; therefore will I hope in him.

Principles for Reflection

*God is in control. God provides his presence,
his Word, and his vindication.*

NO ONE KNOWS— SHOULD I KEEP IT THAT WAY?

The Impulse of Isolation

The wind stung my face as I opened the car door and stepped onto the asphalt. I had parked in a back parking lot. Yards away stood the building. I pulled my coat tightly around me and prepared to walk briskly to a back entrance. I was chilly, but I was hurrying for another reason. As I made the dash from my car, I said a prayer. *Lord, please don't let anyone see me.* I had scheduled the last appointment of the day in the hope that the coast would be clear and the building all but empty. Under no circumstances did I want to be spotted walking into a counselor's office.

I got to the back door unnoticed and entered the building, stepping into a small waiting area. Then I looked up, and my heart sank. Someone else was there. I thought about turning around and leaving, but I decided against it. The woman had already seen me, so what was the use? I sat down, picked up a magazine, and began flipping through it. I couldn't focus on the pages. I felt jittery, woozy. My hands were shaky. What was I doing here? What would I say? A few minutes later, the counselor called me into his office and motioned toward a comfortable chair. As I took my seat, I noticed a box of tissues on a nearby table. Eyeing the tissues, I smoothed my skirt and made up my mind I would not need them.

⌒

It was autumn in Philadelphia. Ted and I, now married for five years, were settled in our second home. Ted was making a wonderful living for us. Noelle was still a baby, and I was just twenty-three. I was busy learning the ropes of mothering. My life was filled with good things. But the center of my world— my marriage relationship—was off-kilter. Ted and I seemed to argue constantly.

One evening when Ted was out of town, I decided to take Noelle to a friend's house and share a pizza dinner. My friend and I had a pleasant evening with our children, and before it got too late, I packed up Noelle's things and we went home. When I arrived at the house, I was surprised to find Ted had already returned from his trip. As I went to greet him, I could see something was wrong. An argument erupted. His temper flared. My frustration reached a boiling point, and before I knew what I was doing, I grabbed the package of pork chops I had left thawing on the kitchen counter and threw it at my husband.

Ted told this story to friends years later, laughing about the fact that I had been out of character and mad enough to throw pork chops at him. But at the time, I had begun to realize Ted and I had serious problems. I had never seen my own parents express anger toward one another, and I did not know how to respond to Ted when we quarreled. I wanted to learn where I was responsible for conflict. I felt terribly inadequate as a wife. Things simply had to get better.

Reluctantly, I decided to seek professional counseling. Having to pursue outside help with my personal life was, to me, a sign of weakness, indicative as well of a spiritual failure. I was embarrassed and ashamed to need a counselor. Wasn't faith enough? I was the child of a gifted evangelist. Shouldn't I be able to work out my problems by praying and by studying the Scriptures? This approach had been good enough for my parents and grandparents, my role models in the faith. I wanted to be like them—victorious in difficulty, intimate with God, able to overcome the obstacles before me. Wasn't that what the world expected of me? Wasn't that what I expected of myself? Yet here I was failing, first, in my marriage and, second, in my ability to make amends. I felt like a disgrace. In my mind, I was nowhere close to measuring up.

It was clear something needed to change in my marriage, and at this point, I was willing to risk embarrassment to get help. Or, I should say, I was willing to risk embarrassment but would do whatever I could to curtail the potential for it. My name was known in some circles, and I feared exposure like nothing else. I had kept my marriage difficulties from even my closest friends and family members.

After flipping through the Yellow Pages, I ended up contacting a counselor I had heard speak at a local Christian Women's Club luncheon some months earlier. The gentleman's talk at the luncheon had stirred my heart, and I had found myself wishing I could talk to him then. At that point, counseling still was not an option in my mind, but remembering this man now, I decided to look him up. He was discreet in arranging for me to come to his office late in the day, and when I hung up the phone, I felt some relief. Perhaps the counselor would be able to help me after all.

The day of my appointment I asked some friends to keep Noelle and explained only that I was "going to see the doctor." I felt a little guilty for not being entirely forthcoming, but again, I did not want to make myself vulnerable. I felt safer keeping things to myself—though I was sure my friends could read "going to a counselor" on my forehead. Pulling out of their driveway, I felt my heart begin to race. What if it turned out the counselor *couldn't* help? I was afraid. I was risking. I was going to make myself vulnerable to a stranger.

UNDERSTANDING THE IMPULSE OF ISOLATION

By this time, keeping my marital difficulties a secret had become a relatively routine practice for me. Since Ted and I had struggled with our relationship from the get-go, I had learned to hide the truth about my marriage almost from day one. Not that masking my heart's true condition was easy. The transition from schoolgirl to wife was hard on me, even without the quarreling. Being so young, I didn't know the first thing about life, and from the moment Ted and I departed for our honeymoon I was terribly homesick. Seated around me on the airplane to Hawaii were ecstatic young women anxious to see their husbands and boyfriends just returned from Vietnam, while I, a newlywed, sat next to my husband in tears. I was unprepared for married life. I was clingy, insecure, and dependent on Ted to be my whole world. When our marriage proved unstable, I simply did not know what to do. I did not believe I could ask anyone to advise me. Rather, I put on my mask, hunkered down, and resigned myself to tackling my marriage problems on my own. Other than my stint in counseling—which ended shortly after it began because Ted appeared to me to be disinterested—my journal was my only outlet.

Why do we isolate ourselves with our struggles? Pride, fear of being judged, fear we will disappoint those we esteem, to name a few of our reasons. I hid my marriage troubles from even those I trusted, partly because I believed my difficulties with Ted reflected badly on me as a wife. I did not want my loved ones to see me as a failure. I had a poor self-image as it was, and I feared my shame would only increase—or become more real, more defined—if the truth were spoken aloud in the presence of others.

We also mask our hardships for reasons that seem noble to us. So often while trying to work on my marriage, I wrestled with the idea that I was responsible for God's reputation. As a member of my father's family, I felt I had to set an example for others, keep all the rules, and make God look good. My parents never pressured me to uphold any image, but, again, I considered my role models. They seemed able to do all the right things and, when circumstances went awry in their lives, to keep their chins up.

Somewhere down the line I became confused and started believing that keeping my chin up—or making God look good—meant demonstrating I could be perfectly whole even in struggles, regardless of what I truly was experiencing. I wanted to prove I could rejoice in my trials and walk in contentment, irrespective of circumstances. This impulse partly came out of an honest desire to illustrate with my life the truth of Scripture. God told the apostle Paul, "'My grace is sufficient for you, for power is perfected in weakness'" (2 Corinthians 12:9). In every way I wanted my life to exemplify that Jesus was enough, that Christianity really worked. Can you see the trap I fell into?

What I would discover after Ted's infidelity came to light was that masking my hurts and defects—pretending I had everything together—was not the way to honor God or prove that Christianity worked. No one is perfect. The Scripture above from 2 Corinthians reads, "power is perfected in *weakness*" (emphasis mine). Our commendable longing to uphold God's name becomes misguided when we try to do so by acting the part and hiding our weakness. Only by dealing honestly with ourselves and with others do we make room for Jesus to move with power in our circumstances. Only then is he truly glorified in our lives.

Unfortunately, we so often sit in our church pews, pretending that the people who need help are on the outside, as if we on the inside lack nothing and never make bad choices. We smile and look happy and victorious, all the while nursing our broken hearts, afraid to acknowledge our problems because we do not want to make God look bad. We strain and struggle to position ourselves as people who have all of the answers. We fight to make Christianity look like a success. But this is not our job. The premise for entering the church—for deciding to follow Christ—is admitting that we are sinners in need of a Redeemer, that we cannot make it on our own, that we cannot restore our own ruins. We will exhaust ourselves trying to do what only God can do. He wants us to be still and know that *he* is God (Psalm 46:10).

Of course, there are very good reasons to be careful about sharing our personal experiences. If constantly pretending that all is well qualifies as one extreme, then ever exposing our deepest disappointments, hurts, and longings is another. We must strive for balance. The Bible instructs, "Watch over your heart with all diligence, For from it flow the springs of life" (Proverbs 4:23). The New International Version reads, "*guard* your heart" (emphasis mine). To guard our hearts is to be wise with the intimate details of our lives. We wear our hearts on our sleeves at the risk of harm to ourselves and to others. We do not have to tell everything. Privacy is important. The voice of Wisdom in Proverbs says, "I wisdom dwell with prudence" (Proverbs 8:12 KJV). We are to be prudent—cautious and discerning—about what we choose to share.

We need to be particularly mindful to watch out for the privacy of those with whom we are in covenant relationship—especially our spouses. I kept my marriage problems quiet in some measure to protect my husband's name; Ted's reputation was in my hands for safekeeping. Inscribed in his wedding band was a verse from Proverbs: "The heart of her husband doth safely trust in her" (Proverbs 31:11 KJV). I wanted to be the kind of wife my husband could trust. Protecting him, I believed, was my business. The Bible teaches that marriage is sacrosanct. Marriage is bigger than whatever problems arise between two people, bigger than just one couple. As a picture of Christ and his bride—the church—marriage is to be treated as inviolable. My mother often points to a verse from Proverbs: "love covereth all sins" (Proverbs 10:12 KJV). *Love covers.* Love keeps the mistakes of others from view. Love does not expose and make vulnerable. Love creates safety for those who are its objects. This does not mean we cover up abuse, but it does mean we look out to guard the honor of those we love and to whom we are joined in marriage.

So how do we find the balance between wise privacy and healthy openness? I am still learning how. In the early years of my marriage, I had a difficult time of it. I guarded my marriage to my own—and perhaps the relationship's—detriment. I lived the best way I knew how and tried to serve God in the process, but fiercely masking my difficulties eventually took its toll on me. And yet, as

I later came to understand, God honored even my smallest attempts to live for him during this period. Isolated as I was with my hurts and disappointments, God saw my heart. He knew my condition, and his unchanging goal was to make me whole. In his great mercy, he reached behind my mask, put his hand on my deepest hurts, and worked consistently for my good.

GOD WORKS BEHIND OUR MASKS

As I have written, God used my endeavors and daily activities during the years leading up to my birthday conversation with Ted to make me healthier and to prepare me for the crisis in my marriage. One experience stands out as particularly transformative—a Bible study series I taught in Virginia before I learned of Ted's infidelities. Again, I was just living and doing the next thing—teaching Bible as I always had done in one format or another. But unbeknownst to me, God was working through this experience to lay an important spiritual foundation in my life, one I would need, not only to survive the crisis with Ted, but also to begin gradually moving out of isolation and into a more honest and balanced way of living.

In Virginia, I taught Bible to a group of women from our community. This class was the most rigorous of those in which I had been involved over the years, and perhaps the most fulfilling. I spent my mornings and afternoons writing Bible study curricula and preparing for class. Ted worked out of his office in the barn, and we would meet together for lunch. Though I still worked part-time for Harper & Row, the Bible class had come to seem like a full-time job. I started studying when the kids left for school and usually worked until they came home.

The most interesting series I taught in those years, the series I have in mind now, I named "Enjoying God," playing off titles of books by J. I. Packer—*Knowing God*—and Charles Colson—*Loving God*. I wanted to emphasize the enjoyment of God, which implied personal and emotional involvement with him. To me, enjoyment spoke of feeling at home. I realized that if we could not feel at home with God, then we would never feel at home anywhere. We would never feel wholly comfortable being ourselves; and our ability to love freely—even to live freely—would be hindered.

I planned to draw material for the series out of the book of Isaiah. I love the Old Testament, and I wanted to teach my class that the God of the Old Testament was not a harsh being looking for opportunities to punish us, as some people believe. I saw warmth, love, and a reaching out in the God of the Old Testament. My desire for all of us in the class was to explore and more personally experience the depth of God's character as illustrated in this part of Scripture.

For a homework exercise in one of the early weeks, I instructed the women to imagine crawling into God's lap and calling him Daddy. I wanted to stress intimate relationship with God as the key to enjoying him. I have found that Christian believers do not always think of God intimately as a daddy, much less imagine crawling into his lap. To my class, I think, the very assignment seemed peculiar. I remember there being a kind of subtle but perceptible shock when I described it.

In fact, all of us—including me—had difficulty doing the assignment. The struggle to get over the awkwardness made us wonder. Why couldn't we envision God as a daddy? Why were we timid approaching him? What was our understanding of God? Was this understanding incomplete, or even wrong?

In the process of answering these questions, we found that our images of God were colored by difficult perceptions of our earthly fathers. My own memories were of my father being absent much of the time. My father has written about his regret and the deep sense of loss he suffered as a result of having to be away from home so much during our childhood years. Clearly, God appointed him to a special calling in life that put incredible demands on him. My dad did his best to compensate for his schedule during the time he was at home with us. I loved him dearly, and I knew he loved me. I just thought he was busy with the needs of others. Now as an adult, I came to realize I imagined God in much the same way.

The discomfort my class and I experienced trying to do the homework assignment only confirmed for me the significance of the study series. I realized it was vital for us to be able to enjoy God as a daddy and know him intimately as his children. Scripture teaches that through Christ we "have received a spirit of adoption . . . by which we cry out, 'Abba! Father!'" (Romans 8:15). The name *Abba,* an Aramaic word for "father," connotes a level of warmth and intimacy—as does the English word "daddy"—that for Christian believers is critical in our relationship with God. God is not just our father; he is our daddy. Consider the difference. "Father" connotes a role, "daddy" a role plus depth of affection. So much in our Christian walk hinges on that depth of affection. If we view God as distant or disinterested, then we will miss the very message of Scripture: that God came near in the person of Jesus. We will fail to grasp the power of Christ's atonement: that a loving father, a daddy, sent his beloved and only son to die for the love of us, his children. While we must reverence God as our creator, we must also know him personally in an intimate, affectionate relationship. Otherwise we miss out. We miss the point of our faith.

In the weeks following the class's attempt at my original assignment, I walked us through a careful examination of God's character as found mainly in the book of Isaiah. We meditated on God's tenderness, his forgiveness, and his comfort. We learned that God's desire is to set us free. We talked about belonging to God as his children. We came to understand that God loves us so much he chooses us to be his own. We examined his promise to restore us and grappled with the power of his love. As our class was drawing to an end, we tried the homework assignment again. This time some of us—including me—could do it successfully.

ENJOYING GOD

Can you do the exercise I assigned my Bible class? Can you visualize spending intimate time in the arms of God? Can you call him Daddy? Let's try it together. Begin by relaxing. Forget yourself for a few moments. Let go of the cares of the day. Take a deep breath, and allow your mind to become still. Now imagine you are sitting quietly with God in a comfortable place. You are sitting beside him, close to him. He turns to you and smiles affectionately. "How are you?" he asks. You answer him, telling him about your day, your family, and your friends. He listens, gazing into your eyes. You talk for a while and then look to him for a response. But he is quiet. He asks you again, "How are you?"

You are perplexed by his asking a second time. In a moment, you realize you are uncomfortable. You look at him, searching his face. What does he mean? He says nothing. In his eyes you see love and concern. Why doesn't he explain? You become anxious, fearful. Sitting there, confused, you begin to cry. He puts his arms around you and strokes your arm. You rest your head on his shoulder, and your cries become sobs. You find that you are crawling up into his lap and pressing hard against his chest. It feels good to let your emotions go. As you weep, you begin to share your feelings with God. You pour out your heart—your fears, your hurts, memories of when you were rejected, your feelings of insecurity, your sins, your lack of love and joy, your selfishness, your anger and bitterness, even toward God. Even toward him. Where was he when you needed him? Why has he allowed all these hurts in your life? You've tried to please him, but it never seems to be enough. Now you are weary. So weary. Why?

Soon you become quiet. You are exhausted, spent of emotion. Resting now in God's arms, you turn and look up at his face. His cheeks are wet with tears. He says, "My precious one, I love you. I do not reject you. I have always loved you." You glance down at his hands, and for the first time, you see his wounds. Suddenly, a new understanding of his love sweeps over you. God is wounded for you. He hurts for you. His heart breaks for you. Your suffering grieves him deeply. You look into his eyes and see not condemnation, but love—a more profound love than you have ever seen before. Your heart is moved with tenderness. You draw closer to God now and say, "I love you, Daddy." He kisses and embraces you. Peace settles over you. You feel safe with him, at home, secure. Take a moment and rest in that feeling; it is contentment. When you are ready, quietly come out of the exercise and thank God for his nearness to you.

Were you able to visualize and relate to God in an intimate way? In what settings can you imagine experiencing closeness with him? Perhaps you see God as more of a distant figure than you realized. Perhaps your relationship with your earthly father makes understanding God as a daddy seem virtually impossible. If this is the case, then please understand you are not alone. So many people come from broken homes or dysfunctional families. So many people still carry deep wounds from childhood—wounds that resulted from neglect, rejection, or abuse. These experiences make it difficult for us to see God as a warm, intimate, loving daddy, and they can be difficult to overcome. But God longs for you to succeed. He will help you to see him as he truly is; as you try, he will rush to aid you in your slightest attempt.

Depending on the severity of your issues, you may need to seek counseling or begin using books, workbooks, or other resources to help you work through your past hurts. Whatever God leads you to do, pray for the strength to act on behalf of your healing. Do not languish in a relationship with God that is remote and awkward. To grow in God—to become all that we were made to be—we must be intimate with him. He wants you to feel safe with him. He wants you to be whole. He does not want you to be hobbled by the past. He is on your side. He wants you to know him and trust him. Does that seem impossible? God understands. He will lead you as you pursue healing, but you must pursue it. Pray for courage. God will walk with you. He will be gentle. He will always seek the very best for you.

It wasn't until many months after teaching "Enjoying God" that I began to grasp the Bible study's significance in my own life. Prior to learning of my husband's infidelities, I was isolated with my hurts from others, but I was also, in some ways, distant from God. I needed a foundational understanding of God's role in my life as *Abba*. I was not as intimate with him as I needed to be to withstand the coming storm in my personal life. Through the Bible study, God broke down my false perceptions of his character so I could draw closer to him in relationship and dare to trust him with greater abandon. In fact, this increased intimacy with God was also the first step toward balance in my relationships with others. Our movement out of isolation begins with our relationship with God. We must learn to trust him first; only then can we venture to trust people. And it is to our great advantage to learn to do both.

COSTS OF ISOLATION

Though God certainly worked in my life during the years I was isolating myself with my pain, eventually all of the masking and getting by caught up with me, and I began to awaken to the costs of isolation. (This awakening itself was evidence of God's grace operating in my life.) Though I was learning to grow in intimacy with God, at the same time I found myself less and less able to express emotion day-to-day. I got to a point where I rarely cried. I could not feel deeply. I was on autopilot—all of the time. I was doing and saying the right things. But on the inside I felt lifeless. My emotions were locked away; I had nowhere I felt I could safely express them. This is one of the costs of isolation—our emotions shut down. Our hearts become cold.

When we allow our hearts to grow cold, we can unknowingly put ourselves in a precarious spiritual position. For when our hearts glaze over and shut down, when we can no longer feel, we run the risk of our *love* growing cold—our love for others and, ultimately, our love for God. Love is what keeps us connected to God. Jesus told his disciples, "Just as the Father has loved Me, I have also loved you; abide in My love" (John 15:9). Love is the great commandment. We are to love the Lord with all our heart, soul, strength, and mind, and love our neighbor as ourselves (Luke 10:27). God made us for love. He does not want our love to grow cold. He knows that, unable to love, we will fall away from him. We will cease to "abide" in him, and we will lose our ability to succeed in our purpose. As Jesus taught, "I am the vine, you are the branches; he who abides in Me, and I in him, he bears much fruit; for apart from Me you can do nothing" (John 15:5).

Another cost of isolation—one that flows out of our emotionally oppressed condition—is the stifling effect that hiding our problems has on our worship life. During my early years in Virginia, for instance, I began to notice I was holding back in corporate worship at my church, even missing out on opportunities to receive ministry from God, for fear of letting my mask slip. I did not want people to think I might have needs, problems, or weaknesses. At times during the worship service, our leaders would call people with specific needs to come to the altar at the front of the sanctuary in order to affirm spiritual decisions or commitments before God. I remember watching others move forward in these moments and wishing I could go forward too. But each time, the familiar caution surfaced in my mind: I was Billy Graham's daughter. I had to remember the image I had imposed on myself: Life was supposed to be perfect. I was supposed to be victorious in all areas of my life.

Ultimately, I came to see I was withholding myself from God in these instances. *He* was calling me to go forward in worship on various occasions, and I, though not willfully so, was refusing. I did not want to refuse. I wanted to be free to go forward. I wanted to change, and for that I desperately needed God's guidance. I had been living isolated behind a mask for all of my adult life. Getting free and learning to live honestly would be a difficult process. I did not know what to do, and God understood this. Once he put me on the road to emotional healing, he stayed with me for the journey. He did not leave me to figure it out on my own.

BREAKING FREE FROM ISOLATION

During the Virginia years, many things worked together in my life to encourage me out of isolation before I learned of Ted's infidelities. I did not do everything perfectly, but God never quit working. In particular, I now see how significant a part others played in drawing me out of my shell—God used people to aid in my healing. One was my husband. Though still difficult, my relationship with Ted steadily improved during this time, largely due to his efforts. He worked hard to make things better between us. We spent more time together and learned to communicate more honestly. I felt myself softening toward my husband. My heart began to open, and while we still had a very long way to go in our marriage, I dared to trust Ted on a deeper level than before.

I began to soften in my public worship life as well. Here God used my church family to help me. My pastor, for instance, tended to speak freely in church about his own struggles, and in doing so he created an atmosphere of openness. Listening to him week after week, I began to think, *Maybe struggling is okay. Maybe there is nothing wrong with me. Maybe I can express myself here.* If my pastor had been wearing a mask, if he had been afraid, like I was, to be transparent with his weaknesses, then I might have remained as I was. Hesitant. Fearful. Frustrated. Stuck. Alone. Thankfully, however, I was invited by my pastor's example to change. With his honesty, my pastor built a bridge. I was on one side, trapped in isolation; on the other side were freedom, healing, and comfort in God. My pastor's openness inspired me to take hold of the guardrail and start crossing over. Honesty makes a way for ministry; it breeds courage and, after that, release.

One Sunday morning, I finally mustered the strength of heart to walk up to the altar when the call was given. Our congregation did not have a church building at the time; we worshiped at a synagogue in a nearby city, and the sanctuary was small and intimate. I remember sitting in my seat wondering whether I should get up. I took myself through the litany of reasons to stay seated: People would notice me. I would be exposed. But this time, the litany gave way to my need. I *needed* to go to the front of the church and settle some things in my heart with God. I felt that if I did not go, I would miss out on something important God wanted to do in me. Before I could think about it any further, I stood up at my seat. I wondered briefly what others might be thinking, but the fear passed. Though I was terribly self-conscious as I made my way up the little aisle to the front of the room, I felt free to be myself in a public setting, and the experience was truly refreshing. God assured me he could look after my heritage for a few minutes. My part was simply to focus on him.

Around this time, I also began to crave more freedom in my personal life. I wanted to become healthier emotionally and decided to spend some time delving into my personal issues and past hurts. I was ready to feel again, to have my own thoughts and opinions. I wanted to be myself, to know myself. I was ready to be whole. As it happened, a friend from my prayer group wanted to do the same kind of emotional work, and we committed to spend regular time together. She and I took turns talking things out. Then we prayed with one another, correcting our thoughts and memories with the truth of Scripture. I kept index cards of Bible verses in my purse and pulled the cards out often—at traffic lights, in grocery lines, or waiting for the kids in the car pool—to renew my thinking about my life. I prayed Scriptures out of the book of Ezekiel, asking God to give me a new, soft heart (Ezekiel 36:26). As I worked through this process, using books and study guides, my heart did begin to open. For the first time in years, I started to experience powerful emotions, not all of which were pleasant. When I finally was able to cry, a torrent of feeling came flooding out.

Unmasking is messy. It was messy for me, and it certainly was messy at times for my husband. As I let God unpack years' worth of hurt, Ted was forced to keep up with my fluctuating emotions, and I was not always easy to live with. One minute I would be the efficient, unruffled, together woman Ted knew; the next minute I would be insecure, uncertain, and afraid. Imbalance lingered. I withdrew. I am sure the process was tough on Ted. And yet I believe the work ultimately helped us in our marriage. We were able to talk to one another with continued openness, and this strengthened our relationship, even as it aided my healing. I found that while uncomfortable at times, the process of unmasking was very much worth the price.

Can you relate to any of my experiences? Have you been living behind a mask, hiding your pain and disappointment from others, fearing exposure, covering the truth? Are you isolated with your hurts? Have you resigned yourself to "just getting by" with a difficult situation or dynamic in your life? Perhaps you relate to my experience of feeling emotionally shut down. Do you still dream? Does life have savor? Or are you on autopilot, coasting through your days, feeling little if anything from one day to the next?

If God is showing you areas in which you are trapped in isolation and suffering the costs, then you can begin to ask him to release you. You do not need to be afraid. He will do the work in your life gently and thoroughly. At the tomb of Lazarus, Jesus called his friend back to life from the dead and then commanded the onlookers, "Unbind him, and let him go" (John 11:44). We can make this Scripture our prayer. God can unbind us and let us go from the things that prevent our entering into rich relationships with both him and others. If you are willing, then, right where you are, ask God to set you free.

Keep in mind that this kind of healing work takes time. I first had to see the need for change in my life. Then I had to realize I could not get over the emotional mountain by myself. I needed God's help, and I had to ask for it. As God did his part, I then came to a point when I sensed him leading me to do mine: I had to expend energy and practice commitment to do the work required of me.

I cannot overstate the importance of following God's lead and prompting in a process like the one I undertook. As I noted, God used people to help me at various stages and in different capacities along the way. In the Gospels we read that a paralyzed man in need of healing was carried to Jesus by several friends (Luke 5:17–20). I believed that this story illustrated what I was to do—let some trusted friends and loved ones help me out of my emotional paralysis. Among these were the women in my prayer group. You must ask God to show you what he has in mind for your own unique healing process, and then prepare to let the process work. Count the cost as you must do for any endeavor, and do not expect instant results. Simply expect God's results, for his results are always good.

FOR THE ONE WHO CARES

If you want to help a friend or loved one who is endeavoring to work through some tough emotional issues, then I encourage you to review the story of the paralyzed man in Luke 5. Notice that the man's friends did not ignore his need; they did not abandon him to a life of immobility. These friends were committed to helping him receive healing. They were willing to give their time and energy. They were available. Further, the friends knew they had to get the sick man to Jesus. Jesus was the healer; they, the friends, were just helpers. So clear were these friends on the power of Jesus alone to heal, they cut a hole in the roof of the house where Jesus was preaching in order to bypass the crowds and get the paralyzed man inside. The friends persevered. They were undaunted and creative in their caregiving.

Try practicing the principles found in this story. If you see that your friend or loved one needs assistance, then make yourself available so God can use you. Pray and ask God to help you address your friend's need in an effective way. Be committed to seeing the process through until God releases you from it. Dedicate your energy to the task at hand as God leads you. As always, remember that Jesus is the healer. Your job is to lead your friend to him. You may need to find creative ways to do this. You may encounter many obstacles. Be open. Do not yield to the temptation to quit if you believe God wants you to help. Ask God to speak to you and show you what to do. He will direct you. You are his servant, and he will not let you down. You can depend on him.

ONE STEP FORWARD, TWO STEPS BACK

When I think about all of the work God did on my heart leading up to my discovery of my husband's infidelities, I marvel. Had the truth been revealed earlier, when I was closed up emotionally, remote from others, and less connected to God, I do not know what would have happened. Again, God knew what was coming, and he was faithful to get my heart ready to handle it. Of course, I did not feel like I was ready to handle it. I felt like a mess. But I did not self-destruct. I was able to persevere.

Even so, with a lifetime of practicing isolation behind me, I was only in my infancy of practicing authenticity. My most natural response to Ted's admission on his birthday was to isolate myself once again. In the days following our initial conversation, I made a firm decision about how I would handle the crisis in our marriage: I would cover Ted and work things out with him. If I could protect my husband and put a tent of safety over our marriage, I believed, then God would have more room to work in the relationship. Ted and I would not be fielding questions or dodging bullets; we could focus, without distraction, on mending the gash in the fabric of our relationship. As I have written, our pastor and his wife, already our close friends, were the only ones in whom we confided. No one else knew for the next year and a half.

I had other reasons for keeping silent. One was profound humiliation. I felt I had failed as a wife in the ultimate way. I reasoned something about me must have driven Ted into the arms of other women. My insecurities multiplied. I did not want to expose what I began to fear was my fault. I could not bear others thinking of me as poorly as I now thought of myself. Telling the truth to even those I loved and trusted would only magnify my disgrace.

Concern for my family's welfare gave me another reason to conceal the truth. I did not want to cause any problems for my parents, who were older now and still having to cope with heavy ministry responsibilities and stress. I did not want to hurt them. I did not want them to think less of Ted. I did not want Ted to lose his job. I did not want to cast a pall over my father's ministry. In light of all this, I knew I had to stop and assess the situation before taking action. I figured Ted and I could work through the issues and make amends, and no one would be the wiser.

But it was a long time that I did the grueling work of maintaining the facade that all was well. Ted traveled a lot, and I needed more support. Looking back, I wish I had sought professional counseling immediately. I wish I had told my family. I felt very alone, and my sense of isolation began to strain my personal relationships with my loved ones. I found myself withdrawing from my family in a marked way, largely fearing I might blow my cover in their presence and betray the truth of what had happened. Over time, even casual conversation became difficult because my burden was so heavy. I lost my perspective; I was not acting like the person my loved ones knew, and the tension, for a time, affected our relationships. This was another cost of isolation.

Though I felt obligated to my initial tack of secrecy concerning my marriage crisis, deep down I did not want to keep pretending. I knew my isolation was unhealthy. Highlighting my emotional confusion, I often fantasized that somehow my parents would discover on their own what I was suffering—that Jesus would reveal it to them in prayer. I would often imagine their responses. They would be so proud of me, I would think. They would praise me for being brave. Such fantasies showed me just how desperately I longed for my loved ones to know the truth, but I still couldn't seem to break my self-imposed silence.

Are you isolated from trusted friends and family with a heavy secret or significant development in your personal life? A diagnosis of illness? A breakdown in your marriage? A crisis with a child? Are you trying to deal with a crisis by yourself? While we must exercise wisdom when it comes to sharing our personal issues, we were not made to carry burdens alone. Yes, we have the Lord, but he gave us people. We do not live in a vacuum. Someone once said that the longer you carry a secret the heavier it becomes. This is true. We need trusted friends and loved ones to help us shoulder the load. Review the costs of isolation detailed in this chapter, and ask God to help you keep these in mind so you don't become deceived about what you can handle.

If you are trying to resolve serious life issues by yourself and would like to reach out for help, I suggest you begin with a trusted pastor or friend, someone who has proven himself or herself to be trustworthy. Be scrupulous. Have you watched the way this person has lived his or her life? Has he or she demonstrated integrity, purity of heart, and moral character in relationships with others? Does this person have your best interests at heart? Can he or she practice good listening? Ask God to lead you and show you whom to approach.

Some circumstances in life require our immediate action. Domestic violence and spousal abuse, for instance, cannot be left unchecked. If you are suffering in an abusive marriage—or if your children are being abused—then get help immediately. You can begin by contacting a church or a local shelter for victims of domestic violence. Do not jeopardize your physical safety or the safety of your children. God is on the side of your security and well-being, and he has given you the spiritual responsibility to take care of your family.

If seeking help for you is not a question of your physical safety or that of your children, then I encourage you to examine your own motives for getting counsel. Do you sincerely want help, or do you want attention and sympathy? Both of these motives in some measure operate in all of us, and a skillful counselor or friend will help keep you in check; but ask God to reveal your heart's true condition now. If you find other motives outweighing your earnest desire for help, then invite God to deal with your emotions and change your heart. Your goal is not to destroy the person who hurt you. Your goal is to heal. Do not forgo counseling because of concern about your motives; just go in with your ears and heart open. If your spouse does not want to go to counseling with you, then that is his or her prerogative. You can only make decisions for yourself. If you believe you need help, then ask God to show you what to do.

FOR THE ONE WHO CARES

If you are the friend or loved one of someone who has been coping alone with heavy life issues, you can begin to create a safe environment for your friend by openly sharing some of your own disappointments and crises. How have difficult situations in your life affected you emotionally? How have you handled your own failures? How has God turned things around for you in tough times? What good has come out of your most profound hurts? Be vulnerable with your friend. Do not be afraid to share your mistakes and weaknesses of character. Your openness will assure your friend that you are not judging him or her by the circumstances in which your friend finds himself or herself. Remember the example of my pastor. Honesty builds a bridge to the one who is hurting and isolated. Though it is important to be sensitive and to know when to quit talking, your transparency will inspire courage in your friend or loved one; and he or she needs courage to come out of isolation.

You may need to help by being a sounding board as your friend examines his or her motives for seeking your counsel. Ask God to help you lead your friend. You may find it beneficial to share about your own motives during past crises. Perhaps you wanted attention or revenge after being hurt, and God showed you that your approach was misguided— that you, in fact, were the one needing to change. I know I have had such awakenings in my life. Sharing these kinds of things with your hurting friend will help create a nonthreatening atmosphere and promote honesty. If your friend or loved one keeps going over and over the same issues and does not seem willing to move forward, then you may need to back away for a time and wait. As always, ask God to lead you.

I broke the silence about my ordeal with Ted not by choice exactly—it was more like necessity that drove me to change course. I had come to the end of myself. The mounting pressure in my relationship with Ted had become excruciating. There were certain issues and dynamics we simply could not overcome. We were stuck. We had been stuck for a long time, and I knew it.

An argument one November morning finally put me over the edge. I knew I needed to be out of Ted's presence. I knew where I needed to go and whom I needed to see, and I realized I had to go right then. I would have come emotionally unglued otherwise. I couldn't cope anymore. I was out of steam, out of strength. And I no longer had the will to keep up the fight.

After Ted left on an errand, I packed my bags and left the house. I did not tell anyone where I was going. Our three children were aware of conflict between their parents, but they knew nothing of the specifics. I hid as much of my own pain as was humanly possible. On this particular morning, however, I knew I was treading on thin emotional ice, and I realized if I did not leave, we all would suffer for it. The season of covering the truth was over. Restraint was not something I could exercise any longer. Everything, it seemed, depended on my getting to solid ground.

Reminders for Painful Times

⤳ Try the "Enjoying God" exercise. If you struggle to imagine God in so intimate a way, pray for the courage to examine what hinders you. Commit to doing what is necessary to deepen your relationship with God. He wants you to succeed, and he will help you.

⤳ If you have isolated yourself with pain and disappointment and find your emotions have shut down, you can ask God to unbind you and let you go. Follow his lead as you begin to do the necessary emotional work.

⤳ If you are isolated with a serious life issue or crisis and would like to seek help, you can begin by approaching a pastor or friend who has proven himself or herself to be trustworthy. Pray and ask God to lead you to the right person.

⤳ Examine your motives. Do you sincerely want help or do you want attention? Do you want revenge? If negative motives outweigh your desire for help, ask God to change your heart. Do not forgo counseling. Just go in with an open heart.

⤳ If your situation threatens your safety or the safety of your children, seek help immediately.

Tips for Those Who Care

⤳ Practice the principles found in the story of the paralyzed man in Luke 5. Be available to help your wounded friend or loved one. Be committed. Be creative in your approach and depend on God. Lead your friend to Jesus, the Healer.

⤳ Create a safe environment for your friend by being transparent about your own struggles, failures, and disappointments. Your frankness will give your friend courage to be open—if not now, then down the road.

⤳ Ask God to lead you as you invite your friend to examine his or her own motives for seeking help. Be honest about your own motives during past crises.

MEMORY VERSE

Romans 8:15

For you have not received a spirit of slavery leading to fear again, but you have received a spirit of adoption . . . by which we cry out, "Abba! Father!"

Principles for Reflection

The longer you carry a secret the heavier it becomes. We can find a balance between wise privacy and healthy openness as we learn to trust God first, and then others.

DO I HAVE WHAT IT TAKES TO FORGIVE?
The Ongoing Struggle of Forgiveness

Mother knew I was coming. I left the Shenandoah Valley at lunchtime, and when I got as far as Black Mountain, North Carolina, I stopped and called my pastor back in Virginia to check in. Before I left the Valley, he told me he would phone Mother to let her know I was on the way. He now confirmed he had done so, and after we hung up, I dialed Mother's number. She was upbeat. "Are you almost here?" she asked. Only Montreat Road and our steep private driveway separated me from Little Piney Cove. Now more than ever, I needed the comfort of its log walls, my mother's understanding, and my old bed. I needed the familiarity of "home."

The afternoon light was turning dim, and the air was cooler here than in the Valley. Thanksgiving was just days away. I got back into the car, tears running down my face, and prayed. *God, help.* I was afraid, nervous, anxious.

For a year and a half I had imagined this trip, turning it over and over in my mind. Should I tell my parents? Should I tell them the awful truth? What impact would their knowing have on Ted? Would my disclosure permanently damage his relationship with my parents? Would Mother and Daddy think me a terrible failure? Could I bear the shame? Could I bear them showing compassion for Ted?

Until now I had been able to convince myself that shouldering the weight of the secret reflected great strength on my part. I was protecting my marriage, wasn't I? I was working everything out with Ted. We were conferring only with our pastor and his wife. We were working it out with Jesus. Wouldn't my parents commend me for handling my problem this way?

Yet after eighteen months of private struggle with Ted, I no longer could maintain the pretense that all was well. I had hit a wall. I realized I desperately needed my parents, and I was on the way home to tell Mother what had happened. Just to tell her. I was not looking for answers or advice. I was afraid of those things; I was in too delicate a condition to receive instruction. I just needed love and understanding. Like a little girl, I longed to climb into her arms and be consoled.

But at the same time, I was scared. I did not want to burden Mother. "I'm concerned about telling her," I had explained to my pastor that afternoon before leaving town. "She's sixty-eight and physically frail."

"You're thirty-seven and emotionally fragile," he said.

It was true. Depression had overtaken me like a thick fog. Fleeting thoughts of suicide came and went. I struggled just to get out of bed. The weariness, the nearly all-consuming frustration, the self-loathing, the sense of injustice—these were too much to continue to bear.

When I got to Little Piney Cove, Mother greeted me warmly. We sat down to a bowl of soup and chatted. I kept the conversation off of me, and Mother did not probe. I marveled at her. She was so cheerful, calm, and steady; yet I knew she was suffering the intense pain of degenerative arthritis. Talking with her, aware of her condition and the weight of her responsibilities, I found that my problems suddenly seemed less significant. Was my telling her about Ted truly necessary now? The infidelities had ended some years ago. Couldn't I just get over it and move forward?

I convinced myself it would be unwise to say anything about the matter that night, as I imagined Mother would worry and be unable to sleep. In truth, whatever she might have been suffering physically, Mother was anything but emotionally frail. Quite the opposite—she drew on tremendous emotional and spiritual reserves. Over the span of my life, I had watched her commune with God in a deep, unrelenting way. Her life depended on her friendship with Christ, and her formidable strength came from him.

But how would she respond to me when I told her? Mother was not naive—she definitely had seen reality's less palatable side. She was also fiercely protective of her children and would do all in her power to keep them from harm. Then again, Mother had lived her life demonstrating total acceptance toward the many and often wayward individuals she met along her way. I simply had no idea what to expect from her: shock, compassion, sorrow, mercy toward Ted? I did not know.

Nor did I even know what to tell her. I had been the sunny-dispositioned, "good" child in the family. As the middle child of five, I had always tried not to rock the boat or draw attention to myself. I wanted to please my parents. I was easygoing and adaptable, and I kept my true feelings hidden. I had certainly never unloaded anything as burdensome as what I was now planning to share with Mother. However badly I wanted to be nurtured by her, the prospect of such vulnerability, such exposure, made me very ill at ease. It was far outside the bounds of my comfort zone. I retired to my room anxious about what the next morning would hold. And afraid.

Growing up, we children were fortunate enough to have had our own bedrooms. My youngest brother, Ned, was ensconced in what is now a small linen closet until my oldest sister, Gigi, moved out of the house and got married. Then the rest of us—Anne, Franklin, Ned, and me—shifted rooms. I ended up with my older sister Anne's original room, which was situated under the eaves of our cabin-style house and overhung by a beamed ceiling. Mother had since decorated the room in pink and furnished it with an antique four-poster bed, dresser, nightstand, overstuffed chair, and bookshelves loaded with volumes on the British royal family—we shared an interest in all things royal.

That night, I noticed a stack of magazines in the hall outside my room. Unable to sleep, I thought I would distract myself by flipping through some of the issues. One contained a stress test, which I decided to take. The results confirmed what I already knew: that my stress level was off the charts. I made note of the magazine's assessment and prescription in my journal: You are "showing severe signs of distress from overwork and need to change your [life]style drastically. Seek help from a professional if necessary."

Okay, I thought. *My emotional condition is real. My being here to talk to Mother is legitimate.* I was looking for anything to validate my being home at this point. Even a late-night stress test from an outdated magazine brought comfort and the assurance that I was doing the right thing.

Early the next morning, I went downstairs to start brewing the coffee and opened my *Daily Light,* a devotional I had been using since the age of thirteen. I read this Scripture from Isaiah: "And I will bring the blind by a way that they knew not; I will lead them in paths that they have not known: I will make darkness light before them, and crooked things straight. These things will I do unto them, and not forsake them" (Isaiah 42:16 KJV).

Reading this verse, I sensed a quiet inner knowing. I could open my heart to Mother; I would be okay. God was reminding me of a principle he had underscored repeatedly since I first learned of Ted's betrayals—he, the Lord, knew my course. I remembered another key verse God had given me out of Job: "But He knows the way I take; When He has tried me, I shall come forth as gold" (Job 23:10).

He knows the way I take. God knew what was happening in my life, and he knew what I would do. Though mine would be an unfamiliar path—a way I did not know—God would be there with me; I would not travel alone. I thought of my three foundational principles: God loved me. He would lead me. He would bring good out of my circumstances.

After I finished spending time with God that morning, I joined Mother where she was sitting in the bay window area of the kitchen. She was dressed in her robe and gazing out toward the mountain vista to which she awoke every day. The fog had rolled in, and the bare trees were vaguely etched against the all-consuming gray. The flower boxes beneath the window ledges were empty. The fire, blazing in the stone hearth, made the log room seem cozy and inviting.

I poured another cup of coffee and settled into the overstuffed chair beside my mother. Then, gathering my courage, I began.

"Mom," I said. "I've come home to talk."

THE OLDER BROTHER

When I shared my situation with Mother, I sketched out what had happened between Ted and me, telling her of the infidelities and some of the circumstances. I did not color in the lines or give many details. Mother's relationship with Ted was permanent. Ted would have to fit back into the family. I did not want to make that process impossible. I told Mother that the years of Ted's deception had dissolved my ability to trust him, and that in the absence of trust my feelings had dissolved as well. I explained that, to me, Ted had become the enemy. And yet my goal—in my mind, my only option—was emotional healing. I just did not know how to get there. God would have to build back the love.

Mother comforted me; she let me talk and cry. She told me to rest. She tried to help me sort through my emotions and offered her own thoughts. She spoke to me as a mother to her much-loved child. I felt enormous relief.

Yet as I listened to Mother, I realized she and I were on different pages. It dawned on me that, while I had been dealing with the betrayal issue for more than a year, she was hearing about it for the first time. Now I needed to give her time to catch up. Not wanting to leave her alone with the burden of what I had revealed, I gave her permission to tell Daddy and another close family member.

The prospect of more people learning about my situation caused me tremendous anxiety. I had been living alone with the pain for such a long time. Imagining what others might think or feel or say about me once they found out was frightening to me. I had given up the control that isolation afforded me, and now fear of others' opinions became all-consuming. "Will each of them tell others?" I wrote in my journal. "I cannot bear that. It would hurt Ted, undermine, discourage. Have I done the right thing?"

In fact, my family members loved Ted and showed him compassion. My emotions in the face of this response, however, were mixed. Though I wanted my family to forgive Ted, I also felt threatened by that forgiveness. I recognized there was enough love to go around, but at the same time, I felt I needed allies—people who would circle the wagons around me and focus solely on my needs. As if it were possible, I wanted my loved ones both to forgive Ted and to consider him the enemy right along with me. My feelings conflicted all the time. I tried to give people the chance to respond in their own ways, but I found myself defensive and vulnerable by turns, wanting to control everyone's reactions.

Mostly, I felt like the older brother in the biblical story of the prodigal son. Luke's gospel relates the story of a man who has two sons. The younger son asks his father for his inheritance and takes the money to a faraway land. There the son squanders the inheritance with loose living and winds up working as a keeper of swine. Nearly starving, the son comes to his senses, remembers that his father's hired servants are living and eating better than he, and decides to return home. He plans to declare himself unworthy to be called his father's son and then to ask his father to employ him as a hired man.

As the younger son approaches his father's house, we read, "But while he was still a long way off, his father saw him, and felt compassion for him, and ran and embraced him, and kissed him" (Luke 15:20). The son breaks down before his father and confesses his wrongdoing. But the father's heart is full of love. He calls for his servants to bring out the best robe for his son and to put a ring on his finger and sandals on his feet. Then the father announces a feast and orders his servants to kill a fattened calf, "for this son of mine was dead, and has come to life again; he was lost, and has been found" (verse 24).

Meanwhile, the older brother hears the merrymaking and asks the servants about the commotion. On learning the news of his brother's return, the older son becomes upset and refuses to attend the celebration. When his father implores him, the older son says, "Look! For so many years I have been serving you, and I have never neglected a command of yours; and yet you have never given me a kid, that I might be merry with my friends; but when this son of yours came, who has devoured your wealth with harlots, you killed the fattened calf for him" (verses 29–30).

"My child," the father patiently explains, "you have always been with me, and all that is mine is yours. But we had to be merry and rejoice, for this brother of yours was dead and has begun to live, and was lost and has been found" (verses 31–32).

In my mind, Ted was the prodigal who others believed had repented and "come home." He was being loved on and welcomed back into the fold. I was the older brother who had tried to do everything right, who had not strayed from the path—and I did not feel I was getting the attention or care I deserved. Even though I did not want Ted to be blotted out by my family—to the contrary, I wanted to ensure he would keep his place among us—at the same time, I did not think Ted merited a shower of compassion. I thought *I* needed a shower of compassion. Like the older brother, I believed the discrepancy to be unfair. I was deeply frustrated, and I had a lot to learn.

"FORGIVENESS COSTS SO MUCH"

Soon after I visited with my mother in Montreat, my father called me from St. Martin in the Caribbean. He and Mother had traveled there after Thanksgiving to vacation with some other family members. I became emotional during the phone call with Daddy and had a hard time holding myself together. He told me how much he loved and supported me. He said he knew I had put the struggle into the hands of Jesus. He then asked if I would join them on the island as soon as I could. I agreed to go and began to make plans.

I was nervous about the trip. I did see it as a chance to receive comfort from a tender father. I recorded Isaiah 32:2 in my journal: "And a man shall be as an hiding place from the wind, and a covert from the tempest" (KJV). Beside it I wrote, "Jesus. Daddy?" I wanted my father to cover and protect me.

But I also considered the trip a risk. I was emotionally strung out. I had never related to my family on this level, never brought a major problem to them. I was angry with Ted for putting me in such a vulnerable position. I wrote, "I just need [my family] to hold me, let me bleed."

When I arrived at the house in St. Martin, we all changed into our swimsuits and headed out to the beach to relax in the sun. That night we went out for dinner; and when we got home, we gathered in the living room for evening prayer and Bible reading. Daddy led a special prayer for Ted and me. I began to cry. After my father finished, I told my family that God had been working in Ted's life, that my husband was growing. "But," I explained, "forgiveness costs so much."

We talked about how much forgiveness had cost Jesus—his very life. We discussed examples of former torture victims forgiving their torturers. "Yes," I remarked, "but they did not have to *live* with their torturers." I wept through the whole discussion. My father held me while I cried. "Felt so good," I wrote of his embrace. "Like a sponge being watered."

Over time I discovered that if any aspect of my crisis with Ted seemed insurmountable, it was the issue of forgiveness. The revelation of my husband's betrayal forced me into a personal battle with forgiveness that continued for the next several years. I made a decision to forgive Ted from the moment he admitted he had been unfaithful. But as weeks and months turned into years; as anger raged, then died; as my heart sat vacant of trust, respect, and compassion for my husband, I wondered, *Have I really forgiven him? Wouldn't I feel differently if I had?*

What did forgiveness really mean? What did it look like? As I struggled over the years, at times I saw forgiveness standing like an open door beckoning me with the promise of release. At other times I saw it standing like a wall condemning me because I could not climb over. Then again, once news of my situation became known, forgiveness also seemed like a bludgeon used by some to punctuate their "shoulds" and "oughts." I was discovering that if I did not exhibit the right attitudes or say the right words, then my testimony was negated in the eyes of others because I did not *look* like I had forgiven. I struggled to be real and honest while trying to do what to some people was clearly inadequate. What was forgiveness? I did not know. Everyone seemed to have a definition.

I read somewhere that forgiving meant wiping another person's slate clean as though nothing had happened. My pain was real and still fresh. Something terrible *had* taken place in my life. The fabric of my spirit had been torn, and I could not deny it. Denial is a wonderful thing. But it only works for so long. I couldn't wipe the slate clean—the pain was just too real. Did that mean I hadn't forgiven?

I remembered the adage "forgive and forget." I read a book by that name— *Forgive and Forget: Healing the Hurts We Don't Deserve* by Lewis B. Smedes (New York: Harper & Row, 1984). It is one of the best books I have encountered on forgiveness, and I credit Smedes for influencing much of my thinking on the subject. In his book, he argues that if we forget, we will not forgive. He writes, "You need to forgive precisely because you have not forgotten what someone did. . . . Forgetting, in fact, may be a dangerous way to escape the inner surgery of the heart that we call forgiving" (page 39). Reading these words brought me relief because I knew I needed to forgive. And I could not forget.

I was told I needed to forgive "as God in Christ" had forgiven me. What did *that* mean? I considered this Scripture: "And be kind to one another, tenderhearted, forgiving each other, just as God in Christ also has forgiven you" (Ephesians 4:32). I wanted to forgive God's way, but what did it look like? What did "as God in Christ" amount to in practical terms?

Then I read 2 Corinthians 5:19: "God was reconciling the world to himself in Christ, not counting men's sins against them. And he has committed to us the message of reconciliation" (NIV). This verse explained that God had forgiven *and* reconciled the world. Was that what forgiveness meant—reconciling with the one who has hurt or betrayed? Did forgiveness and reconciliation go hand in hand? Was reconciliation an outward sign of the inner work of forgiveness? Did forgiveness mean not only wiping the slate clean but also continuing to live in an intimate marriage relationship with my husband?

It seemed that if I had truly forgiven Ted, then I should be able to reconcile with him. I wanted to be obedient, but I also knew my life would never be the same. I knew I was a different person. Forgiveness was one thing; reconciliation was beginning to seem like another. I could reconcile with a friend for gossiping about me or excluding me from a social gathering. I could forgive her and then reconcile with her. I could also forgive an employee for embezzling money. But would I put that employee back in charge of my finances? Would I reconcile with him? Would that be wise? Eventually, I came to understand the difference: Forgiveness is unconditional; reconciliation is conditional—it depends largely on the other person.

I wrestled with these issues. I truly did. I wanted answers. But they did not come easily. One day I was on the phone with my uncle Clayton Bell—my mother's brother and a pastor in Dallas. I trusted his depth of insight, so I asked, "How do we forgive as God in Christ forgave us?" Expecting a thoughtful discourse, I heard instead his gentle voice offer just a single word: "Freely."

I felt as though a weight had rolled off my shoulders. I could forgive freely. I had made that choice. When my husband first told me of the infidelities, hadn't I decided right then to forgive him? I struggled with the question of reconciliation, but forgiving freely made sense to me. I honestly could do that. I could forgive and ask nothing in return.

FORGIVENESS IS A "GOD THING"

When we forgive as God in Christ did—freely—we experience freedom. We abandon revenge, even the secret desire for revenge. We give the one who hurt us the opportunity to make a new beginning. We let go of our right to get even. Forgiving freely unties us from the wrong that has been done to us; we no longer have to drag it around with us year after year. As Smedes writes, "Only a free person can choose to live with an uneven score" (*Forgive and Forget,* page 142).

Several years ago, I heard Desmond Tutu, retired Anglican archbishop of Cape Town, South Africa, and 1984 Nobel Peace Prize winner, speak at the University of Virginia. He was in a room with several other Nobel laureates, and I was keenly interested in him. His life's work had been dedicated to opposing—through nonviolent means—South African apartheid and all of its rapacious manifestations. After apartheid's collapse, he chaired South Africa's Truth and Reconciliation Commission and later wrote a book called *No Future Without Forgiveness* (New York: Doubleday, 1999). The archbishop's life stood as a testimony to the freedom available when we forgive. I was captivated by his response to the events of his life and wanted to observe him firsthand.

Watching Archbishop Tutu, I hoped to see if what I thought was real truly *was* real. What kind of a man could this be, I wondered, to have forgiven the grossest human rights violators—murderers, torturers, and conspirators—living in his midst? I studied the archbishop's behavior and body language, watching as he moved about the room and interacted with people. And I was not disappointed. I noticed as he conversed that his face radiated joy. He deferred to others. He laughed easily. This was a man who *lived* in the freedom of forgiveness. I admired him all the more and aspired to experience this same freedom in greater measure than I previously had known.

There is not only freedom but also power in forgiveness—spiritual power. Look at what God's forgiveness through Christ unleashed. It literally changed the world. It started a revolution. No longer was the rule an eye for an eye and a tooth for a tooth. Now the standard for living was this: turn the other cheek, give your cloak also, go the extra mile, love your enemies. Forgiveness isn't easy; it isn't the coward's way. It is the Savior's way.

Why is it so hard to forgive? Why am I slow to do it? Because I am selfish. I am prideful. I do not forgive because I like wallowing in self-pity. I like to play the martyr. I like to nurse my pet injuries. It is easier to complain than it is to forgive. I would rather blame others than take responsibility and do my part. I would much rather blame others. I find it easier to be the self-righteous older brother than the prodigal's forgiving father.

Are you struggling to forgive someone in your life? Are you resisting the struggle? Are you holding on to blame? Let's consider some symptoms of unforgiveness. Ask yourself: When the name of the person who hurt me comes up in a discussion, am I critical? Do I have to take a dig? When I see that person, what is my first thought? Do I think of what he or she did to me? Am I quick to withdraw? Have I built a wall that he or she cannot overcome? Do I cling to *my* view of the hurt, not even trying to see the situation from his or her perspective? And this is the most important question: Can I worship God fully and freely, without any hindrances or issues of conscience blocking me?

I have a friend who once struggled with unforgiveness. One day she asked me to pray with her. I said, "First we're going to have to deal with forgiveness. To experience emotional healing, you're going to have to dig out some issues and work on forgiving." She said, "I can't do that. I won't do that." And because of her hard stance, she was unable to take the next step in her relationship with the Lord. She was still living in unforgiveness. We get stuck when we refuse to forgive. We only harm ourselves. Unforgiveness is like a hot coal. The longer we hold on to it, the deeper and wider it will burn.

Forgiveness is not simply an option to consider. It is a command. "And whenever you stand praying, forgive, if you have anything against anyone; so that your Father also who is in heaven may forgive you your transgressions" (Mark 11:25). Notice the latter half of this verse. We learn that when we forgive—when we obey God's command—we release God to forgive us. Now consider what the consequences can be for one who refuses to forgive. He or she blocks the operation of God's forgiveness in his or her own life.

Forgiveness isn't natural; revenge is natural. Forgiveness is not complacency, though complacency is a very good counterfeit. Forgiving is not excusing or denying the wrongs done to us. So what is forgiveness? Forgiveness is a "God thing"—it is an act of God. When we choose to forgive, we follow the Savior, who when being nailed to the cross said, "Father, forgive" (Luke 23:34). *Father, forgive.* The Savior's forgiveness was not blind or frivolous. Forgiveness is realistic. It looks the offense straight on and calls it what it is—sin. God looked at our sin, named it as such, and said, *Somebody has to die.*

Forgiveness is simple, but it is hard. It is costly, and God knows just how costly it is. He watched as his Son was rejected, abandoned, beaten, humiliated, spit upon, tortured, mocked, and then crucified, suffering one of the most horrible deaths ever imagined by humanity. God did not have to sit by, but he did. Why? So he could forgive me. So he could forgive you.

THE PROCESS OF FORGIVENESS

There is an often-overlooked process of forgiveness. My son, Graham, used to own a state-of-the-art gymnasium in Asheville, North Carolina. People would go to the gym and ask Graham to help them develop workout plans. Graham would customize the plans to suit his clients' individual needs, and before long these new clients would begin showing up regularly at the gym in their workout gear. They would exercise, and they would leave feeling good about themselves for getting with the program.

Then they would try to get out of bed the next morning. Perhaps these novices each asked themselves, *Why did I do this? Why did I start this program? I don't feel any better—only worse!* But if they continued to go to the gym—if they committed to the process—then, yes, pain and soreness would persist, but soon their muscles would become more flexible. They would find themselves getting stronger. And eventually they would be able to gaze with admiration in the gymnasium mirrors, recognizing themselves no longer as novices but pros.

God has given us a workout program called forgiveness. The first time we try it, we do not feel very good. We are stiff, unused to the regimen. But the more we exercise by practicing forgiveness, the less difficult the workout becomes. You may find yourself having to address the same issue in your heart with the same person over and over. I cannot recall how many times I had to say of my husband: "I forgive him for adultery. I forgive him for adultery." I had to live by that mantra for a long time—and I never felt comfortable with it. But the process of forgiveness did become easier. And it will become easier for you. As you practice, you will get better at forgiving. You will find yourself moving in forgiveness—living in it. You will discover the power of it, and the freedom. But you have to exercise. You have to exercise your will.

How do we actually work through the process of forgiveness? I find it helpful to think of the process in stages. My particular stages derive from my own experience, along with an amalgam of teaching I have absorbed over the years.

Step 1: Recognize That You Are Forgiven

The first step is to recognize that we are totally forgiven. If we hope to forgive another person, then we must realize God has forgiven us. Realizing God has forgiven us is not a simple, intellectual acknowledgment. We must be able to receive God's forgiveness in the depths of our being. We need to register this forgiveness on a heart level so the reality of God's grace becomes a part of us. How do we do this? First, we ask God to impart the understanding of forgiveness to us. Once we have prayed, we take action to further internalize the truth of God's forgiveness. For example, I recommend meditating on the crucifixion, on the price God paid to forgive us. We can go to the Scriptures and spend time allowing our emotions and imaginations to engage in the narrative of Christ's passion. I found this practice helped me a great deal. In recent years, I have chosen to hang a crucifix in my room as a constant reminder of the cost of my forgiveness.

Step 2: Make the Choice to Forgive Another

After we recognize that God has forgiven us, we can make the conscious choice to forgive others. Christ's work on the cross was complete; God forgave us completely. So must we forgive those who hurt us. We choose to release the offense altogether. Any offense for which we need to forgive another person is only a shadow of the debt Jesus paid for our forgiveness. Being forgiven so much, we have no right to withhold forgiveness. God's way is the way of forgiveness, and I want to follow him.

Our choice is a matter of our will. We must *decide* that we will walk the way of forgiveness. Once we make the choice, God inhabits our decision and empowers us to fulfill our commitment. If we do not make the choice, then God will not force us. But once we make the commitment, he enters in—and we do need his help! On our own we cannot create a lasting, powerful forgiveness. Only as God activates our choice, as he enables us in this choice, can we effectively forgive. The choice opens a door, inviting God to do the work in our hearts. It is not our work; it is God's work in us. Paul wrote, "I can do all things *through Him* who strengthens me" (Philippians 4:13, emphasis mine).

Keep in mind your imagination can be a huge hindrance to the process of forgiveness. Once my private life became more exposed, I constantly imagined what other people might be thinking or saying about me. I lived my life in the minds of others, obsessed by their opinions. I carried a world of imagined exchanges and confrontations in my head, which only stoked my anger toward my husband. But not everybody was talking about me. They had too much else to do. I had to go back to the principles I learned from Jeremiah and remember that God was going to be my vindicator. He was going to make it all fair; he was going to make it right in the end. My part was simply to forgive.

Our emotions also can get us in trouble. I might make the choice to forgive, but then the offender walks through the door—and I feel that anger, I feel that resentment. I found I had to return time and again to my original decision to forgive my husband. My emotions were so erratic I constantly wondered if I really had forgiven. To help myself, I recorded in my Bible the date I chose to forgive Ted. When negative emotions tempted me to believe I had not forgiven, I went back to that date and purposefully remembered my decision.

When I consider my battle with my emotions, I picture in my mind one of those blow-up clowns children play with—the kind that is weighted at the bottom. Every time you punch the clown, it rights itself. Why? Because of the weight in the bottom. Forgiveness is like that weight. Emotions will come and knock us off-balance. But the decision, the choice, to forgive will right us again. Anger will come, but our decision will bring us back to center. With every blow, we will become more adept at regrouping. We will learn not to hit the floor every time our emotions surge.

Step 3: Use God's Word to Correct Your Thinking

Third, we must use God's Word to correct our thinking. This too is a process, and it takes time. God's timeline is eternal, remember? I remember thinking that, once I made the choice to forgive my husband, our relationship would snap back to normal and we would go on with our lives. It didn't happen that way. I had to stay in the Scriptures and choose to believe what they said: that God was with me, that he knew the way I would take, that he would not fail me or forsake me, that he had good plans for my life. So often my own thoughts and feelings ran contrary to Scripture. But the Bible explains we are to take "every thought captive to the obedience of Christ" (2 Corinthians 10:5).

Making the choice to forgo my own opinions where they deviated from God's Word was hard work, but doing so paid off. For example, Scripture instructed me to pray for my husband and ask God to bless him. In 1 Peter 3:9 I read, "not returning evil for evil, or insult for insult, but giving a blessing instead." The more I prayed for Ted, the more difficult it was for me to withhold forgiveness from him. I learned to work on accepting my husband for who he was. I began to quit expecting him to respond to me in the ways I wanted. By applying God's Word to my thinking, I was learning to forgive *freely*. And this brought relief.

Step 4: Now Consider Reconciliation

Finally, when we understand that we are forgiven, when we have made the choice to forgive, when we have renewed our mind with God's Word and can recognize change in our hearts, then perhaps we can reconcile with the person or persons who hurt us. Much will depend on what has happened in the heart and life of the offender or offenders. Again, forgiveness and reconciliation are not synonymous. Friendship is not necessarily a by-product of forgiveness. We need to be able to see signs of true, lasting repentance and change in those with whom we may reconcile. But forgiveness will clear the way for reconciliation if reconciliation is going to occur. You cannot fully reconcile if you have not forgiven.

CONFORMED TO CHRIST'S IMAGE

Does this process seem easy? It isn't. The process of forgiving my husband was messy. I did not do it well. Most of the time I did not do it right. My life has not progressed in a straight line. But over time, I have begun to see the ways God used the trial in my marriage to make me more like Christ. Christ endured. Christ forgave. I was deficient in these "skills," and through suffering, I changed. Though still grossly inadequate in so many ways, I learned how to experience more of Christ in my heart.

I now understand my trial, not just as a mountain to get over so I could move on with my life, but also as an opportunity for me to be "conformed to the image of [God's] Son" (Romans 8:29). What a different perspective—to see that God is fulfilling his purpose in our lives through those whom we must forgive! This is a hard perspective, but once we take hold of it, once we see the beauty in it, we experience more freedom. Now that I see how God used Ted's offense to accomplish his, the Lord's, purpose in me, I can praise God with a greater depth of gratitude. It took me a long time to get to this point, but I did get there. You can too.

Where are you with the issue of forgiveness? Be honest with yourself. What stage are you working on? Are you asking God to help you realize how much you have been forgiven? Making the decision to forgive someone who has hurt you? Or using the Scriptures to correct your thinking? Perhaps you realize you truly have forgiven an offender in your life and are ready to consider the possibility of reconciliation. Wherever you are in the process, ask God to help you persevere in it. We need perseverance and patience to walk this road, and we cannot produce these ourselves. Patience, or longsuffering, is included in the Bible's description of "the fruit of the Spirit" (Galatians 5:22). That means it grows and ripens over time as we live a life connected to God.

Once you recognize where you are in the process and what is required for you to keep going, pray for what you need. Perhaps you realize you do not really believe God has totally forgiven you. Ask him to help you understand on a deep level just what he did for you on the cross. Remember, if you are going to be able to forgive another completely, you must take hold of the complete forgiveness God extends to you.

If you are resisting making the choice to forgive, then acknowledge your resistance. Tell God about your feelings. Be honest with him. Let him expose the true condition of your heart. Invite him to change your position and help you commit to forgiving. Again, this is a decision you will have to make purposefully. If you have not committed to the hard work of forgiveness, then you will waver back and forth. You will do the work halfheartedly. Your efforts to move forward in life will be hampered. As Scripture teaches, "A double minded man is unstable in all his ways" (James 1:8 KJV).

Maybe you have made the choice to forgive and are trying to renew your mind every day with the truth of Scripture, but you are discouraged. You do not feel you are making any progress in your heart. You feel cold, unwilling, and disgusted. Stop and invite God to open your eyes to the little things he is doing to help you. Go back and look for his involvement in your daily life. Put your situation aside and take some time to worship God for who he is. He is in control. He is making provisions for you. You are his child. He loves you. Praise him in faith, in spite of your emotions. Ask God to help you experience his presence so you can be refreshed.

If you are praying about reconciling with someone who has hurt you, then ask God to lead you. Pray for wisdom. Seek counselors who will guide you in biblical truth. Stay in the Scriptures. Be aware that unconfessed sin in your life will separate you from God. Keep your heart clean before him. Surround yourself with practicing Christians. Maintain your daily devotional time with God. Remember, you need to hear God's voice. You cannot afford any erosion of your intimacy with him.

FOR THE ONE WHO CARES

As a friend or loved one of someone who is struggling to forgive, you can help by simply being aware of the stages of forgiveness. Ask God to help you understand the difficult process your friend is working through as he or she struggles to forgive. Keep in mind that this work is demanding, and it takes time. Recognize there is more going on in your friend's heart than what you can see. Do not assume that, because your friend seems bitter one day, he or she has hunkered down in unforgiveness. Resist the temptation to judge. One day your friend may seem very peaceful when talking of the offender; the next day he or she may be irate. Let the process take its course.

Pray for and support your friend through the stages of forgiveness. I was able to share my struggles with a confidante who let me wrestle with tough questions and say what was on my mind. She loved me through the process, prayed with me, and cried with me. She did not take on my prejudices about Ted but tried to stay objective. As you offer support, remember to bring your friend's focus to the Scriptures—but do not bludgeon with the Scriptures. Ask God to show you the difference. At times we need to draw a line with those we love when they let their emotions fuel beliefs that contradict God's Word. At other times we need to be gentle. Ask God to help you. Remember the words of Jesus: "Abide in Me. . . . I am the vine, you are the branches" (John 15:4–5). As a helper to your friend you must continue to "abide" in Jesus. He is your source. He is the true Helper.

If reconciliation is an option for your friend, then he or she will need a lot of prayer for wisdom and may come to you for counsel. You need to be prepared, and you can begin to get prepared by studying the Scriptures. You always want to direct your friend to the truth. Additionally, you may need to direct him or her to a pastor or trained counselor. Again, do not try to be the rescuer. Remind yourself that God is the Rescuer. He has not left you alone to support and advise your friend. Use the resources around you—the church, counselors, books, older Christians who can act as mentors in your friend's situation. God has not appointed you to provide everything in the care of your friend. Beware of your own pride, lest you find you are contributing to your friend's isolation.

As you work through the stages of forgiveness—leaning on God for strength, support, and help—you will find your hope restored if you can learn to praise God in advance for what he is doing in your life through your offender and the offense. We have reviewed the importance of looking back and thanking God for what he has already done in our lives. We have considered the power of praising him in the midst of present difficulty. But it is equally vital to make a point of praising God for what he *will* do. He knows our end from our beginning (Job 34:21; Psalm 139:1–18). Everything that happens to us God already intends to use for his good purposes, the chief of them being to make us like Jesus. This is worth praising him for! In Christ we are never stuck, never doomed. With him we always have a future. As Jeremiah wrote, "'For I know the plans that I have for you,' declares the LORD, 'plans for welfare and not for calamity to give you a future and a hope'" (Jeremiah 29:11).

Take a moment now to lay your fears, hurts, and frustrations at the feet of Jesus and to thank him for his love. Thank him for caring about you. Tell him you want to believe what Scripture says—that he plans to give you a future and a hope. Whatever you may feel, praise God for that future. In your hopelessness, praise God for hope. Take the verse from Jeremiah if you need to and say it back to the Lord with praise:

Lord, I praise you because you know me and you know the plans you have for me. You are an all-wise, all-knowing God, and I praise you for that. I praise you for your goodness. Everything you have planned for my life is good, because you are good. I thank you, God, that you have a future for me. And though I feel hopeless and despairing at this moment, I know that this is not your plan for me. Your plan is to restore my hope! I praise you for that, and I wait for it with faith and anticipation. Please give me the grace to wait expectantly. I want to please you.

By praising God for your future in this way, you are exercising faith. You are showing God you desire to trust him. You are saying you want to believe him. And that is enough. He will take your little bit of faith and enlarge it. He will help you. You will be able to trust him. Do not fear. As with everything we try to do for God out of a pure heart, he responds immediately to our slightest move in his direction.

Reminders for Painful Times

- ↜ Consider the symptoms of unforgiveness. Do they apply to you? If so, ask God to help you commit to the work of forgiving.
- ↜ Where you are in the process of forgiveness? Which stage are you working on? Recognizing that God has forgiven you, making the choice to forgive, or using the Scriptures to renew your mind? Pray for perseverance and patience, asking God to give you what you need to stick with the process.
- ↜ If you are praying about reconciling with someone who hurt you, ask God for guidance. Seek godly counsel. Stay in the Scriptures. Surround yourself with practicing Christians. Maintain your daily devotional times with God. Keep short accounts with him.
- ↜ Take time to praise God for what he is going to do through your battle to forgive your offender or offenders. Thank God for making you more like Christ, for giving you a future and a hope.

Tips for Those Who Care

- Be aware that forgiveness is a process. Be patient with your friend or loved one. Learn to listen. Do not judge him or her or presume you know his or her heart.
- Be available to listen to and encourage your friend during this time, and ask God to show you how. Remain objective but supportive. Depend on God to help you.
- Pray for your friend as he or she walks through the stages of forgiveness. Bring your friend back to the Scriptures if necessary.
- If your friend is praying about reconciliation, be prepared to point him or her to biblical truth. Be willing to direct your friend to a pastor or trained counselor. Do not try to be the rescuer. Use the resources around you.

MEMORY VERSE

Mark 11:25

And whenever you stand praying, forgive, if you have anything against anyone; so that your Father also who is in heaven may forgive you your transgressions.

Principles for Reflection

Forgiveness is a "God thing."
It is a process — one that requires hard work
and perseverance;
but God will enable us at every stage.
He does the work in our hearts
so we can do what he requires.

HOW DO I MAKE PEACE WITH GOD?
Choosing to Trust Him

Two years into my crisis with Ted, he suffered a heart attack. We had worked determinedly at our marriage with the help of a counselor but did not seem to be getting anywhere; and by this time, we had separated informally, hoping we could resolve our challenges if given some space. After the heart attack, Ted returned to our farm in the Valley to recover, and he did not look well. He looked older, gray, and stooped; he lacked vim and vigor.

I sincerely hoped the heart attack would serve as an opportunity for fresh love to surface between Ted and me, but not long into the recovery process, our old dynamics were in full swing. I continued to encounter patterns of behavior in my husband that kept me from feeling it was safe to trust again. In fact, trust had all but evaporated. Our struggle for healing in the marriage continued, with reconciliation seeming as remote a prospect as ever. I was discouraged. "I wish I had more compassion," I wrote in my journal. "I have a cold heart."

Soon after Ted's return to the farm, and once I was assured he was in stable condition, I made an already planned trip to China with my mother and two sisters, Gigi and Anne. I desperately needed more hope, and I prayed the trip would provide some refreshment. If only God could give me a sign of assurance that reconciliation was possible—if he could change my heart toward my husband—then at least I would have something on which to build. As it was, I agonized over what the future might hold, not knowing how much longer I could maintain my resolve to work on the marriage. I believed only God could stir my determination at this point; I had little strength to keep doing so myself.

The trip to China turned out to be the trip of a lifetime. Mother had waited all of her nearly sixty-nine years to take her daughters to Tsingkiangpu—today part of the larger metropolitan area of Huaiyin in Jiangsu Province—her first home. Sharing this very special sentimental journey with her brought to life for my sisters and me the exotic stories of our childhood. We gained a deeper understanding of our mother—her love for old things, her attention to detail, her pack-rat tendencies, and her artistic eye. I will never forget seeing the expectant faces of the Chinese Christians, testament of the lasting work of the missionaries; or looking up at the window of the room where my mother was born; or standing atop the Great Wall with my mother and sisters. These moments are priceless, irreplaceable.

As it happened, we arrived in China in May 1989 as pro-democracy demonstrations in that country were mounting toward a crisis. We kept abreast of the rising tensions by watching CNN in various hotels; and from our rooms in Beijing, we could hear the roar of the demonstrating crowds. Being a child of the 1960s, I found the political developments profoundly moving. My sisters and I walked up to Tiananmen Square to show our support for the demonstrators and were confronted with an overwhelming mass of people fanning out as far as the eye could see. Standing alongside these brave citizens, I felt part of an event of great historical significance—a people's will resoundingly being expressed. Though the atmosphere was one of celebration, Mother feared a government crackdown was imminent, and she, of course, was right. We ended up cutting our trip short and leaving the country only days before government forces massacred Tiananmen Square demonstrators. My heart shattered for the hopeful Chinese with whom I had stood side by side. Lives had been taken. Had hope also been crushed? What would become of this nation?

Throughout the trip, difficult personal questions about reconciliation with Ted dominated my thoughts and prayers. While visiting Shanghai, we attended a large prayer meeting at the Mu'en Church, where Mother, my sisters, and I each gave a brief talk. At one point during the meeting, we were invited to go to the altar, get on our knees, and pray. I went forward, and kneeling there at the crowded altar, I told the Lord I was determined to do my part to hold my marriage together. I pleaded with him to change my heart toward my husband. I wanted to be able to reconcile and was afraid of what I was feeling. This moment with God stands out as an important one of resolve, or as close to resolve as I could get. "I hope I drove a stake concerning the choice to rebuild our marriage," I wrote in my journal, "—to not consider divorce."

Meanwhile, my heart remained as empty as ever, and I continued to ask God to repair, strengthen, and restore me—to change me so I could make a fresh start with my husband. But as the weeks of travel went by, my prevailing sense was that something inside of me had died. When I reflected on Ted's betrayal, I could not imagine living with him as a wife without withholding much of my heart. I could not imagine trusting him again. I simply did not know how to put a marriage back together with one who had wounded me so deeply.

By the evening of Ted's forty-fourth birthday, two days before my return to the States, we were in Paris. I did not want to go home, and I cried myself to sleep. It now had been exactly two years since I first learned of Ted's affairs. Our lives had been so altered since then, and I was so weary. "I'm not strong enough to hold up under it," I wrote in my journal. "But I feel as if everyone, including God, expects me to."

Boarding the plane for home, I was at a complete loss. The future seemed like an abyss. Dread was all I seemed able to feel. China had been a good vacation from the reality of the marriage; otherwise nothing in my heart concerning my personal life seemed to have changed. I had asked God to give me new love for my husband, to give me a flicker of hope. Now, en route back to the States, I felt neither.

Weighing the Repercussions

In the months after returning from China, I fought to keep from sinking emotionally. Hadn't I prayed with everything in me, asking God to do something extraordinary in my heart? Why had no miracle taken place? I knew stories of how God healed other people's hearts, other people's marriages. Yet nothing seemed to have changed for me. God seemed not to have answered my prayer. Perhaps he had not seen fit to help me. Or, I thought, maybe I was hindering God. Was something wrong with me? Was my heart stubborn? Was I hard-hearted?

Every so often, the desire to permanently check out of life drifted into my consciousness. I wept often. Exhaustion was my constant companion. I felt like I was dying a slow, excruciating death. As the months dragged on, I became overwhelmed by the futility of my position and concluded I could not keep living like this—just waiting for something to happen.

Finally, I recorded this assessment of the marriage: "The spiritual fabric of our union is gone and no matter what I try to put on it or over it, it is torn and [it is] God's responsibility to weave it together. I cannot do a spiritual healing—only God can. . . . It's over."

At this point, cutting my marital tie with Ted had come to seem the only workable option for us. While I observed some change in Ted, I did not see the kinds of changes that would invite me back into an intimate relationship with him. I did not perceive the depth of change necessary to convince me to let down my guard and trust Ted with my heart. I had forgiven him, but entering into intimacy no longer seemed possible.

I understood I had biblical grounds for divorce. Ted already had broken the union and sanctity of the marriage through adultery. Divorce in our case would amount to the realization that reconciliation seemed beyond attaining. But I did not want to be divorced. I did not want to hurt or displease God in any way. God was on the side of marriage. He instituted marriage as a picture of Christ's sacred relationship to his church. Knowing that men and women would have difficulty adapting to one another, God gave us principles so we could make marriage work. Yet my marriage seemed to have failed. I knew the failure was not all on me, but I feared I had displeased God in feeling unable to reconcile. I feared God would have no further use for me if I divorced. I worried he would look on me as a has-been—that I would be cast aside, put on a shelf.

I also dreaded the stigma of divorce. I realized that, until I learned of Ted's infidelities, I had considered divorced people second-class citizens. I dreaded having other Christians think of me that way. My life was somewhat high-profile in Christian circles because of my father's ministry, and I recognized that my revised marital status, were I to divorce, probably would not escape notice. I would be identified as "Billy Graham's divorced daughter." To someone who for years had fought to get free from concern about others' opinions, "divorced" seemed the most repugnant label out there. I felt as though "failure" would be tattooed on my forehead for all to see and judge.

Then there were the major lifestyle changes a divorce would entail. I had been married all of my adult life. I feared being alone—without a companion, without the special, intimate connection and prerogatives afforded by marriage. I could not imagine what life as a divorcée would look like. Despite our difficult dynamic, I could not imagine what life without Ted would look like. After all, we had grown up together. What would my days be like in his absence?

Divorce would mean insecurity in every way. Living on the farm had been a dream come true; it was an ideal place for the children, and I had made a home for us there. If Ted and I divorced, I would have to leave it. My financial situation would change. I would be responsible for managing my income. I would have to do things like file my own income tax return. Ted had managed all the business and financial areas of our life together. I simply had no idea where I would begin.

The most distressing aspect of weighing the repercussions of divorce was considering the effect it would have on the children. How I ached for them. Though I believed the family unit already had been damaged by Ted's infidelity, the children knew nothing of what had happened. Certainly they could pick up on some strife between their parents, but Ted and I had hidden our struggle fairly well. To the children, the family was basically as intact as it had ever been, and I experienced real heaviness when I thought of what divorce might do to them. What issues would they carry in life as a consequence of divorce? Would they suffer deep wounds that would take years of counseling to process? Would they be unable to find happiness in marriage? Would they see marriage as cheapened? When the children were little, I had promised them their mom and dad would never divorce. Every child needs that security. What would it do to them now if the promise was broken?

I considered these matters very carefully and over a long period of time. I did not try to soften the potential consequences; I knew I had to be realistic. In the end, however, I concluded divorce was the course I needed to pursue. I shared my decision with Ted one day while he and I were talking in the kitchen. Sitting at the table, I explained I no longer had hope our marriage could be saved. I told Ted that while I did not want a divorce, I saw no other way and would seek one. Ted's face, which I knew how to read so well after all our years together, reflected pain and dismay. His eyes filled with tears. My heart broke. We held each other and cried. Soon afterward, we made preparations to take the legal steps toward divorce.

Wrestling with Blame

When I considered what Ted and I were about to undertake, my thoughts often tended in the direction of blame. First I would blame Ted for the infidelities; then I would blame myself for not being able to reconcile. I felt like the weak link in a long line of Christian leaders and wondered if, as a result of my choices, the future of a great heritage now was at risk. I also at times blamed God for my situation. I felt like God had let me down. I was out there doing what I thought he had called me to do. I was being faithful to him—rearing my children, serving my husband, serving in ministry. Couldn't God have prevented the infidelity? Couldn't he have intervened? For whatever reason, he did not. And now the marriage was a shambles, seemingly beyond repair. Ted and I were locked into a destructive dynamic. Years had gone by, and there seemed no real, viable way to resolve our issues and stay together. I could not deny I was angry with God.

I wrestled with God about the way my life had turned out. I did not want to blame him. I wanted to embrace what I had claimed to believe all of my life: that he was good; that he was on my side. I wanted to believe what the Scriptures said about him. Again, I considered my role models—my parents and grandparents. They seemed able to trust God when trouble came. What was different about me? What in me was hindering a real depth of faith?

I desired the level of faith that enabled the biblical character Job, who lost absolutely everything, to declare of God, "Though he slay me, yet will I trust in him" (Job 13:15 KJV). But this kind of faith, I learned, had a price. If I wanted this level of faith, I was going to have to do something other than flounder when the waves of emotion and doubt crashed against my life. I was going to have to exercise the little bit of faith I did have and take a stand. What did that mean exactly? It meant that even if God did nothing else for me, I needed to let go of my anger toward him. I needed to give up the struggle. I needed to make my peace.

How did I do this? Ultimately, I made a decision in the face of my circumstances to accept what Scripture teaches about God. The Bible says, "The LORD is righteous in all His ways, And kind in all His deeds" (Psalm 145:17). I did not understand God's ways. Returning to the questions of my youth, I did not understand why Darlene Deibler Rose was forced to endure the agony of a Japanese prison camp and the loss of her husband when she had served God so faithfully. Now I did not understand why I, who had tried to be faithful in my life, was having to endure this breakdown in my marriage. But I came to a point where I saw the need to let go even of my questions. I would not have all the answers in this life. I knew that. In the meantime, I would have to make peace with God. I would have to choose to trust him and believe in his goodness without knowing the answers. That was the only way. Otherwise, I would not be able to go on.

YOUR CHOICES

How do you feel about God right now? Are you angry with him? Are you frustrated? Do you feel like he has left you to fend for yourself? Do you feel let down by God? Betrayed? Remember Jeremiah. He was honest with God. You can be honest with God too. Let God know what is on your heart. Tell him what you feel. You can do that. You can be real. God can handle the truth. But once you have finished, once you have expressed the hurt and frustration, you will come to a point of decision. You will find yourself faced with a choice. You can choose to believe that God is either for you or against you. That he is either good or not good. That he either loves you or rejects you. At the end of your emotions, you will arrive at this fork in the road. Like Job, you will be presented with the opportunity to choose what you believe.

Consider what Scripture tells us about God. The psalmist wrote, "The LORD is on my side" (Psalm 118:6 KJV). And again, "The LORD is my light and my salvation. . . . the LORD is the strength of my life" (Psalm 27:1 KJV). Jeremiah wrote, "The LORD is good unto them that wait for him, to the soul that seeketh him" (Lamentations 3:25 KJV). Remember the beautiful words Jeremiah penned in the midst of his grueling life experience: "It is of the LORD's mercies that we are not consumed, because his compassions fail not. They are new every morning: great is thy faithfulness" (Lamentations 3:22–23 KJV).

Do you believe these testimonies about the Lord? Do you believe that God is for you? That he is the strength of your life? That he is good? That his compassions never fail? Can you say to the Lord in your situation, "Great is thy faithfulness"? I encourage you to spend some time in prayer, asking God to renew your will to believe what his Word says about him. Pray for the courage to trust him. Pray for faith. You do not need much. Jesus said we could do a great deal with faith the size of a tiny mustard seed (Luke 17:5–6). Ask God to help you make the decision to trust in his goodness. Once you do, you will find that—as with your decision to forgive those who offend you—God will step in and empower you in your decision. The decision will anchor you when the storms come. And God will do his part to make sure the anchor holds.

You also will need to acknowledge to God that you have blamed him and then repent of that blame. The Bible says of Job that through all of his losses, he "did not sin nor did he blame God" (Job 1:22). I was not as pure as Job. At various points in life, I have had to tell God I was sorry for doubting him. I have asked his forgiveness for my distrust, for my attitude of blame. Though I have not understood his ways, God has been faithful to me at times when I was anything but faithful to him. I did not trust him, but he still loved me. He was still good to me. In moments of clarity about God's unwavering love, I have wept tears of shame, even as the apostle Peter wept when he realized he had betrayed Jesus.

You too might experience such moments coming out of seasons of anger toward God. If you keep your heart open and let God show you the truth about his love, you will experience some heartbreak over your own faithlessness. Do not fear these moments—welcome them. Cleansing comes when we bring our sins and failures to God in a spirit of humility. He will not turn you away. He will heal you. He will forgive you and draw close to you. As Psalm 34:18 proclaims, "The LORD is near to the brokenhearted, And saves those who are crushed in spirit."

FOR THE ONE WHO CARES

If your friend or loved one is struggling with anger toward God, remember that he or she is walking through a process, perhaps a long and grueling one. God will deal with your friend. God will bring him or her to a place of decision, and he or she will have an opportunity to choose to trust him. Your job is to encourage your friend along the way.

In conversation, sprinkle reminders of times when God demonstrated his goodness in your friend's daily life. Your friend may not seem to welcome everything you say, but always endeavor to bring your friend back to the Lord's faithfulness and love. Take time also to listen. Your friend may feel like his or her emotions represent a betrayal of God. Your loved one may feel ashamed of those emotions. Be sensitive. Don't be easily shocked. Give your friend permission to say what is on his or her mind and gently lead him or her back to the truth. Continue to pray daily for your friend. Ask God to give your friend the courage to trust him when he or she comes to that place of decision.

SINKING

As Ted and I prepared to take steps toward divorce, I braced myself, anticipating what I would have to face when the news became known. I feared others would condemn me because I had not been able to reconcile with Ted. I feared they would think me a failure and accuse me of not forgiving Ted. I dreaded others' responses, but I tried to remind myself that I was doing what I believed was best. I knew I was the only one who could decide ultimately whether reconciling with Ted was truly possible. No one else could evaluate the relationship from the inside. Only Ted and I knew what was between us.

I came to consider the failure of my marriage this way: I had taken my marriage vows very seriously. I had worked hard at the relationship. I never dreamed my marriage would suffer betrayal. I did not want my marriage to be destroyed. I hated what had happened. But I could not seem to change it. In the aftermath of destruction, I would have to trust God to look after my children and me. I had committed the kids to God before they were born, so they belonged to him. He was responsible for them. He was responsible for all of us. I had to believe—I chose to believe—that God would be faithful as Ted, the children, and I walked into the unknown.

Perhaps this is the juncture at which my relationship with God became wholly my own. I had to hear from God myself. I had to know what he was saying to me. Whenever I quieted my heart, I believed that God was confirming my decision. I might have been wrong in thinking I was hearing from God, but I experienced relief in these moments, and peace.

Let me note here that a marriage damaged by adultery does not have to end in divorce. Though Scripture seems to release from marriage a man or woman whose spouse has committed sexual immorality (Matthew 19:9), God can mend what has been broken and enable reconciliation. If your marriage has suffered betrayal, then I strongly urge you to establish boundaries with your spouse—determining what you can and cannot give—and seek out godly counsel right away. Put yourself on a path toward healing. Remember: do not isolate yourself with the information. God *can* save your marriage. You do your part, and let God do his. In my situation, having weighed things very carefully and prayerfully, I believed God ultimately released me from the relationship. But that may not be so for you. Seek to hear what God is saying about your circumstances.

After I made the decision to divorce, with great trepidation I called my parents. I was very nervous and afraid they would condemn me. I wanted them to hear me and recognize that I had done everything I could to preserve the marriage. I had wrestled with the issues from all angles. I had prayed. I had looked deeply into the Scriptures. I had sought counsel. I had worked for years to reconcile. I explained these things to Mother and Daddy, and, in fact, they did not condemn me. They repeatedly assured me of their love. I was their hurting child. They wanted me to be whole. Though I cannot tell their story, I can imagine the pain the divorce must have caused them. I am sure their hearts were broken as well.

As expected, once the news of my pending divorce became public, well-meaning people began to urge me to forgive and reconcile with Ted. I heard about the "new Ted." Ted had changed. He was pulling his life together. I needed to make the relationship work. I needed to forgive. I felt like a circle had been drawn, and I, the faithful wife, was on the outside.

Yet while I came under enormous stress as others contacted me and wanted to know what had happened to the marriage, I recognized that, to some extent, the stress was of my own making. My decision not to let others know the truth about Ted and me early on meant the people closest to us now had to scramble to catch up in the face of a divorce. Loved ones certainly had the right to question my judgment, but I was so fragile and exhausted I hardly could keep going. The sense of obligation I felt to keep justifying and explaining nearly broke me.

On one occasion, I became so frustrated I just about lost my grip on reality. Some weeks after I had made the decision to divorce, as I remember, my pastor planned to preach a sermon addressing the issue of repentance. He was going to use an illustration about infidelity. Knowing I was in rough shape, he called me on the Saturday evening before church to warn me ahead of time about the subject and illustration. I thanked him for his sensitivity but thought I could handle the sermon. I could not. My journal entry after the service is terse: "[The] sermon [was] all about the goodness of God to those who repent—What does God say to the one sinned against?"

My pastor likely preached a rich message, but I only heard one thing: When wronged, one simply needed to forgive. Then one's problems would be solved. Conflicts would be settled. Peace would be available. Healing would take place. Yet there I was, having struggled for years to determine what forgiveness looked like, still fighting daily to maintain a forgiving heart toward Ted, listening to others' admonishments to forgive and to reconcile with him, and knowing my heart was as cold as a stone. Sitting in the pew, I became totally convinced I was beyond rescue.

For a moment, I believed a lie. I had the horrible sense that God had passed me by—that he was finished with me, that I had failed to rise to the occasion, that he had tried to heal me but had become weary of my weakness. Maybe I hadn't forgiven after all. Maybe forgiving just wasn't something I could do. Maybe I would have to live in this embattled, miserable condition for the rest of my life. Maybe there was no hope. It didn't seem God was going to give me what he promised everyone else. Maybe I had outsinned God's grace.

For perhaps the only time in my life, I felt separated from God in an ultimate sense. I had tried so hard to forgive, and finally, it appeared that my efforts were in vain. I thought God had rejected me and was no longer on my side. At that moment, I was blind to all but my pain and what appeared an endless struggle. I ran from the church when the service was over.

Shaking, I drove myself home, parked the car in the driveway, and went straight for my bathroom, looking for razor blades. I anxiously searched my bathroom drawers, then Ted's drawers, fumbling with items and products. Thoughts of the children passed through my mind. I knew they depended on me and would be deeply affected by a suicide, but I was in such pain. I was blinded by pain. I kept looking and looking, but there were no razor blades anywhere. None. Anywhere. I finally gave up and sank into a chair. I took a deep breath. Then a friend came by.

In retrospect, I see it is unlikely I would have followed through, even if I had come across razor blades in the house. Again I realized I was the mother of three children who were going to have a much harder time in life if their mother committed suicide. I wanted to see them grow up. I wanted to know what tomorrow would bring. But such an incident did stand out as an alarm, a signal for help. It pointed to my utter desperation and need. I needed help and support. More than ever. Thankfully, my friend came over to check on me and helped bring me back to center, at least in that moment. The corrective influence a loving person can have on our distorted perception of reality is very great. We need people. Never underestimate the healing that God can administer through a friend.

Has something like what I experienced ever happened to you? Have you ever seriously contemplated ending your life or made an attempt to end it all?

Has the pain ever been that bad? If so—and if you have never gotten sufficient help concerning the issues that drove you to the edge—then I recommend you seek counsel immediately. Find a pastor or professional counselor who can help you walk out of your dark place and into the light. You must not endure such intense pain by yourself. Make sure to inform trusted individuals about your situation. Ask these friends to stay in close contact with you. Do not hide your pain from them. Be honest. God will use others to help you. Go back to the story about Jesus and the paralyzed man. Remember, this man never would have gotten to Jesus without the help of his friends.

FOR THE ONE WHO CARES

If you are the friend or loved one of someone who has tried to commit suicide or who has talked about the possibility, then consult immediately with a professional counselor or a pastor who is experienced in handling such situations. Help your friend arrange to seek professional or pastoral counseling without delay. Track down the necessary phone numbers. Make the appointment yourself if needed. Go with your friend if he or she wishes.

Meanwhile, continue to pray for and with your friend. Reach out to your friend or loved one in simple ways. Bring a meal to his or her home. Call frequently to check in. Plan an outing—take your friend on a walk in the sunshine. Give your friend or loved one little things to look forward to. Make sure to listen to your friend sympathetically as he or she talks about the pain and struggle in his or her life at this time. Remember, your friend is overwhelmed by his or her circumstances and cannot see things as they really are. Be patient. Keep loving your friend, and continue to connect him or her with people and resources as needed.

Did my sinking low enough into despair to search my bathroom for razor blades mean God had dropped me? Did it mean he had failed to uphold me in my decision to trust him? Was he proving himself untrustworthy? We will always face temptation to believe the enemy of our souls, the one the Bible calls "the accuser" and "the father of lies" (Revelation 12:10; John 8:44). But the presence of temptation does not evidence a failure on God's part. On the contrary, temptation provides an opportunity for God to be our Rescuer and show us the way out. The Bible declares this:

No temptation has overtaken you but such as is common to man; and God
is faithful, who will not allow you to be tempted beyond what you are able, but
with the temptation will provide the way of escape also, that you may be able to
endure it.

1 CORINTHIANS 10:13

God knew I was vulnerable during that sermon in church. He knew what my response would be. He knew I had taken my eyes off of him to focus on what seemed to be overwhelming circumstances. He also knew there were no razor blades in my home. And he knew what it would take to bring my mind back to the truth: the love and support of a friend who was willing to help me get myself together.

I am not trying to give pat answers concerning the very complex and difficult issue of suicide. I can only speak from my own experience. I know that God came through when I was sinking, and he brought me back to reality. The reality of his love. The reality of his goodness. The reality of my decision to trust him. If you have faced the temptation to end your pain by ending your life, then I pray that God will show you where he was in the midst of your situation and point out the "way of escape" he provided. May you recognize his great love for you and his determination to rescue your feet from what the psalmist calls "the snare of the fowler" (Psalm 91:3 KJV). God is for you. When you get tired in the struggle and want to give up the fight, remember, "underneath are the everlasting arms" (Deuteronomy 33:27). God will never let you go. He will not leave you. He will not desert you. Never.

Reminders for Painful Times

↳ Are you angry with God? Do you believe he has let you down? Tell God how you feel. Express what is bothering you.

↳ Consider what the Bible teaches about God and his love—meditate on verses that describe his character.

↳ Ask God for the courage to believe what Scripture says about him. Make a conscious decision to trust in his goodness.

↳ Tell God you are sorry for your attitude of blame toward him. Ask him to forgive you. Allow him to cleanse you.

↶ If your marriage has suffered the betrayal of sexual immorality, recognize that God can save your marriage. Seek to hear what God is saying about your situation.

↶ If you have ever contemplated ending your life and have not sought or received sufficient counsel, then do so immediately. Find a pastor or professional counselor to help you. Let trusted friends know about your pain. Ask them to stay in close contact with you.

Tips for Those Who Care

↶ Remember that your hurting friend is walking through a process. His or her feelings about God may vary. Do not condemn your friend for feelings of anger.

↶ Encourage your friend by sensitively pointing out examples of God's goodness in his or her daily life. Gently lead your friend back to the truth of God's love.

↶ Listen to your friend. Give your friend permission to share his or her heart.

↶ Pray for your friend daily. Ask God to give your friend courage to make the decision to trust him.

↶ If your friend has attempted or considered suicide, seek advice immediately from a pastor or professional counselor. Help your friend seek counsel right away. Pray for and listen to your friend. Stay close to him or her. Connect your friend with people and resources.

⌒

MEMORY VERSE

Job 13:15 KJV

Though he slay me, yet will I trust in him.

Principles for Reflection

We will come to a point in our personal struggle where we must make the decision either to trust God or to disbelieve him. By choosing to trust him, we make our peace with him.

HOW DO I LIVE
IN TRANSITION?
Learning to Be Still during Times of Uncertainty

The divorce was final in March 1991, a few months after I turned forty. Noelle was the only one living at home with me during that school year. I had enrolled Windsor, who was in seventh grade, at a nearby boarding school. Graham, a high school sophomore, had moved to Dallas, where Ted was living. All at once I went from having three children at home to just one—and she with little more than a year remaining before college. The legal process with Ted had come to an end. Confusion gave way to calm. Finally I was afforded a respite, but I now struggled with loneliness. I missed my children.

"It is so quiet," I recorded in my journal. "Noelle is gone [for the day]. The refrigerator hums. This is the kind of time I hungered for but now it seems so empty—interminable."

Life as I knew it had changed utterly. I was no longer a wife. My children were growing up. Who was I? How was I to spend my time? How was I to redefine myself? I tried to get excited about the future but was more often daunted by it. Some days I was so exhausted I could hardly get out of bed. At other times I became restless and overcome with anxiety. A doctor pictured my state of mind this way: behind me I could see the storm that had caused destruction in my life; up ahead I could see the beach I wanted to reach, but my feet were bogged down in the mud. The description could not have been more apt. I was living in the uncomfortable zone of transition.

Very gradually, a new life began to unfold. Believing I needed to invest in myself, I applied to the adult degree program at Mary Baldwin College in Staunton, Virginia, and soon resumed the undergraduate degree I had abandoned years ago in order to get married. Mary Baldwin agreed to give me credit for some of my documented "life experience," like my trip to China and my work with Harper & Row (by then HarperCollins). I studied hard, and my first semester managed to earn a 4.0 GPA. What a wonderful boost for my faltering self-confidence!

Noelle, too, applied to colleges, eventually settling on a Virginia school, and she graduated from high school in the spring of 1992. Windsor returned from boarding school that summer, and I enrolled her in the public high school for her freshman year. Graham, who spent part of the summer at home with us, talked of wanting to attend a small college or a Bible school after his own high school graduation in Dallas the following spring. The kids were making plans, and I tried to adapt to the change.

Meanwhile, I focused on trying to sell the farm, which already had been on the market for some time. Though the thought of doing so pained me, I was well aware wisdom was on the side of letting go of all or part of the property. My finances would abide no other course of action. I had cut corners as best I could to run the farm on my reduced income, but managing the staff and maintaining the property proved too great a strain. I needed a buyer. After ultimately years of waiting for the farm to sell—what felt like an epic transition—I finally had a contract at the end of 1992. Once again I began to make preparations to step into the unknown.

This was a difficult stretch of months for me. I had virtually no vision for life after the farm. I was trying to organize the family, deal with our grief over the loss, and recover from recent surgery complications. As a temporary fix I rented a nearby farmhouse, figuring the kids and I could stay there until I found something permanent; and almost immediately, locating a permanent home became my all-consuming passion. My aim was to get us out of this next phase of transition as quickly as possible.

I looked at houses from one end of the Valley to the other and even briefly considered leaving Virginia altogether as a way of starting over. All along I prayed that God would show me where he wanted us to go, and finally, in the spring of 1993, I located a home near the Valley that I thought would suit us. I fell in love with the house, a beautiful Williamsburg Colonial, and began to picture us living in it. Never having bought a home on my own, I did not know much about negotiating a fair price, but I made what I believed was a reasonable offer and trusted that God was leading me.

Then came a surprising turn of events. Before I could get to my realtor's office to sign the papers, another would-be buyer stepped in and made a higher offer. I increased mine—but not by enough. I was too nervous to commit to spending any more money, and I felt I had to let the house go. I was stunned. It was hard to believe that after all of the months of racing around, I was back to square one. I felt overwhelmed, confused. I thought God had been involved in these plans. Had I missed him? How would I locate the energy to begin all of the looking and planning again?

Every life contains pivotal moments that alter one's course in significant ways. Losing this house to another buyer stands out as one such moment in my life. From time to time, I look back and reflect on how differently my life would have turned out had I gone higher on my offer and purchased that home. Given all that followed, I see I would have spared the children and myself a world of hurt. I would have maintained my financial security. I perhaps would have healed from the divorce more quickly.

Of course, such musings are not very productive. I remind myself still that during this period I was trying to follow God as best I knew how. My heart and intentions were pure. I wanted God to select our home. I wanted him to chart my course. I trusted the Lord to lead me. Though I did not understand why I had lost the house, I realized I now would have to trust that God knew better than I. What transpired over the course of the next twelve months, much of it thanks to my own bad judgment, ended up breaking me. But, again, I had decided to trust God, hadn't I? As I would soon learn, this meant trusting him even with my most shameful mistakes.

MAKING DECISIONS ON THE FLY

The weekend after the house deal fell through, I went to Fort Lauderdale, Florida, to visit my oldest sister, Gigi, and her family. I felt directionless, deflated. What was I to do now? I had looked at so many houses in the Valley to ultimately no productive end. I didn't know if I had it in me to give all of those homes another look. Perhaps God wanted me to live somewhere else entirely after all. I was open to reconsidering that possibility—actually, I was so exhausted I was open to just about any possibility.

"I am so frustrated . . . ," I wrote in my journal, "—here I thought I had direction but I don't now. So disappointed. . . . If only I could hurry, fall in love, and marry and move wherever to be with him—simply settle all the issues!"

I wrote these remarks flippantly, but I was partly serious. I did want to be married eventually. While recognizing differing views on the subjects of divorce and remarriage, I believed I had the freedom to remarry. Because my marriage to Ted had been dissolved as a result of adultery, I believed that from a scriptural standpoint, remarriage was possible for me. In my insecure position, I began to long for the security marriage could bring. Lonely and tired, I found myself yearning for the friendship available through marriage. Perhaps more than anything I just wanted to feel settled; and from this perspective, sharing my life with a companion seemed appealing.

Meanwhile, I went around Fort Lauderdale with Gigi to look at houses. A life in that city would have much to recommend it, I reasoned. Living near family would benefit both the kids and me. I knew of a good church where we could become involved. I also wondered if I might prefer Fort Lauderdale's faster pace to the Valley's small-town experience. Perhaps moving to Florida was the course I needed to pursue. I did not know, so I approached house-hunting as I had in the Valley—as someone trying to discern God's will—and I remained open. Maybe too open.

Of the several homes I saw, one especially stood out. I knew I could get it for a reasonable price, bring in a contractor to make renovations, and treat the property as an investment. In fact, this idea gained momentum almost instantly, and I decided to pursue it. Giving myself essentially no time to step back and reflect at any length on this course of action, I met with a contractor, who provided a reasonable quote for the renovations I had in mind. Then I made an offer on the house, and the offer was accepted. A week after I lost a house in Virginia to another bidder, I owned a home in Florida. I had curtailed the limbo. I had found somewhere to go. But my head was spinning. Was this the way God was working? "How on earth will I explain it all?" I wrote in my journal.

The kids, it turned out, were not at all happy about my decision. After all, only the week before, I had convinced them that the house I lost in Virginia was ideal. Noelle told me my purchase of the home in Fort Lauderdale overwhelmed her. Graham said he hated Florida. Windsor was upset, as she would be the one most affected by the change in plans. For my part, however, I thought I was doing the best I could to manage our lives. I had tried to keep both the kids and my own future in mind. Of course, I had not had time to keep much of anything in mind for long—things seemed to move so fast. But I was trying. I had no template, no blueprint, for getting out of transition. I just prayed and kept going.

In truth, I was beginning to look forward to the Florida move. I felt empowered by having purchased a house on my own. I found hope in the idea of beginning anew. I was ready to create my own nest, and my creative juices began to flow. I started to comb decorating stores in the Valley, consider fabric samples, sketch room charts, and scour antique shops. I bought decorating books. I sent some of my furniture out to auction. I got busy. Very busy. I seemed to have more energy, and I used it.

But as my days filled to capacity with tasks and to-dos, a concern started to nudge the surface of my thought life: Was all this busyness a natural outgrowth of my newfound excitement, or was it an effort to keep from questioning what I was doing? I thought about the kids' negative responses to my change in plans. Should I have paid attention? Was the dismay of my children a sign I should reconsider my course? I did not know. And for whatever reason, I did not opt to slow down at this point so I could pray and find out. Perhaps I even avoided praying deeply about it. I simply asked God to block my plans if they were not in his will. My modus operandi was to keep walking through doors until God shut them. Now that I had set myself in a direction, I just continued to move forward.

Further, by this time I had left HarperCollins and signed on as an acquisitions editor with a new publishing house, McCracken Press; and between trips to Florida to meet with the contractor renovating my house, I worked with my sister Gigi on completing a book project. The pace of my life escalated to an almost unmanageable level, but I felt locked into my obligations. How was I to slow down? It seemed impossible. Not that busyness was an altogether unfamiliar, or unpleasant, mode of living for me. In part, I was accustomed to maintaining a full schedule. I responded to stress by getting busy. This time, however, I was beginning to worry that my frenetic pace was a bit much.

THE BUSYNESS TRAP

My pace leading up to the Florida move *was* a bit much, as I would later realize. In the midst of my transition, I could not seem to evaluate my behavior with a great deal of clarity. Busyness was my coping mechanism. I stayed busy to keep my mind off the pain, fear, and uncertainty I was feeling about the future. I did not want these emotions to hold sway over me. I did not want to bog down in loneliness. These were worthy desires, but in the course of things,

I also kept my mind off important points that needed to be raised as I prepared to uproot my children—mainly Windsor—and myself. Eventually, the busyness knocked me off-balance. And knocked off-balance, I became vulnerable to making further mistakes and suffering further devastation, both of which transpired in short order. The busyness helped me cope with my circumstances up to a point, and then it became a trap.

Undoubtedly, busyness can be a virtue during difficult times. So often when we are hurting, we become self-focused—to our own disadvantage. We continually review in our minds the unfairness of our situation, the actions of our offenders, and the frustration, loneliness, and apprehension we feel. We routinely get stuck as we imagine hypothetical scenarios: if only our lives had played out this way or that way, we think. We become preoccupied with our wants, disappointments, and hurts. Ultimately, our self-absorption makes us unproductive. We suffer further. Our relationships suffer. We wake up after weeks or months and find we are in a rut.

On the other hand, having something to do helps us take our minds off ourselves. Activity lends normalcy to our lives. As we put our energy and skills to use, we begin to feel human again. We realize we have purpose, even if that purpose on a given day amounts only to purchasing materials for a household project. Ultimately, though, excessive busyness can hinder us in discerning God's plan for our lives during times of transition. Busyness can also keep us from recovering fully in the wake of personal crisis. While it is unprofitable for us to dwell on our pain, there is a time for evaluating, with an ear to hear God, what has happened to us. We need God's perspective on the past so we can better understand what he wants to do with, in, and through us in the future. Seeking God's perspective takes focus and resolve. It takes time. I wish I had known that back then. I would have spared myself and others a great deal of heartache. My prayer is that the following insights will help you avoid making the kind of painful choices I'll soon describe.

CULTIVATING STILLNESS IN TRANSITION

Looking to God for clarity of purpose and direction requires more than a few moments here and there; in times of significant change, it requires more than just the time we have allotted for daily devotions. Seeking God is not an easy, one-step exercise. When we seek him, we must slow down for a period of time so we can listen. Hearing God's voice can be difficult when we are still vibrating from upheaval or heartbreak. After a crisis or major life change, we need to cultivate stillness. The Bible says, "Be still, and know that I am God" (Psalm 46:10 NIV).

How do we cultivate stillness? We cut back our schedules where possible, eliminating activities that either are unnecessary or unduly drain our energy. We schedule downtime for ourselves. We maintain our devotional time with God. We prioritize relaxing. So often we get locked into a frenzied pace, believing there is no way out—and at times in life our schedules do fill up for good reason. But we can always find some pocket of time for ourselves. If an activity or obligation interferes with our ability to take care of our personal needs, then we may need to let go of that activity. Stillness, rest, quiet—these are important to God. Even if we can only take small steps toward cutting back on busyness, we will do a great service to ourselves.

Beyond setting aside time for relaxation and quiet, we can further cultivate stillness during our devotions with God. To vary my time with God, for example, I often practice meditating on the Scriptures. Stillness, of course, is not ultimately about doing, but quieting our minds in order to focus on a few principles or characteristics of God can transform us. When I engage the Scriptures in this way, I usually choose a verse—or a portion of a verse—and think about what it says, what it means in my life, and what it tells me about God. I often stretch out on the floor while doing this, allowing my body to relax and my mind to become clear of any distracting thoughts. In the stillness, I let the content of the Bible verse become my sole preoccupation.

Out of one of these meditation times came my deep conviction that God was at work in my ruins. I began by reading Isaiah 51:3 (NIV):

> The LORD will surely comfort Zion
>   and will look with compassion on all her ruins;
> he will make her deserts like Eden,
>   her wastelands like the garden of the LORD.
> Joy and gladness will be found in her,
>   thanksgiving and the sound of singing.

Lying on the floor in my room, I tried to imagine God's look of compassion. I tried to picture his face. What did it look like? What depth of emotion did his eyes convey? I stayed with this image of God's face for some time.

Next I expanded my meditation to include the concept of ruins. The verse said that God looked with compassion on my ruins—*all* my ruins. What were my ruins? My broken marriage. Our splintered family. My hurting children. The loss of the farm. The loss of stability. The death of my dreams. My failures. I imagined God's heartbreak over what had happened in my life and his great sorrow over my woundedness and pain. Now God's compassion seemed more personal—I realized his look of compassion was directed toward me.

Once I began to grasp the depth of God's compassion for me, I expanded my thinking still further and considered his promise to restore my ruins—to make my deserts like Eden, to give me joy and a new song. Staying with these ideas, I gained confidence that I was safe in God's care, that he had a plan, and that I could have hope for the future. I became peaceful inside. Quiet. Content. Now I could incorporate all of these concepts into prayer and praise:

Thank you, Lord, that you have compassion and do not hold my ruins against me. Thank you that you hurt over the things that hurt me. I am so grateful you are going to restore me and build back what has been torn down. I want to experience your joy. You have promised it, and I thank you.

Do you see how practicing this kind of meditation during our devotional times can positively affect us when we're living in transition? We come away from such moments renewed in our outlook. Our thinking about our situation changes, and a change in our thinking paves the way for change in other areas. The Bible teaches, "For as he thinks within himself, so he is" (Proverbs 23:7). Part of God's restorative work in us during transition involves an overhaul of our thought life. While God wants to give us specific direction to move us eventually out of transition, he knows that, for us to receive this direction, we must be thinking correctly. Cultivating stillness—whether specifically during prayer to God or on a large scale by altering our schedules—will enable us to hear what God is saying about our assumptions and habits of mind so we can make the necessary adjustments.

LEARNING TO CULTIVATE STILLNESS

Are you currently living in transition? Are you filling up your calendar with work, activities, and events? Are you impatient to get past the transition and move on with your life? Do you find yourself running from one thing to the next, with little or no downtime each day? Has your daily time with God diminished or evaporated altogether? If you find you are answering yes to these questions, then I encourage you to step back and reevaluate your current direction. Remember, busyness in itself is not bad—*excessive* busyness is what causes us to lose our footing. Think about what you can cut out of your life for the moment. Ask yourself what activities are truly necessary and valuable, and stick with those. Put the others on the back burner. You can always return to them. Right now it may be more important for you to be still.

As you take steps to adjust and unpack your schedule, I encourage you to make a point to schedule downtime for yourself. Take walks, listen to music, work out at the gym, or give time to a favorite hobby. Regular intervals of unstructured time promote relaxation. We become calmer, more centered as we learn to slow down. Anxiety recedes. We are no longer as quick to become angry or provoked. We are less easily knocked off balance. This is a gradual but important process. Once at rest, we are in a better frame of mind to hear God's voice.

If you have neglected your daily time with God, then recommit to it now. Do not condemn yourself for having drifted off course. Begin again. Approach your devotions with a mind to understand God's plan for you. Beware of interpreting Scripture to fit your own plan—we can spend countless hours with God and still come away having missed what he was saying to us. Remember to seek *his* mind.

Try meditating on the Scriptures during some of your devotional time. You can use my own example as a model if you would like. Choose a Bible verse that speaks to your heart. Get comfortable in a place where you will not be distracted. Relax your body and let all the thoughts and to-dos pass from your mind. Quiet yourself. Now consider a phrase or concept in the Bible verse you have chosen. Meditate on the phrase. What does it mean? What does it say to you personally? What does it tell you about God? Do not rush while you think on these things—stay very relaxed. Invite God to show you something new, to change you in some way. You can add phrases or concepts from the Bible verse to your meditation as you go. Allow God to increase your clarity about what the verse is communicating specifically to you. As you gain understanding, begin to thank God for what he is showing you. Praise him for what you have learned about his character, and ask him to help you apply to your situation whatever you have learned.

SOMETIMES GOD WAITS TO GIVE DIRECTION

There are times in life when we may seek God for direction and hear very little in response. God does not always talk when we seek him. Sometimes his only response is silence. God's decision to be quiet does not mean he has abandoned us—he is as close to us as ever. It just means he has chosen to wait. So often in transition we believe we are waiting on God to show us what to do, but, in fact, he may be waiting on us. What is God waiting for? Perhaps to see how badly we want to be with him. Will we keep seeking him, even when we do not hear or feel him, or will we give up the effort? God also may be giving us time to become whole in some area of our emotional life. We are not always ready to receive direction from God when we think we are. God is interested in our well-being. He wants us to succeed in our future endeavors. He wants us to be prepared for what lies ahead. He is for us, not against us.

Consider the prophet Elijah. After being used by God to discredit and kill the prophets of Baal on Mount Carmel, Elijah learned of threats being made against him by the king's wife, Jezebel, and he fled into the desert. There he collapsed under a juniper tree and asked the Lord to take his life. Elijah was exhausted, without hope. He had been through an intense ordeal. A chapter in his life had closed. Now he was in transition, and he was telling God how he felt: he was giving up; he was ready to quit; he wanted relief. Perhaps you have felt like this.

But God did not answer Elijah right away. God waited until after his prophet had slept, and then he sent an angel with only a simple word: "Get up and eat" (1 Kings 19:5 NIV). Elijah did as the angel instructed and lay down again, only to be touched by the angel a second time and given the same command. As he was told to do, Elijah ate and drank; then he commenced a forty-day journey to Mount Horeb, "the mountain of God" (verse 8 NIV).

Once on the mountain, Elijah did not get direction from God immediately. God first asked Elijah to share his concerns: "What are you doing here, Elijah?" (1 Kings 19:9 NIV). The prophet answered, expressing his feelings more fully than he had when under the juniper tree. "I have been very zealous for the LORD God Almighty. The Israelites have rejected your covenant, broken down your altars, and put your prophets to death with the sword. I am the only one left, and now they are trying to kill me too" (verse 10 NIV).

God's response to his prophet at this point was another simple directive. Elijah was told to go and stand on the mountain and prepare for the Lord to come by. We read:

> Then a great and powerful wind tore the mountains apart and shattered the rocks before the LORD, but the LORD was not in the wind. After the wind there was an earthquake, but the LORD was not in the earthquake. After the earthquake came a fire, but the LORD was not in the fire. And after the fire came a gentle whisper. When Elijah heard it, he pulled his cloak over his face and went out and stood at the mouth of the cave.
>
> 1 KINGS 19:11–13 NIV

Now, at last, God was going to address the prophet's concerns and give him instruction.

Can you see the different stages highlighted in this story? God brought Elijah out of his transition gradually. The prophet was depressed, despairing, afraid, and ready to die when he fled to the desert and collapsed under the juniper tree. God knew he needed to rest. Elijah needed simple nourishment, not the pronouncement of a grand plan for his future. Once the prophet was strong enough, he was able to take a journey to the mountain of God. On the journey, Elijah regained his confidence. He was no longer fleeing *from* Jezebel but moving *toward* God. He was operating out of healthy motivation and purpose. He was walking in wholeness, not running in fear.

Then, from a position of strength, Elijah shared his frustrations with the Lord, not only concerning Jezebel's specific threats, but also concerning the context of those threats—Israel's spiritual demise—and the fear, disappointment, and isolation he, Elijah, felt as a result. Elijah could better understand his own heart now that he was stronger, and he could articulate his feelings more completely to God. In fact, his prayer had expanded and changed while he was learning to be still and wait in transition. From this perspective, God's decision to delay addressing his prophet's original request was an act of mercy. God knew that Elijah's first prayer, a petition to die, was not his real prayer. God wanted to answer the true concerns of Elijah's heart, and he waited until Elijah was able to express them.

Finally, notice the manner in which God made his presence known to Elijah: in a gentle whisper, or as another translation relates, in "a still small voice" (KJV). God was not in all of the drama—the wind, earthquake, and fire. His voice was quiet, nearly imperceptible. But not imperceptible to Elijah. The prophet now was able to pick up on God's whisper, because he himself was quiet. He had been still before God for more than forty days—first beneath the juniper tree, then as he walked alone in the desert toward Horeb. He had recovered during that time; anxiety and fear no longer consumed him. He still had an issue to bring before God, but that issue no longer caused him to be incapacitated. He was back to center—expectant and calm. God did not need to speak to his prophet with fireworks; he could reach him with the slightest stirring. Because Elijah was ready. Because he was still.

LET GOD LEAD YOU OUT OF TRANSITION

You too can expect God to speak to you during your transition, but be patient, understanding that he will speak when he chooses. How does God speak to us? He speaks through the Scriptures, our circumstances, and godly counsel. He speaks to our minds. Sometimes God's word is an "aha!" At other times, it comes as a gradual awareness. Be open to whatever God has to say, even if it is entirely different from what you anticipate. Perhaps you want God to confirm your plans—he may have something else in mind for you.

As in the story of Elijah, God may want to say something simple. Do not be disappointed if God says "Get up and eat" for a stretch of days, weeks, or months. Just do what you think God is telling you. You might need a simple word. You might need to be encouraged to rest. You might need to hear God say "Trust me" or "Stop!" You do not really know what you need. Only God does. He made you. He knows where you are. Remember that he is in control. Have faith in the pace he sets for your time of transition. If he keeps you in this quiet, simple place for a while, then thank him. Don't chafe against the stage you are in. Don't rush to get out of it. Again, God is interested in your wholeness.

Perhaps you are stronger than you were several months or even years ago. You might be strong enough, like Elijah on his way to Horeb, to begin walking forward. But if you have not yet heard from God concerning his plans for your future, then I urge you not to make a move. Elijah was walking, but he was walking toward God in order to hear him—he was not setting off on a journey of his own design. Do not be deceived. You may be stronger than you were but not yet ready in God's estimation to receive direction about the next stage of your life. It is not your job to get yourself out of transition. God is the one who ordains the stages in our lives—he will move you when he is ready.

I wish I had better understood this myself, but I was too busy wanting to get my life settled.

If you have been seeking God for some time now and are becoming frustrated, let me encourage you: tell God about your frustration and ask him to give you peace. Ask him for the patience to keep waiting. Transition is a time to grow in our dependence on God—don't miss out! Lean on him. Tell him what you feel. Let him slow you down and teach you how to live peacefully where you are. Yes, you will experience times of frustration, impatience, anxiety, and discouragement. Make no mistake—you will want out. You will be tempted to do something to get yourself out. But rather than yield to those emotions—rather than take matters into your own hands and act impulsively without clear direction—learn how to bring your emotions to God. Tell him honestly how you feel. Find the Scriptures that speak to your need and pray those Scriptures as prayers. Stay close to God and wait for him to tell you what to do.

Maybe, like Elijah when he got to Horeb, you are now sharing your feelings about your past experiences more freely with God. Take heart in knowing that God will address your desires in time, and in the interim, enjoy the benefits of simply expressing your heart to him. As you share your feelings in prayer, you will grow closer to God. You will better understand your own heart. Often we do not know all that is in our hearts until we begin to articulate our feelings to God. You may find that your understanding of your needs and desires has changed or expanded during your transition. You may begin to see patterns in your life that need correction. You may realize that God wants to address not just the patterns but also the root causes of those patterns. He has much bigger plans for us than we do!

Maintain your faith that God will show you what to do when he is ready. God spoke to Elijah and gave him very clear, specific direction once the time was right (1 Kings 19:15–18). God will do the same for you. He may or may not speak to you in the same way he spoke to Elijah, but he will give you the guidance you need when you need it. Remember, you do not know what God has planned for your future. You have no idea what this plan requires in the way of preparation. God never takes on anything before it has been prepared, and our destinies depend not only on the work God wants to do in us personally but also on the coming together of people, events, and opportunities. God must prepare all of these as well, so he can lead us into greater maturity in Christ and toward the fulfillment of his purposes. Paul wrote, quoting Isaiah, "No eye has seen, no ear has heard, no mind has conceived what God has prepared for those who love him" (1 Corinthians 2:9 NIV). In your transition, God is preparing something beautiful and extraordinary for you, something you in your limited human thinking cannot imagine. Do you trust him? Ask him to help you. He loves you. He will lead you. He will bring good out of your circumstances.

FOR THE ONE WHO CARES

If you are the friend or loved one of someone who is living in transition, first remember there is no prescribed length of time for recovery. God may release your friend from transition quickly, or he may keep your friend there for some time. In order to encourage your friend or loved one to be patient and at rest for any duration, you need be patient and at rest yourself. Remember, God is in control of your friend's situation. He will provide everything your friend needs to move forward in the proper time. Even if you cannot see evidence of God's leadership in your loved one's life from day to day, thank God anyway. Praise God for having a plan for your friend and for overseeing that plan.

By encouraging yourself this way, you will foster your own faith, cultivate peace in your heart about your friend's life, and, in turn, be able to communicate this peace readily. On the other hand, if you are impatient with your friend's circumstances—if you are anxious that God fix everything on *your* timetable—then you will struggle in giving your friend the kind of support needed. Ask God to use you as an advocate of stillness, patience, and faith in the life of your friend. Ask God to *make* you an advocate of these things.

If you notice that your friend or loved one is living at a pace that does not promote reflection, if he or she is racing through each day, each week, not seeming to have any real downtime, then gently encourage your friend to consider what activities he or she might be able to drop for the time being. If your friend seems afraid to slow down for fear of having too much time on his or her hands, then emphasize the need, not for immobility—certainly not for isolation—but for balance. Encourage your friend to find the time to deal with his or her issues.

Be aware that your friend may come to you repeatedly during this time of transition to voice the same frustrations and fears about his or her current position in life. Take time to listen. Do not become impatient. Remember, you want to create an environment in which your friend is comfortable being honest. But do guard your time and energy.

Sometimes our friends and loved ones get stuck in certain emotional patterns for a time, and if we are not careful, we can become stuck too. Determine what time and energy you will give your friend in order to be supportive, but maintain balance in this so you don't become drained.

As you sense your friend or loved one becoming more able to receive guidance from you, gently encourage your friend to take advantage of the benefits of transition. For instance, you can urge your friend to see this time as an opportunity to rest and to practice healthy eating and exercise habits. Like Elijah, your friend may need time to recover from a difficult experience. Or perhaps your friend is expressing a desire to spend more time seeking God but doesn't know what to do. Encourage your friend to cultivate his or her daily devotional life and to take more time to relax whenever possible. Point out to your friend that if he or she can practice stillness, this time of transition will yield greater understanding about God's purposes and prepare your friend for what lies ahead.

Finally, make sure to be sensitive as you encourage your friend in these ways. Your friend may not be able to hear you—his or her anxiety or despair may be too intense. Again, your sensitivity will stem from your own ability to trust God and to be patient with his process in your friend's life, no matter how long that process may take. Be gentle with your friend and look for opportunities to build his or her expectations for the future. Assure your friend that God is in control and has good plans in store.

THE CHILDREN'S ISSUES

If anything made me slow down, even a little bit, and reflect, it was the children's issues; for as moving day approached, those issues surfaced more intensely than before. To prepare the kids for the move, I planned a trip to Fort Lauderdale for Mother's Day so they could see the new house and get acquainted with the city. Noelle and Windsor accompanied me. They were not sold on our future environment, and on our return, they and Graham—from where he was in Dallas—seemed to come unglued. Graham and Windsor fought with one another by telephone. Windsor snuck out with a friend one night, only to have the car they were using break down on the side of the road. I got a call from the sheriff after five o'clock in the morning. Meanwhile, Graham was set to graduate from high school in a few weeks and had no plans lined up either for the summer or the following school year. I wondered why he seemed so aimless and unmotivated.

For her part, Noelle planned to transfer to another college but could not decide which school she preferred, or even where to spend her summer. She insisted she did not want to go with me to Florida. She seemed at loose ends, and I was concerned about her. Then I received some difficult news. At about this time, the girls' counselor informed me that Noelle was battling bulimia. This was a huge blow. It seems that Noelle had spoken to the counselor about her condition because she knew bulimia was dangerous. Frequent vomiting can cause internal damage, and Noelle, who I learned had succumbed to the disorder her senior year of high school, was looking for help.

I was heartbroken by the news of Noelle's struggle, but I was not wholly shocked. Bulimia is a disorder related to control. Noelle had lost control of so much in her young life; it somehow made sense that she was striving to exert control over her body. I hurt deeply for her and with her. I was angry at the bulimia. We talked openly about it, and yet I knew I could not pressure Noelle. Bulimia cannot be overcome by confrontation alone; it is a "secret" disorder. The one affected needs time and, I believe, professional help in order to dismantle the disorder from within. I felt helpless, responsible, grieved.

I wrestled a great deal with guilt over the children's issues at this time. Their father and I had divorced. I had sold the farm and thrust the kids into a transitional environment. Now with no warning I was moving our home base to another state. Had I caused Noelle's eating disorder? Had I provoked Windsor's behavioral troubles? Had I consigned Graham to a life with little direction by sending him to live with his dad, who maintained a hectic schedule? I hurt for the children. I second-guessed my decisions. I tried to keep us going in the direction to which I had committed—Florida—but at times I wondered what in the world I was doing.

Ultimately, I realized I was going to have to renew my commitment to trust God with the children's lives. I needed to be present for my kids and invest my energy in their futures. Getting stuck in regret would not help them. I continued to search my heart to determine where I truly was responsible for the children's pain—I had been trying to do that since the divorce. But now, as the children began to hit the skids, I recognized it was time to let regret go and look to God as never before. I had entrusted the children to God before they were born. I had put their lives into God's hands before the divorce. Now I was going to have to believe God for their emotional healing and protection as they entered young adulthood. I found it was one thing to put my faith in God before trouble surfaced in their lives. It was quite another to reaffirm that faith on a daily basis once the trouble came. At times I was afraid for my children, but I remembered what Jeremiah wrote of God: "great is thy faithfulness" (Lamentations 3:23 KJV). I claimed this truth for the kids day after day.

ACTING ON IMPULSE?

In the stretch of weeks before my move to Florida, Noelle finally decided she would remain in the Valley for the summer before transferring to a college out-of-state in the fall. I took comfort in Noelle's remaining behind, even if for just a few months. I had begun to feel melancholy about leaving home, leaving friends, leaving the familiar. Knowing that Noelle would stay in Virginia awhile made the thought of moving seem less final. I could return. I could visit.

Even so, nostalgia for Virginia escalated. I grieved the loss of my life as I had known it and began to feel the loss acutely. At a certain point, my grief culminated in another decision. In those last days, I became convinced that relocating to Florida was a mistake. Moving away suddenly seemed an irrational proposition. We had lived in the Valley for about eight years. The girls were happy there. We had many friends. After consulting with some confidants, I decided to call everything off. I contacted the contractor and the realtor in Florida and told them to quit working. I did not have peace about going forward.

But almost as soon as I changed my direction, I began to wonder if I should go back to my original plan. I did not know which was more impulsive—the decision to move to Florida in the first place or my newest decision to retract. Which decision did I need to reverse? My emotions put me in a tailspin. Making major decisions on my own was foreign to me. I was extraordinarily vulnerable and easily influenced. I did not trust my own instincts.

This is where my inability to get still before God really hurt me. The Florida decision may have been the right one all along. I had purchased the home in Fort Lauderdale quickly and without planning for it; but I did want to hear from God and was trying to hear him in a way that made sense: by getting out and looking at houses. I was not sitting at home waiting for a thunderbolt to indicate where I was to go. I was trying to be practical. However, my peace about the decision never had a chance to take root because I did not put in the necessary time with God to clarify my course. I was too busy. Had I been able to slow down, I would have received from God the understanding I needed about where he was taking me in life and what I needed to do to get in line with his purposes. Without that understanding, I had no idea if in going to Florida I was in the will of God or not, and so I wavered. In the end, after listening to the rationale offered by supporters of the move, I changed my decision again. I called the realtor and others and told them to resume work on the house. I would go to Florida, I supposed. But I was a real mess.

Because I had not cultivated stillness, I was also unprepared for the unseen challenges that were about to arise in my life. I found I was doing to myself what I had done to my family after my marriage to Ted broke down. Just as I had not given my loved ones enough time to catch up with the reality of my marital situation before they had to adjust to the divorce, so I was not giving myself enough time now to catch up with all the changes in my life before making life-altering decisions. Even if moving to Florida was God's will for me, by the time I got there, I was unstable due to all of the busyness. My failure to get still and seek God before this new chapter of my life opened made me vulnerable. As a result, when the wind began to blow—and it blew hard—I stumbled, and then I fell.

Reminders for Painful Times

↶ Are you in a transition? Is your schedule packed with activity? Determine what activities are necessary and valuable, and cut out the others for the time being.

↶ Schedule downtime for yourself. Have quiet time with God every day. Try meditating on the Scriptures.

↶ Expect God to speak to you, but remember that he will speak when he chooses. He may be silent for a while, or he may say something other than what you expect. Even if he gives you a simple word, do what you believe God is telling you.

↶ Do not make major decisions if you have not received direction from God. Turn over to him your frustration with transition and ask him to give you the patience to wait for his timing.

↶ Have faith that God will show you what to do when the time is right. He is preparing a good future for you.

Tips for Those Who Care

- Remember that God is in control of your loved one's healing process. Ask God to renew your hope for your friend's future.
- Encourage your friend to cultivate stillness during transition. Emphasize his or her need for balance in daily life. Carefully encourage your friend to adjust his or her schedule to allow for downtime.
- Be patient when your friend comes to you repeatedly with the same issues and concerns, but guard your time and energy. Encourage your friend to make use of the benefits of transition.
- Point your friend toward God and encourage your friend in his or her devotional life.
- Be sensitive as you offer guidance. Be a good listener. Remind your friend that God has good plans for him or her.

MEMORY VERSE

Psalm 46:10 NIV

Be still, and know that I am God.

Principles for Reflection

Excessive busyness can be a trap.
Make time for rest during transition. Learn to be still.
Spend time with God.
He will give you direction when he is ready
and when he knows you are ready.

I DON'T WANT STAMINA— I WANT OUT!
Aborting God's Healing Work

I moved to Fort Lauderdale in July 1993. I put Windsor on a plane so she could meet up with Gigi's kids for a trip to Colorado. Noelle moved in with friends and stayed in the Valley for the remainder of the summer. For the first time, I made a move alone. My nest, indeed, was empty, but I was hopeful my little house and a new environment would inspire me as I started over.

Life had thrown me an unexpected, though not unwelcome, curve in the weeks preceding the move. On one of my trips to Florida to prepare for my relocation, Gigi and others had decided to introduce me to an impressive widower. The widower, whom I will call Frank, came highly recommended by reliable sources. He was well-thought-of in his church and was said to have given his life to Christ at one of my father's evangelistic meetings years earlier.

On our first date, Frank took me to dinner and treated me with respect. His manners evinced a familiarity with the finer things in life, and he came off as quite charming. I enjoyed myself but determined that Frank and I were not a good match. His personality seemed too strong for me. I wanted to be careful.

People around me, though, believed I should at least give Frank a chance. He was billed as an established, respectable person who could make plans, provide for, and take care of me. I listened and considered, still not trusting my own instincts.

Frank then asked me on a second date—this time, as I recall, for a tour in his boat. Again, I had a nice time, but I did not find myself particularly drawn to my companion. He appeared to be a powerful man in control of his life. He was physically attractive. He served faithfully in his church. But I was not overly interested.

Nonetheless, once I moved into my Fort Lauderdale house, I began seeing Frank on a regular basis. Being new in the area, perhaps I was too insecure to refuse his invitations. He seemed to be a spiritual man, and I became more attracted to him with every exposure. He was well mannered and gracious. He also possessed a remarkable presence. The dynamics of a room changed when he entered. I was flattered by his attentions.

In August, Windsor returned from her trip to Colorado with her cousins, and Noelle moved in with me temporarily before heading off to school at Samford University in Birmingham, Alabama. In the meantime, Frank invited us to join him on a cruise in the Bahamas. The girls did not seem terribly excited, but we accepted. I thought it would be a fun, new experience for us; and the trip would give us a break from the renovation work still going on at the house.

Windsor and Noelle did not take to this "new experience." They spent much of the time arguing and squabbling with each other and did not seem to enjoy themselves. The girls were not enamored of Frank. I, on the other hand, found myself caught up in the romance of the excursion. Frank's sense of confidence intrigued me. He seemed a man who could take care of the children and me, and I noticed my original resistance to his strength of personality dissipating. In a total reversal, I now found I was beginning to count on his strength to make me feel safe.

During the trip, Frank and I spoke more than once about the prospect of marriage. Looking back, such conversations were obviously incongruous with the depth of our relationship. Frank and I had known one another all of a couple of months. Even so, I told him that when he asked me to marry him, I would be ready to give him the answer he wanted. What I meant by this reply, I myself was not even certain. I truly did not expect a proposal to be imminent, but the very idea was exciting. I was swept up in the moment. Unsure of myself, I was hungry to feel settled. Frank had quickly become more important to me, and it felt good to be wanted.

On the last night of the cruise, the girls stayed on the ship while Frank and I disembarked. We walked on the beach and talked awhile. Then, standing in the moonlight, Frank turned to me and asked me to marry him. I remember feeling awed that he had proposed so soon after our exchanges on the subject, but as promised, I gave him the answer I thought he wanted. I said yes. And with that answer, I believe I aborted God's plans for my near future.

I still do not know how to account for this impulsiveness on my part. Yes, I wanted to be taken care of. I wanted a settled life. But obviously this brand-new relationship had not been tested. I suppose the votes of confidence from people in his church were enough to convince me Frank would make a good husband. How easily influenced I seemed to be! Why didn't I maintain some reserve, wait, and watch the relationship unfold for myself?

Clearly, I was vulnerable. I was still in transition, trying to acclimate to a new environment and build a life. This was not easy. After years of living in the largely rural Shenandoah Valley, I now had taken up residence alone in a strange city. I expected a change of this sort would challenge me in positive ways, but the unfamiliarity of my new surroundings left me feeling unsure of myself. I was now conscious of personal safety, for example. I kept the doors locked, even while at home, and tinted my car windows for security—an approach to life unfamiliar to me.

Other practical aspects of living remained unfamiliar. Though I had now been divorced from Ted for roughly two years, I still struggled in trying to figure out how to manage my finances. In fact, rather than conquer my apprehensions by learning the ropes of financial management, I simply had hired someone else to handle my money. This was a mistake. Taking care of my own finances, even if I had started off doing a poor job, would have given me a new measure of self-confidence. The independence would have anchored me and spilled over into other areas of my life. At the time, however, I gave power away, largely out of fear and a sense of inadequacy.

Looking back, I see that, ultimately, I did not believe I was capable of building my own life apart from a husband. I had known no other life, and I must not have trusted God enough to believe he could teach me a new role. Though opportunities to flourish in singleness were cropping up, I lacked the courage to take hold of them. Preferring to settle the matter, I gave someone else—in this case, someone I hardly knew—the authority to build my life for me. I allowed myself no time to adjust to my new environment and allowed God no time to cultivate the strength and self-sufficiency I required at this stage in life. I did not set out to abort God's plan. But through my bad choices, I did just that.

Where are you in your life right now? Are you still in a transition of some kind? So often, in our efforts to alleviate the frustration of waiting in transition, we end up making things worse. How can we avoid this? How can we protect ourselves from ourselves? A key, I have since learned, is to establish a circle of trusted confidants, including—if possible—friends, family members, and a pastor or counselor who all have your best interests at heart. Together, these trusted individuals comprise your safety net. Do not ignore their advice. Make yourself accountable. Trust these friends and loved ones to help guide you through your period of instability. Even if you feel that your supporters do not fully understand you or your situation, listen to and carefully weigh their counsel. They likely can see the big picture in ways you cannot. Conversely, stay away from people who do not know you well or are not committed to your long-term welfare. They might steer you in the wrong direction entirely.

FOR THE ONE WHO CARES

If you are a friend or loved one to someone who is living through an unstable time, recognize your friend's current vulnerability to making wrong decisions. Your friend may seem "normal" in his or her interactions with you, but your friend is still recovering from crisis and processing a loss. He or she is not operating at full strength. Understand your friend may be battling emotions that, if left unchecked, can prompt him or her to do the wrong thing. Consider what you can do to build up your friend when he or she is dealing with these emotions—loneliness, frustration, insecurity, impatience, and despair.

Pay attention to your friend's habits. Is your friend spending a lot of time alone at home? Is he or she locked into a routine with little variation? Where could your friend's daily life use a lift? Reach out in ways that will make your friend feel special, loved, and protected. Invite him or her to go out with you to a movie. Ask your friend to share a meal with you and your family. Your friend needs to keep getting exercise— invite him or her to take a walk. Send your friend a card in the mail. Let your friend know specifically what you are praying about for him or her each day, and be sure you are, in fact, praying! Your small, out-of-the-ordinary efforts will make your friend feel loved. Though your friend is ultimately responsible for his or her own choices, you can help your friend incline toward the right ones just by taking the time to reach out.

If it looks like your friend is going to make a major decision that could take him or her in the wrong direction, you may need to step in and offer strong advice. Begin by asking your friend questions about his or her decision. Why does your friend believe the decision is the right one? What are the gains and losses? Ask your friend to articulate what he or she believes will be the ramifications for the significant people in his or her life. How will your friend's spouse be affected? Your friend's children? Siblings? Parents? Challenge your friend to think about the decision from different angles. Encourage him or her to carefully weigh the pros and cons.

When you engage your friend in this manner, use a loving tone. Do not be afraid to be bold with your advice if you feel your friend is headed down the wrong road, but remind your friend that you are taking such a strong interest in his or her affairs because you love him or her and want God's best for his or her life. You will likely need to bring in other confidants from your friend's inner circle, though you may want to ask your friend's permission; otherwise he or she may feel betrayed or ganged up on. You may also come to a point where you want to involve the leadership from your friend's church, but seek good advice and step carefully before doing so. Finally, recognize that you cannot prevent your friend from doing something if he or she is determined to do it. At some point, we have to let go and allow our friends and loved ones to make mistakes.

In my situation, I had wonderful friends and family members who gave me good, sound advice. I was just too stubborn and willful to listen. And am I ever sorry! I was in a hurry to get my life going in the direction I wanted. Resist the urge to be in a hurry. Relationships, if intended by God, will work out eventually. God will make things come together in his timing and will not rush you through your healing process. If you feel rushed, then step back and ask yourself why you feel that way. Ask God to show you the source of your anxiety. But do not act while you are anxious.

God indicates his direction by giving us peace. If you do not have peace, then stop. As is true following the death of a loved one, I would advise against making any significant decisions for at least a year after your crisis. God has all the time in the world. If your heart is to do his will, then he will make his direction so clear you will not be able to miss it. In the meantime, remember that he wants you to be whole—totally healed.

Perhaps you have already made a decision that has altered the terrain of your life for what looks like the worse. You may be devastated about your choice. Take comfort in God's promise to use even your mistakes to advance his greater purpose for your life. Remember that failure is never final. Ruins are where God begins. His Word promises that he will make "all things to work together for good to those who love God, to those who are called according to His purpose" (Romans 8:28). Do you love him? Are you seeking his purpose?

If so, this promise holds true for you. We may have to live with consequences, but God still loves us. He still wants to redeem us. Go back to your decision to trust in his goodness. God will bring life out of what looks dead. He will make our mess ultimately into something beautiful. He promises, "I will repay you for the years the locusts have eaten" (Joel 2:25 NIV). I was about to learn this truth the hard way.

MELTDOWN

My daughters were distressed about my engagement to Frank. Both girls adamantly opposed it. Living in Dallas, Graham was not as immediately affected by my decision. He just wanted me to be happy. As I saw it, the children were moving on with their lives. Again, rather than be cautioned by their responses, I reasoned that, as a single woman living on my own, I needed to make choices keeping the kids in mind, but not allowing their needs to dictate what was best for me. Such was my logic, though evidently my ability to judge what was best for me was less than adequate.

After the cruise, the girls and I began to make preparations for the school year. Ted arranged to take Noelle to Samford. I already had enrolled Windsor at a school in town, but she was not happy with that choice; so I investigated boarding school options, and we settled on a school in South Carolina. After Noelle left for Birmingham, Frank and I drove Windsor to her new campus.

Taking Windsor to boarding school proved a painful experience. While she had seemed willing to go as we drove there, once we arrived on campus she had misgivings about staying. She had endured so much change—transition, in fact, had encompassed all of her formative and young adolescent years. Ted and I first separated when she was in fifth grade; now she was in tenth. In between had been the divorce, the sale of the farm, the departure of her sister and brother, and my relocation to Florida. Now that we had gotten to South Carolina, and yet another school, Windsor was weary and emotional. I did not blame her. She said she did not want me to leave, and it took a good deal of strength for me to go through with it.

Driving out of the campus gates, however, I could not help but feel a wave of relief. At least the girls were settled. I knew I badly needed to rest, and Frank pulled out all the stops to make me feel special. I convinced myself I was about to gain security and enter a long-awaited season of enjoyment.

But it wasn't long before I began to notice some red flags in my relationship with Frank. At different junctures, he made comments to which I should have paid closer attention. A close friend of mine from Virginia visited me in Florida and told me outright that marrying Frank would be a mistake. This friend knew me well. She had walked with me through the divorce from Ted and its aftermath. She knew my kids. After spending time with Frank and me, she expressed unadulterated alarm.

Listening to my friend share her concerns about the prospect of a marriage, I found myself in agreement. Her admonition to call off the wedding resonated with me. Canceling my plans seemed the right thing to do—I felt peace when I considered doing so. But once my friend boarded her plane, I reverted to my former mind-set. Perhaps I was afraid of letting Frank go. I had become dependent on him for stability. He now was a vital part of my new identity. The thought of things not working out frightened me. I would be alone. I would be in transition yet again. While hearing the warnings, I deceived myself into believing everything would be fine.

Then the rubber met the road. During a heated exchange late in the fall, Frank made some statements that caused me enough distress to pull out of the relationship. I was crushed. Friends and loved ones were fully behind me in my decision to break things off. I flew to my parents' home in North Carolina to clear my head and to take comfort in the embrace of family.

But some time later, Frank and I began to communicate again. We discussed the breakup, and Frank renewed his pursuit of my affections. I wanted to resist, but in the end, his strength won the day. He exuded confidence, and I was unsure of myself. Before long, I agreed to resume the relationship and, unbelievably, to move in the direction of marriage.

Throughout these hectic months, I continued to pray and to spend time each day reading the Scriptures. In my eyes, nothing I read seemed to indicate I should put on the brakes. But did I earnestly want to hear from God concerning my marriage plans? Probably not. Was I crying out in prayer to God in search of his direction? I doubt it. I did ask God to speak to me, but when all was said and done, I suppose I only heard what I wanted to hear. I probably picked and chose the Bible verses that confirmed my own agenda.

Are you in a time of decision? Are you really seeking God about it? Be brutally honest with yourself. Perhaps you are particularly vulnerable to making the wrong decision at this time. If so, then acknowledge your vulnerability. Do not deceive yourself. Maybe friends have warned you about taking a course of action, and you find you are not inclined to heed their advice. Maybe that course of action looks like it will take care of a lot of your problems in one fell swoop. Are you intent on going down the road that looks good? Or do you really want to hear from God? Your road may be the right road. But it may be a distraction—a costly distraction. Do not be tempted to grab hold of what looks like a quick fix. Remember, God is never in a hurry. His work is not superficial; it is thorough and deep. If you find you are praying and looking into the Scriptures with less than an open heart, ask God to change your heart. You do not want to take matters into your own hands. The Bible teaches, "There is a way which seems right to a man, But its end is the way of death" (Proverbs 14:12).

I often wonder if I would have welcomed a firm, reasoned intervention to the marriage to Frank. Not likely. The important people in my life tried to stop me. My parents called me and urged me not to go through with a wedding. Other loved ones voiced opposition to the marriage. Obviously, I did not listen. Again, I heeded only the signs that confirmed my own agenda. People at church seemed excited for Frank and me, and though these individuals were only casual acquaintances, I read the enthusiasm of fellow believers as a sign that God was sanctioning my course. In my mind, I suppose, my plan was set—I already could envision the ceremony.

While the kids were away at Christmastime, Frank and I spontaneously set our wedding date for New Year's Eve. I phoned the children and told them the news. Graham seemed nonchalant, perhaps thinking his mom would make the right choice for her life. Windsor was angry. Noelle was upset and insisted she would not come for the wedding. In the end, however, all three kids came to Florida and were with me for the ceremony.

The wedding was a simple affair held in my living room with only a few guests in attendance. After Frank and I said our vows, my daughters went back to Windsor's room in tears. I encouraged the girls to try to be happy for me. I told them they would get used to the new alignment in our family. Meanwhile, I was truly excited about my new life and remember sharing my joy with one friend by saying I was so thrilled "I could bust!" Here I was with a man who was going to take care of me, a man who was in charge. The house looked beautiful. The guests were happy. It all seemed dreamy—at least for those moments.

When Frank and I got ready to leave the house, however, I began to see hints of another reality. I learned that Frank had not made dinner reservations. Because it was New Year's Eve, finding a restaurant with available seating became quite an ordeal. Once we got to a place that looked like it might have room, Frank got out of the car and, as I recall, proceeded to walk toward the restaurant; he did not come around to my side and open the car door, as was his gallant custom. After dinner, we checked into a dreary hotel. I no longer felt protected or cherished.

The next morning I opened the *Daily Light* and read a familiar verse that had sustained me throughout the divorce from Ted—one I also had read as a prayer for the children from time to time: "I know whom I have believed, and am persuaded that he is able to keep that which I have committed unto him against that day" (2 Timothy 1:12 KJV). This passage also was printed there: "I am persuaded, that neither death, nor life, nor angels, nor principalities, nor powers, nor things present, nor things to come, nor height, nor depth, nor any other creature, shall be able to separate us from the love of God, which is in Christ Jesus" (Romans 8:38–39 KJV). These verses were a comfort to me. They spoke of God's faithfulness, and at this particular moment, I needed to be reminded that God was with me. I did not know what to do. Even now, I was beginning to sense that my life with Frank might not turn out as I originally imagined, and I was dismayed.

My anxiety about the marriage only increased in the following weeks. As days passed, Frank's treatment of me seemed to change. Before the wedding, I believed he was a man who loved me and would take care of me. Once we were married, however, I began to have a different impression. Scenes and conversations from our dating days—things to which I should have paid attention at the time—began to surface in my mind; and gradually I came to some conclusions about my new husband that I had not arrived at before the wedding. Again, I had been so intent on getting what I wanted, I had seen only those things that coincided with my plans. Now my observations added up to a disheartening picture of both my circumstances and the person to whom I had entrusted myself. I was crushed and bewildered. I wondered how I could make the relationship work.

In fact, a little more than a month into our marriage, my relationship with Frank completely fell apart. We had an argument one afternoon, and Frank said some things that caused me to feel concerned for my personal safety. This particular scene took place at his house. I still owned my house in Fort Lauderdale, and after Frank made the comments in question, I got into my car and began to drive there.

I did not intend to leave Frank permanently at that time. Before I could get to my destination, however, my thinking changed. Frank called me on my car phone and made assertions that only furthered my apprehension. After the call, I knew I could not go back to him. I was convinced that to do so would be unwise and might jeopardize my well-being.

Once I hung up the phone I shifted into crisis mode. I dialed my mother's number from the car, hoping she would help me at this time of panic, but Mother was in a meeting and unavailable. When she finally called back, I explained my sense of urgency.

"Mother," I said, "something has happened with Frank. I can't go back."

Without hesitation, she spoke to me in her firm but tender voice. "Come home," she urged. "Come home."

Reminders for Painful Times

- Are you in transition? Establish a circle of trusted confidants and rely on them to help guide you. Listen to and carefully weigh their advice. Make yourself accountable. Do not rely on people who don't know you well or who don't have your best interests at heart.
- Do not be in a hurry to make life-altering decisions. Do not make decisions based on anxiety. Wait for God to give you peace.
- If you have made a significant decision you now regret, remember that failure is never final. God still loves you. You may have to live with consequences, but God promises to make something beautiful out of your ruins.
- Are you in a time of decision? Are you really seeking God about your choices? Be honest with yourself. If you find you are more interested in your own agenda than in God's plan, ask him to change your heart. You do not want to take matters into your own hands.

Tips for Those Who Care

~ Is your friend or loved one in transition? Recognize your friend's vulnerability to making wrong decisions. He or she is still recovering from crisis. Gently talk to your friend about your concern for him or her.

~ Consider what you can do to build up your friend. Pay attention to your friend's habits. Reach out in ways that will make your friend feel special, loved, and secure. Encourage him or her to share. Listen patiently.

~ Is your friend about to make a major decision that could take him or her in the wrong direction? You may need to offer strong advice. Ask your friend questions about the decision. Challenge him or her to think about the decision from different angles.

~ Use a loving tone when engaging your friend. Do not be afraid to be bold with your advice, but remind your friend of your love and that you want God's best for him or her.

~ If your friend is about to make a life-altering decision, you likely will need to bring in other confidants from your friend's inner circle. You also may need to involve church leaders at some point. Seek counsel before acting, and realize that you may have to let your friend make a mistake.

MEMORY VERSE

Proverbs 14:12

There is a way which seems right to a man,
But its end is the way of death.

⌒⟩

Principles for Reflection

God is not in a hurry.
If you feel rushed to make a decision,
then stop and ask yourself why.
Listen to your close friends and advisers.

HAVE I OUTSINNED GOD'S GRACE?
Experiencing God's Healing Embrace

After our conflict, Frank left town for a few days. I wanted to be on the road to Montreat before he got back, and making that happen required a near herculean effort. I retrieved my belongings from Frank's house and left him a letter of explanation. I hired a locksmith to change the locks on my own house. Then I put my house on the market and collected estimates from moving companies. I located a tenant to occupy the house until it sold. Finally, I packed all of my important valuables into my car and drove away. How I managed to organize myself so quickly is beyond me. My sister Gigi was an enormous help.

En route to Montreat I picked up Windsor at her boarding school in South Carolina. I already had phoned Noelle and Graham; both were anxious about my safety and well-being. And I had spoken to Ted, who was kind and solicitous. When I told Windsor I had left Frank, she reacted strongly. We were sitting in my car, and Windsor became so upset she got out of the car wailing. She had just begun to get used to the idea that her mother was remarried. Now in less than six weeks everything had changed. With no warning. It was a lot for a fifteen-year-old to handle. It was a lot for me to handle. I tried to hold myself together in the face of my daughter's grief, but I worried about the harm I undoubtedly had caused her.

Gigi had phoned ahead to Montreat to let my parents know when to expect Windsor and me. I felt wrecked. I was coming home with my life in pieces. The transition I so badly had hoped to curtail by marrying Frank was now upon me in a fiercer way than ever before. Shame weighed me down. I dreaded having to meet my parents' gaze—I didn't think I could handle what their eyes might communicate. Disapproval? Embarrassment? Condemnation? I wanted to run and hide. But I could not. I had nowhere else to go.

I look back now, overwhelmed by God's tenderness and timing, for it was at this, my darkest hour when God stepped in with one of his most powerful metaphors in my life. I climbed the mountain to Little Piney Cove, my grieved daughter beside me, questions racing through my mind, fear welling up inside, and humiliation all but stamping out my hope. Yet still I climbed. I could not undo my mistake. I knew I had to face it. I felt unworthy to go home, but I needed my parents. I had only reached the top of the driveway when I spotted my father waiting in the parking area. Opening the car door, I barely had time to set foot on the asphalt before he was at my side. This dear father, who had every reason to rebuke, wrapped his strong arms around me, pulled me into a warm embrace, and greeted me with those simple words: "Welcome home."

My father's embrace at that moment was one of the most profound gestures of acceptance I have ever experienced. To be utterly broken and still accepted. To feel ugly and yet be loved. To feel like an outcast and still be welcomed. Unhesitatingly welcomed. I marveled at the contrast between my heart, full of shame and self-loathing, and my father's, so full of love. I must have felt many things at once in his arms: shock, relief, gratitude, safety, disbelief. One thing I most definitely felt was shattered. And through his embrace, my father let me know I had permission to feel that way. He was not condemning me. No defense or explanation was required.

My parents' love extended far beyond the welcome home. I stayed in Montreat for about two months, and Mother and Daddy lovingly supported me. They never sermonized or blamed me for what had happened; they exhibited God's mercy. I was refreshed by their compassion and also surprised by it. Leaving Fort Lauderdale, I had imagined that my impulsiveness in marrying Frank, my willfulness, and my hard-heartedness—my sins—would damage my family relationships. I was prepared for my parents to express grave disappointment in me. I, the middle child who always sought to please, now had created havoc that would touch not just my own life but also the lives of others. How could my loved ones forgive me for all I had done?

During those months in Montreat, I wrestled with an almost overpowering sense of guilt. If I had struggled in blaming myself for the kids' issues before all of this, then after the ordeal with Frank, my struggle escalated far beyond what I previously had experienced. I would lie in bed and condemn myself, knowing that six months earlier none of this mess had happened. Less than a year earlier I had not even left Virginia. Now my life was suddenly upside down. It was more than just upside down; it was no longer intact. I had destabilized my children and now felt untrustworthy as a parent. How could I regain my kids' respect? How could I persuade them they could count on me? How could I ever forgive myself? This new reality was very hard to face. My pride came crashing down around me. I had no self-respect to stand on.

I realized that, whereas I once had felt like the forgotten older brother in the story of the prodigal son, I now squarely inhabited the place of the prodigal. I was the one who had squandered my opportunities; I was the one whose life had fallen to pieces; I was the one having to come home. I remember feeling I could understand Ted better in the wake of my own wrongdoing. Years earlier I had condemned Ted for being the prodigal, and I had stoked my own indignation over having been victimized. Now I was the prodigal, and, indeed, there were new victims.

After Ted's infidelities had come to light, I resented the open arms my friends and family offered him. But in the wake of Florida, I saw how desperately I needed those same arms to open up to me. I found that my life depended on receiving what I did not deserve—the warmth and unconditional love so beautifully pictured by my father when he greeted me in the driveway, caring nothing about my faults but only for the child who had wandered away and now had come home. The story of the prodigal, I discovered, was not about the sons after all—it was about the incomparable, embracing love of the father.

The months at Montreat were months of recovery. I spent a lot of time resting and praying. I wrote in my journal daily in an effort to process my whirlwind experience in Florida. I wrote a newsletter to family, asking my loved ones to forgive me for bringing shame on them. I especially sensed God helping me understand myself at this time; and I learned more about the depth of his love for me than ever before.

One Sunday morning I was sitting with Mother in the sanctuary of Montreat Presbyterian Church. A friend of Mother's had joined us for the worship service, and, as always, we sat toward the back of the church on the right-hand side. The sanctuary was crowded, and our dear, decades-long friend and pastor

Calvin Thielman was preaching on the gospel account of the woman and the alabaster box.

In the story, a woman of ill repute visits a home where Jesus is eating, bringing with her an alabaster box of very costly perfume. Standing behind Jesus, the weeping woman begins to wet Jesus' feet with her tears, kissing and wiping his feet with her hair as she anoints them with the expensive ointment. Observing this, the religious leader in whose home the scene takes place says to himself, "If this man were a prophet He would know who and what sort of person this woman is who is touching Him, that she is a sinner" (Luke 7:39).

Jesus then tells a parable about debt and forgiveness, explaining that one who has been forgiven much loves much, while one who has been forgiven little loves little. "Do you see this woman?" Jesus asks the religious leader. "I entered your house; you gave Me no water for My feet, but she has wet My feet with her tears, and wiped them with her hair. You gave Me no kiss; but she, since the time I came in, has not ceased to kiss My feet. You did not anoint My head with oil, but she anointed My feet with perfume. For this reason I say to you, her sins, which are many, have been forgiven, for she loved much. . . ." Jesus then turns to the woman and says, "Your sins have been forgiven" (Luke 7:44–48).

As I took notes and listened intently, it began to seem as if Calvin were addressing his message to me. I remember him explaining that the aroma of the woman's costly perfume could be released only after she had broken open the alabaster box. Calvin used the illustration to explain that our brokenness releases a sweet fragrance to God as well; that when we come to the end of ourselves and turn to God, offering him what we have, he honors our offering and begins the process of changing us. At that moment, I had the overwhelming sense God was speaking directly to my heart. I felt a desire to come clean—to acknowledge my sin and have a fresh start. It was as if I was breaking open right then, and God was changing me with his love.

Once Calvin had finished preaching, the organist began to play, and we prepared to sing a final hymn. Then something unexpected happened. As I remember, the organist looked at Calvin, and Calvin gestured to him to stop playing. A tall Texan with silver hair, our pastor stood formidably in his long, black robe and explained that he felt it necessary, rather than close the service, to give people the opportunity to come forward to the altar and do business with God.

I do not remember Calvin's exact words. I only recall knowing that I was supposed to step out of the pew and walk to the front of the church. As soon as this occurred to me, I was assailed by the familiar onrush of doubts. *I'm Ruth Graham's daughter. The whole congregation will see me. What will they think? How can I do this?* But the pull to walk forward proved stronger than my desire to hide. I thought, "This is between God and me. I've got to unload this burden. I want to be whole."

I stepped into the aisle and began to walk. No one else in the sanctuary had moved. I gathered my small courage and, looking up, saw Calvin standing at the front of the church waiting for me. When I got to him, he opened his arms and warmly embraced me. I collapsed onto him and wept. He then asked his assistant to close out the service, and he led me into his study.

When we got to Calvin's study, I cried without reservation. I was so completely broken. I had hit bottom. Calvin understood my condition and let me say whatever was on my heart. He did not question or criticize me. He prayed with me. He was sweet and gentle. Calvin had witnessed some difficult episodes in my life. He knew what I had endured through my divorce from Ted; he knew how I had struggled with my children's issues. Now here he was comforting me, allowing me to pour out the depth of my emotion as I confessed my sins before God, repented, and asked God to forgive me. Calvin's gentleness and acceptance were like a balm.

I let go of all the pent-up emotion—the fear, guilt, anxiety, condemnation, shame, and humiliation. I had left Florida in such a hurry. I had tried to hold myself together and be strong. In Calvin's office, I felt as if the floodgates of my soul were opened. I did not have to hold myself together. I did not have to be strong. I could let go of the sins and mistakes. I experienced an almost physical sensation of release, as if God himself were taking the weight off of me.

Calvin told me he did not know why he had been compelled to make such an altar call at that time; he did not regularly call congregants to the altar. Nor did he know why the organist had happened to glance his way and afford him a chance to change the course of the service so naturally. Listening to Calvin, I realized that *God* had stopped the service—and that he had stopped it for *me*. God was reaching out to me. He was going to redeem me. I was important to God. Even in my failure, he loved me enough to alter the plans of my pastor in order to touch my life. My own father had welcomed me into his arms on my return home. Now God, with his everlasting arms, was doing the same.

GOD'S OPEN ARMS

This message of God's love was a crucial one for me to receive at that time. Going through the divorce from Ted entailed brokenness, but what I suffered after leaving Florida was a true and complete breaking. I did not know if I would ever be able to forgive myself. I did not know if I would ever recover. As I walked to the altar that day, God showed me the power of his love to transform. His love redeemed my sins and mistakes. His love lifted my burden. His love renewed my hope. Though the days ahead would include much difficulty and effort, I do not think I ever condemned myself again about the marriage to Frank. I felt washed. I was more secure in God's love for me than ever before, and I had a greater understanding of his unbelievable grace. I still had to live out a process, but something in me had changed. Restoration could begin.

Do you identify with the role of the prodigal son? Have you blown opportunities in your life? Have you made costly mistakes? Have you alienated those who love you? Have you sinned? Do you want to return to God, ask his forgiveness, and make a new start? Remember, God sees you—he knows your situation, and he wants to redeem you. You may not have experienced a reception from others like the one given by the prodigal's father in the gospel story, but God waits open-armed to receive you. You may not have been shown mercy by loved ones, but God is showering you with mercy. Do not hide from God in shame. His arms are open. He stands ready to forgive.

When you decide to come back to God and repent of your sins, he responds immediately. His heart is rejoicing over your return! He forgives you! He has removed your sin far from you—in the words of the psalmist, "As far as the east is from the west" (Psalm 103:12). You are free to go, free to live, free to recover! In God, you always have a second chance. Thank him for that from your heart. Remember the openness with which the woman in the religious leader's home expressed her gratitude to Jesus for his love. She took a risk by even coming to him. But there must have been something about Jesus that drew her. She poured out her costly ointment on him and worshiped, wiping his feet with her hair. He is drawing you to himself as well. Thank God and worship him for the love he offers, for the opportunity you have to start again!

Very often in moments like these, God asks us to do something to affirm our repentance and our love for him. I had to step into the church aisle and walk to the front of the sanctuary. God knew that stepping out in front of a crowd was not an easy thing for me to do. Though I had responded to altar calls in church settings before, my tendency was to retreat with my deepest emotions to a private place. But obedience is a sign of our love. Jesus said, "If you love Me, you will keep My commandments" (John 14:15). God asked me to go against the grain of my personality and step out. I obeyed, and he met me there.

God also knew it was an important part of my healing to publicly repent and show emotion. I had spent my life trying to look right and do the right things. I had gotten used to hiding. I was comfortable hiding. But it wasn't good for me. Hiding was unhealthy. God wanted me to be free. My test of obedience was also an opportunity to experience freedom—to love God openly, to be vulnerable before others. And with that obedience came my healing.

Perhaps you identify more with the older brother in the story of the prodigal son. You are frustrated. You do not feel you are being treated fairly. Maybe you feel invisible, taken for granted, while a prodigal in your life seems to be getting all the attention and accolades. Maybe you feel bitter about the difference in the ways you and the prodigal are being treated. Maybe you feel outright betrayed. Tell God what you feel. Be honest with him—it is good for you to express yourself. Let him know you feel hurt by what looks like injustice.

Now think back to the message of the boiling pot in the first chapter of Jeremiah. God is a just God. He is your vindicator. He will make all things fair one day. Circumstances may not look fair to you at this time, but God sees your end from your beginning. He is not partial to the prodigal. God loves all of us with the same total, extravagant love. Recall your decision to believe in God's goodness. A good God will not forget or neglect you. He sees you. He loves you. Your feelings and issues are important to him.

What do you feel toward the prodigal in your life? Are you envious? Resentful? Angry? I encourage you to confess any wrong attitudes and ask God to change your heart. Remember what the father in the prodigal story told the older brother: "My child, you have always been with me, and all that is mine is yours. But we had to be merry and rejoice, for this brother of yours was dead and has begun to live, and was lost and has been found" (Luke 15:31–32).

God is pleased with you for having remained steadfast. You have enjoyed the unbroken fellowship and pleasure of the father. He has never stopped being delighted with you. Enjoy his delight. What is happening in the life of the prodigal—the welcome he or she is experiencing—is not about you. Regardless of the actions of those around you, God is giving you the opportunity to forget yourself for a moment and rejoice that someone who was headed down the wrong road has turned back and has been redeemed. You don't want to miss the chance to rejoice with heaven! Ask God to help you rise above your difficult emotions. Ask him to help you let go of your anger toward those who may be focusing their attention on the prodigal. Let God change your heart so you too can open your arms in welcome.

FOR THE ONE WHO CARES

Maybe you have the honor of playing the role of the prodigal's father in the life of a friend or loved one. What an opportunity! To have the chance to show God's grace and mercy to a broken person! God has entrusted you with a privilege at this moment. Thank him for choosing you. Thank him for trusting you with the heart of another. The psalmist wrote, "The LORD is near to the brokenhearted, And saves those who are crushed in spirit" (Psalm 34:18). Now God is giving you the chance to demonstrate this same nearness and love.

Ask God to help you lovingly accept the one who is humbly returning to you. Ask God to give you his love for that person. Remember what the father in the story did when he saw his son on the road. Jesus said the father "felt compassion for him, and ran and embraced him, and kissed him" (Luke 15:20). The father did not wait for his son—he *couldn't* wait. His heart was so full of love, he ran to his son in welcome. This is the way the Lord responds to returning prodigals. His heart overflows for those who have been lost and then return.

Don't let hurts from the past or frustration with your friend or loved one rob you of the chance to extend grace now that he or she is repentant. Let the offense go. Don't miss your opportunity to show God's love. If you make up your mind to take the part of the prodigal's father—to welcome a friend back into your life and demonstrate God's grace—then God himself will step in and give you the ability to do it. He will enable you to give yourself to the one in need. As you do so, you will experience an enlarging of your capacity to extend grace and to restore. The more we give, the larger will be our capacity to give until our hearts, like God's, are overflowing. Nothing has the power to change us like love, and the Bible says, "It is more blessed to give than to receive" (Acts 20:35). Exercise your faith and open your arms.

GOING HOME

There were yet many decisions to be made during those months in Montreat. Not the least of them involved what I was to do about the marriage to Frank. I knew that God had charged me to guard my personal welfare and look after my children. I believed that going back to the marriage would jeopardize my ability to fulfill those responsibilities. Still, I studied the Scriptures and sought godly counsel from trusted individuals concerning what to do. After a lot of praying and searching, I concluded I should not go back to the marriage and that I had grounds to end it. I hoped I was interpreting the Scriptures properly. I had submitted myself to counsel from those who were more impartial, older, and wiser than I. I thought my trepidation about returning to the marriage was founded, and so did my counselors. In the end, I threw myself on God's mercy and moved on.

My next major decision, a difficult one for me, was determining where to live. Since arriving in Montreat in February, I had been living in our family's first house, called the Old House, at the bottom of the mountain; and I wondered if perhaps Montreat was where I needed to be after all. A solid, God-loving community, Montreat was much closer to Windsor's boarding school, and I knew I would have a good church to attend. By March I was leaning toward staying, and I spontaneously signed a contract on a little yellow Victorian cottage. I saw another opportunity to fix up a charming house and reasoned that the purchase would be a good investment. But I was acting somewhat impulsively yet again.

Then came the storm of indecision. A few weeks later, I found myself homesick for Virginia and my friends there, so I changed my mind about Montreat and told Mother I was "going home" to look for a place to live. In the Valley, I located a promising condominium but did not commit to buying it right away. North Carolina might turn out to be a good thing, I figured, and I did not want to reverse those plans too quickly. Of course, at this point, the meaning of "quickly" was relative. Everything seemed to move quickly.

In April, my house in Fort Lauderdale sold at a profit, and I went down to pack up my things. Where the movers would take the things was still in question. Actually, I am convinced the movers thought me one of the flakier individuals with whom they had to deal. On loading day, I still did not know whether to send the furniture to North Carolina or Virginia—I even considered storing it in Florida.

"Is there any other state you want to go to?" one mover asked.

"No," I said, laughing. "It'll be North Carolina or Virginia." The whole episode was starting to feel like a repeat of my wavering over whether to move to Florida.

In the end, I decided to return to the Valley. "The principle I'm operating on," I wrote in my journal, "is: to go back to where I started making mistakes." I referenced the angel's command to Hagar, Sarah's maid: "Return to your mistress, and submit yourself to her authority" (Genesis 16:9). Later I recorded, "Perhaps to go back to a place of defeat & have victory." The divorce from Ted and subsequent sale of the farm had pulled the rug out from under me and thrown me off-balance. It was then that my life began to spiral out of control. I reasoned that now was the time to go back—back home to Virginia—and begin again there.

By going back to Virginia, I did not feel like I was starting my life over exactly. I had been absent from the Valley for only nine months. But I did feel like I was returning with my tail between my legs. I told myself I was probably worth just one social gathering's worth of gossip, and I tried to hold my head high. After all, God had forgiven me. What were the comments of others when my heavenly Father had erased my sin? He would pave the way for me and make everything right eventually. He was my vindicator. My job, I reminded myself, was to trust him.

Trusting, I realized now, would mean more than saying simply, "Okay, God, I'll trust you," and then going merrily on my way. Trusting was about sticking with my choice to trust and hanging on to God for dear life. When Jacob wrestled with God at Peniel, he said to the Lord, "I will not let you go unless you bless me" (Genesis 32:26). Jacob trusted that if he could just hold on to God, then God *would* bless him. I knew this had to be my posture as I headed back to Virginia.

Trusting might be messy—it might be tough to go back to the place where I had begun making mistakes. But I could do it, knowing that God's ultimate purpose for me as I returned to the Valley was good. With my recent decisions in Florida, I may have aborted God's purpose for my life in some ways, but his larger purpose for me took even my sin into account. He had a plan to weave my mistakes into something he could use. I had to believe that. And I was determined not to let go of God until he blessed me.

Reminders for Painful Times

꙾ Do you identify with the prodigal son? Have you sinned or made mistakes that cause you to believe you have wrecked your life? Do not hide from God in shame. His arms are open to you. It is the enemy of your soul who condemns—not your heavenly Father.

꙾ Thank God for his grace—for giving you a second chance. Remember how openly the woman with the alabaster box expressed her gratitude to Jesus for his love.

꙾ Is God asking you to do something to affirm your repentance at this time? As you obey, you will grow and begin to experience healing and joy.

꙾ Do you identify with the prodigal's older brother? Do you feel you are being treated unfairly or taken for granted while a prodigal in your life gets all the attention? Talk to God about your feelings.

꙾ Remember that God is just. His love is impartial. He loves you just as much as he loves the prodigal. If you harbor negative attitudes toward the prodigal in your life, confess them to God and ask God to change you.

꙾ Recognize that God is giving you an opportunity to rejoice with him over the return of someone who was headed in the wrong direction. Let go of your anger, and let God change your heart so you can open your arms in welcome as well.

Tips for Those Who Care

꙾ Has God given you the opportunity to play the father to a returning prodigal in your life? Recognize the great honor with which God has entrusted you—the chance to express his love to a broken person.

꙾ Ask God to help you see this person as he does and to give you his compassion for the returning prodigal. Don't let past hurts or frustration with this person rob you of your opportunity to demonstrate love and grace.

꙾ God will give you the ability to welcome the prodigal with compassion as well as the freedom to do so with genuine joy.

꙾ Exercise your faith. Open your arms.

MEMORY VERSE
Deuteronomy 33:27 KJV
The eternal God is thy refuge, and underneath are the everlasting arms.

Principles for Reflection

*God stands ready to forgive and
to welcome us in his embrace.*

WHO AM I?

Learning to Be Authentic

Feeling very timid and unsure of myself—not to mention afraid—I stepped up to the microphone to speak. An auditorium full of people stretched out in front of me. Nearby were the organizers of the ministry event. I wondered what they knew of me. Did they know my recent history? What might they be thinking? Why was I even here? Why had I agreed to do this?

I had traveled to Owen Sound, Ontario, to give my testimony at this meeting because John Wesley White, a veteran associate evangelist for the Billy Graham Evangelistic Association, had invited me. In truth, the invitation had come as a shock. Having only just returned to the Valley after my experience in Florida, I had prepared myself to live quietly. I knew God had forgiven me for my mistakes. I knew he loved me. But I did not expect him to use me in any public ministry venue. Hadn't my choices disqualified me? I felt totally inadequate. His forgiveness and love were enough. I expected little else.

And yet I wanted to believe that God had something more for me. Windsor, who by then was home from boarding school, urged me to accept the invitation to the meeting. I had no idea what of value I could offer. I feared being judged, shunned, and criticized. Still, the mere fact that I had been asked to speak stirred up the faintest hint of anticipation. Perhaps God did have something for me to do. Perhaps I did have a purpose, however modest. In my heart I dared to hope.

Now, standing at the podium, I wondered what I had been thinking when I said I would do this. How could I give a testimony? What could I say except that I had failed miserably? I had blown it—what could God do with that statement? Surely, the people were expecting me to tell them something of significance: I was Billy Graham's daughter. But standing there, I realized all I could do was be myself. I would have to be honest, or I would not honor God. And I desperately wanted to honor God. I had lost so much. What else really mattered?

I began to speak on a passage of Scripture I had been reading during my devotional time that morning. Originally I had planned something different, but at the last minute, I sensed God leading me in another direction. The familiar passage I now read came from the book of Psalms:

> He makes me lie down in green pastures,
> he leads me beside quiet waters,
>   he restores my soul.
> He guides me in paths of righteousness
>   for his name's sake.
>
> PSALM 23:2–3 NIV

One phrase at a time, I walked the audience through the passage, sharing what I believed God had shown me during my time in the Scriptures. I explained that sometimes, through circumstances and life events, God makes us lie down. We need to lie down, and if we don't do it voluntarily, then God will make us—for our own good. I pointed out that when God makes us lie down, he gives us green pastures in which to rest. Green indicates the presence of life. God's purpose is to renew. He doesn't make us lie down in the dust. Then God leads us—goes ahead of us and shows us the way—beside quiet waters. Water speaks of refreshing, of cleansing. God cleanses us of sin, guilt, and shame.

I told the audience of my own love for the gentle lapping of quiet waters more than for the roar of the ocean. In a quiet place, I said, God cleanses my heart, and then he restores me. He takes the broken pieces and puts them together again. The regrets. The hurts and shame. He builds out of my wrecks, my ruins. Finally, once he restores, God guides me in paths of righteousness. Why? For his name's sake. My restoration is not ultimately about me. God wants to receive the glory for the good that comes out of my life. He is the reason I live. My renewal, my recovery—these are for him.

As I spoke, I looked out at the audience, having no idea what lay ahead for me. I only knew I was where God wanted me to be at that moment. I spoke of my experience with the brokenness of divorce and the depression I had battled.

I was not at a place emotionally where I could share much detail about these things, but I knew I had to be honest and transparent on some level. In being so, I could talk about God's life-giving, restorative love with a measure of authenticity I had not experienced before. For I was in the midst of God's renewing process right then—I was in it. And from that place I could speak with conviction.

The audience seemed to respond to my vulnerability, and as far as I knew, this was all God wanted from me. I was content that God had used me in some way to help others and relieved I had not been rejected. On my way to the Toronto airport after the event, however, I caught a glimpse of something more that God wanted me to see. A married couple graciously drove me, and as we traveled, I shared some of my difficult life experiences in greater detail with them. I noticed a beautiful progression. As I opened my heart, this man and woman were moved to share some of their own heartaches and struggles; and in that atmosphere of mutual vulnerability, we were able to comfort and encourage one another. Honesty built a bridge for ministry. I was back to the lesson I had learned years earlier from my pastor in Virginia. I remembered how his honesty about his own life struggles had given me the courage to become more open about some of my own, which in turn facilitated my personal growth and some important emotional healing. This lesson seemed an important one for me to relearn at this time. What did God want out of my life? Honesty. Authenticity. He wanted these. So he could use me.

STILL MASKING

Back at home, rebuilding my life in the Valley took its toll. Overworking myself in a new job as a donor relations coordinator with Samaritan's Purse, the international Christian relief organization my brother Franklin serves as president and chairman, I felt overwhelmed by exhaustion; I was rudderless and emotionally numb. "I must admit that much that I do is sort of habit," my journal reads. "My one passion isn't God—I don't have a passion about anything. I'm too tired. I feel beaten, defeated. I don't know how to get above it but just put one foot in front of the other."

My children seemed off-kilter as well. Soon after Windsor got home from boarding school, she became difficult and argumentative. She started summer classes at the public high school and began to spend time with a group that did not seem to bring out the best in her. She became increasingly self-critical, and we constantly butted heads. Volatility was the order of the day.

Noelle also lived at home that summer, and to my great distress, she continued to suffer from bulimia. She and I discussed her condition. I tried to be sensitive and encourage her to talk about what was bothering her, and she kept up her visits with her counselor. But I was worried. I desperately wanted my daughter to be healthy. Once again I felt responsible.

Graham experienced some difficulties of his own during this period. After spending a year at Bible college, he decided he would try a four-year school. I took him to visit several, but he acted ambivalent about where he wanted to go and what he wanted to study. He seemed unfocused, disinterested, and distant. I wondered if some of his aloofness had to do with his having been away from his sisters and me for so long. Evidence of our family's breakdown seemed ever-present in the lives of my children, and the battle to move forward with my life became fierce indeed.

"I'm at . . . 106 lbs!" I recorded in my journal. "I wake up shaking!"

And yet I continued to behave outwardly as though my life were smooth sailing. Though I had learned how to become more open over the years—and I had seen the way God used my honesty in Ontario—I still seemed inclined in daily life to mask my true feelings. One friend told me she was amazed to learn I had emotional difficulties. "People expect me to be a certain way and I'm good at it!" I wrote. I did not want to keep living this way—behind a mask. I desperately longed to discover the person God had created me to be. I wanted to understand his plan for my life. I wanted to be useful in the lives of others by living honestly and authentically. But I couldn't seem to do it. I did not know how.

In the Potter's Hands

By midsummer, and at my physician's urging, I started seeing a professional counselor on a regular basis. My physician believed the stress, anxiety, and strain I had experienced in recent years were caused in part by some unresolved emotional issues in my life. She believed the counseling process would help me sort through those issues and recommended an excellent local professional, who proved to be an important contributor to my overall recovery.

One of the most important things I learned through personal study and other means during this period was that becoming authentic—growing into the person God envisioned when he made me—was not up to me. One of my favorite Bible verses reads, "for *it is God* who works in you to will and to act according to his good purpose" (Philippians 2:13 NIV, emphasis mine). I realized I did not have to make myself whole. I did not have to muster up the wisdom or the energy or the know-how. I did have a part to play in my recovery and personal growth—my job was to love God and to do what I believed he was telling me. But I came to see that God was the healing Creator. I was his wounded creation.

As our Creator, God takes responsibility for us. In Jeremiah, God uses the analogy of a potter working with clay to describe our relationship with him, the Lord. The prophet writes, "Then I went down to the potter's house, and there he was, making something on the wheel. But the vessel that he was making of clay was spoiled in the hand of the potter; so he remade it into another vessel, as it pleased the potter to make" (Jeremiah 18:3–4).

Like so much else in life, becoming who God wants us to be—and learning to live authentically as ourselves—is a process; and it is a process directed by God. God is the potter; we are the clay. If we are lacking in areas, we need not fear. We are in the hands of the potter. Though we must do our part to cooperate with God, he will remake us as it pleases him.

He is doing so right now. We might not see his hand—and if we do, we may not like it—but he is at work. Even at this very moment God is adding to our ability, giving us more patience, maturing us in our emotions, strengthening our resolve, and developing our endurance. He constantly is making us into the people he intends. He is incorporating all of our mistakes, relationships, circumstances, and plans gone awry. He uses everything in our lives—nothing is wasted. We get so distracted with life at times, we start to believe God has taken a vacation; but he is always working. We are his art, his pride, and he is ever about the business of perfecting us.

What Do I Say to Myself about Myself?

As I studied and worked with my counselor, I came to understand that a key to becoming authentic was developing a healthy self-image. The Bible teaches, "For as he thinks within himself, so he is" (Proverbs 23:7). Our self-image influences every area of life. Our decisions, our relationships, and our preferences in large part stem from what we say *to* ourselves *about* ourselves. If we think poorly of ourselves, then we remain vulnerable to making choices in life that jeopardize our best interests. We might sell ourselves short in relationships. We might make the same unwise commitments everybody else is making because we lack the courage to be true to God's word in Scripture. We change ourselves to fit into whatever group we are with. A poor self-image keeps us from seeing, and being, who we really are. It can keep us from hearing and obeying God's voice, and it can frustrate the purpose of God for our lives.

So how do we develop a healthy self-image? If a healthy self-image is vital to our becoming authentic, how do we overcome our insecurities and move in the direction of wholeness? First, we need to understand what a healthy self-image looks like. As I learned over the years, a healthy self-image consists of at least three things: a sense of belonging, a sense of worth, and a sense of competence.

We all need to feel that we belong—that we are loved, wanted, and accepted. We were designed for community, for relationship. The Bible says, "God sets the lonely in families" (Psalm 68:6 NIV). God said at the very beginning, "'It is not good for the man to be alone" (Genesis 2:18 NIV). We were not meant to live isolated from others. Again, this is why isolation affects us so adversely.

We also need to believe we are valuable. Jesus said he came to give us abundant life (John 10:10). How can we live full lives if we believe we are of little value in the world? Everyone needs to feel significant. Wanted. Valued. Cherished. We need the confidence that we have something to offer others. Otherwise our motivation diminishes, and we shrink back from living. We miss out on the level of joy God wants us to experience.

Finally, we need the assurance that we can cope with our circumstances, handle what life gives us, and meet challenges head-on. We lose hope when we become overwhelmed by the affairs of life. That is why Jeremiah wrote, "It is of the Lord's mercies that we are not consumed" (Lamentations 3:22 KJV). Jeremiah knew that God did not want him to live defeated by anxiety and fears.

Sadly, all too often we allow the wrong sources to have undue influence on our self-image. We try to build belonging, value, and competence into our lives by using the wrong materials. We depend on our relationships, accomplishments, and status to define us. We look to our professions or our possessions. There is nothing wrong with feeling proud of our achievements, children, spouses, or professional success. Acknowledging success and position is not in itself the problem. The problem comes in making these things the foundation of our identity. I am Billy Graham's daughter. My relationship to my father is part of what I am. But it is not *who* I am. That relationship is not enough to stand on.

I have found that if we depend on relationships to give us identity, then we likely are asking others to be what only God can be for us. We are asking others to meet all of our needs, to make us whole. No human being can do that. If we derive our self-worth from our children, then we will only stay frustrated. Our children were born to make us feel inadequate! If we are looking to our families for our sense of belonging or for validation, then we must recognize that most families are dysfunctional! If our worth and competence depend on our accomplishments, then we constantly will fall short. We will never be able to accomplish enough to satisfy our need to feel valued, accepted, and competent. There always will be someone waiting in the wings to do us one better.

Often we look to the outward trappings and the accomplishments of others to gauge our progress and success on life's road. For a long time, I compared myself to my two beautiful sisters, Gigi and Anne. In my case, the result always seemed to be unfavorable. My sisters had received acclaim in ministry and had written award-winning books. By contrast, I felt unattractive and unsuccessful. I never did seem to have any significant ministry call. I had experienced divorce. Using my sisters' lives as yardsticks caused me to feel even more discouraged—and at times hopeless. My self-image suffered. What did I have to show for my life? Not much, I believed.

But Scripture teaches that comparing ourselves with others is a waste of time: "When they measure themselves by themselves, and compare themselves with themselves, they are without understanding" (2 Corinthians 10:12). Comparing ourselves is unwise; it is unproductive. Ultimately, it is a distraction from God's healing process in our own lives. Everyone, whether they recognize it or not, has problems. Everyone hurts. So often we exalt people based on appearances. But no one is immune from struggle of some kind.

A friend of mine from my early married days in Philadelphia has since told me she used to envy my life. At the time I had a charming pre-Revolutionary War house, a brand-new car, and a handsome husband. He and I got to travel. We seemed to lead an exciting life. To my friend, my world seemed all but perfect. Little did she know I was trying to make my faltering marriage work as best I could and having a very difficult time of it. My friend found the surface of my life appealing—she saw the mask; but if she could have seen further in, would she really have wanted the whole package? I do not think so.

Not only, as I can attest, is envying unproductive; but it is also harmful. The last of the Ten Commandments is "You shall not covet" (Deuteronomy 5:21). Coveting—excessively longing for what does not belong to us—is sin; and sin always hurts us. We open a door for coveting when we become discontent and quit trusting God. We stop believing that God is for us. We begin to doubt he has good plans for our lives. We start to believe instead that repairing our lives is up to us. Longing for a quick fix, we begin to covet someone else's life, marriage, situation, or position. This is discontentment at its worst.

The Bible tells us to be content with what we have and to trust God, "for He Himself has said, 'I will never desert you, nor will I ever forsake you'" (Hebrews 13:5). Being content does not mean settling for less than what we desire in life; it means learning to flourish where we are, while trusting God to lead us to the next stage when he is ready. Remember, God is the potter. He is *always* at work, making us into the people he created us to be. We do our part in the process, but we are not left to make things happen on our own. And that should give us hope.

How do you answer the question "Who are you?" What do you tell yourself about yourself? How do you define yourself? Are you the wealthiest woman in town? The most successful lawyer in your firm? The most active mother at your children's school? Do you live in the largest house on your street? Are you the wife of a prominent politician? Or the husband of an award-winning entrepreneur? Are you so-and-so's mother? So-and-so's brother? What are your choice labels of identity? Have you accepted a label given to you by others, and allowed others to define you?

Consider these labels for a moment. Do they really give you a sense of significance in the world? Or—and this is a difficult question to answer honestly—do you wear them, like I often have done, to make yourself feel better about the broken places in your life? It can be difficult to step away from our labels and acknowledge that we have been hiding behind them; but we must be honest with ourselves. And are our labels really adequate anyway? Do they give us the sense of worth we so desperately desire? When we look at the big picture, are we really satisfied with the identities we have pieced together, or do we long for something more? Take a moment to answer these questions in your own heart. Ask God to help you understand what living an authentic life means for you.

Conversely, you may feel that you have nothing to show for your life at all—that you have no positive labels of identity whatsoever. You may feel worthless, pitiful, and hopeless. Perhaps you believe your only hallmarks of identity are your failures. Failed marriage. Failed business. Failed relationships. Share with God what you say to yourself about yourself. Tell him your frustrations, disappointments, and hurts. He understands.

Now let him show you the way *he* sees you. God sent his only Son to die for you—that's how much he values you. He longs to be close to you. You are fascinating to him, always his first choice of company. Whatever has happened in your life, God does not condemn you. The Bible says, "There is therefore now no condemnation for those who are in Christ Jesus" (Romans 8:1). God loves you. His desire is to put you on his potter's wheel and make you whole, a vessel lacking nothing.

Perhaps you are considering your failures and shortcomings through the lens of another's successes. Would you like to trade your life for someone else's? Have you envied another person to the point of wanting his or her life? Have you excessively desired another's possessions, status, marriage—or anything belonging to someone else? Pause and give God a chance to bring such longings to your mind. Ask God to forgive you for coveting, and tell him you want to change. Ask him to make you content with where you are in life right now. Commit again to trusting God, and ask him to give you the courage and ability to *keep* trusting him. Losing faith is so human. God knows our weaknesses. Again, as David wrote, "He is mindful that we are but dust" (Psalm 103:14). Remember, God is not chiding you for being dust. He loves you all the more for your weakness, and he longs to give you his strength (2 Corinthians 12:9–10). Your job is to keep a right attitude and to continue cooperating as God does his work in you.

FOR THE ONE WHO CARES

Does someone you love struggle with a poor self-image? It can be painful to watch those we care about flounder in life, uncertain of themselves and dominated by insecurity. How we want to fix it! If only they could see how special and significant they are! Unfortunately, helping a friend with low self-esteem is not simple. A person's self-image is a complex tapestry of threads unique to his or her life and personality. To be effective instruments of healing, we must depend on the Creator for direction; we will only be helpful insofar as we are guided by him.

Begin by acknowledging your own insufficiency in your friend's healing process. Remember that you are God's instrument—only he can touch your friend deep within and bring lasting change. You can try to encourage your friend by sharing how much God loves him or her; but until your friend grasps the truth of God's love in his or her own heart, your words will not have the effect you may desire. Changing the heart of your friend is God's responsibility. God alone can access the deep recesses of the heart and speak peace to the one you love. Remember, God is the healing Creator; your friend is his wounded creation.

Practice your dependence on God by spending time in prayer before you spend time with your friend. Praying for your friend is the most important thing you can do for him or her. Pray that your friend will be open to the changes God wants to make in his or her heart. Listen for God's voice and be open to God's instructions. He will tell you what to say, how and when to encourage your friend, and when to step away so that he, the Lord, can work.

Pray too that God will prepare your friend's heart to receive your encouragement. Ask God to open your friend's understanding to the truth of Scripture and what it has to say about him or her. Perhaps God has a specific promise he wants you to share with your friend. Or maybe he wants you to spend recreational time with your friend, demonstrating love rather than just talking about it. Whatever direction you sense from God, the key to your effectiveness will be learning to lean on the Creator. Our adequacy—especially as helpers—comes from him.

OUR AUTHENTIC IDENTITY IS IN CHRIST

While we may endeavor to build our self-image out of the world's materials and dictates, our true identity can only be found in God. He is the one true source. Not a spouse. Not parents. Not position. Not status. Not children. But God alone. The Bible says of Christ, "In Him you have been made complete" (Colossians 2:10). In Christ we are complete. What more can we add to "complete"? A new hairstyle? A new car? A bigger house? When we understand our position in Christ, we realize that accomplishments, possessions, expectations—none of these count at the core of our being. Only in Christ are we the people we were designed to be. We have everything we need in Christ to be authentic. Everything.

In God we find the components of a healthy self-image—belonging, worth, and competence. The Scripture tells us that God "chose us in [Christ] before the foundation of the world" (Ephesians 1:4). Think about this. In God we belong. He chose us to belong. When he flung the stars out in space and put the planets in their orbits and separated the dry land from the waters, God knew your name. He knew where you would live. He knew your parents. He knew whom you would marry. He knew if you would be single. He knew your tastes and preferences. You were on his mind. He chose you. While God was busy with everything else, he was thinking of you. And he loved you right then. How wonderful!

We read in Ephesians 2:19 that in Christ we are "no longer strangers and aliens, but . . . fellow citizens with the saints, and are *of God's household*" (emphasis mine). When I came across this verse in my Bible, I wrote in the margin beside it the words "I belong." I encourage you to do the same as a reminder that in Christ you belong to the eternal family of God. Perhaps you have suffered deep divisions in your relationships with your earthly family. God's family is eternal—his familial love for us is everlasting. The Bible declares that nothing can separate us from the love of God in Christ Jesus (Romans 8:35–39).

Our part is to *receive* this gift of love from God. While God's love in Christ does not fail, we can choose to accept that love or to refuse it. God chooses us to belong to his household, but he waits for us to choose him. Have you accepted the love of God through Jesus? Have you chosen to follow Christ? Have you invited him into your heart? By birth we are God's creations, but we must decide to become his children and join his family. There is a difference, an eternal difference. God does not love us any more or less for our choice—the difference is in the eternal destiny of our souls. As God's creations, we have his love; as his children, we have a personal relationship with him and a home. If you would like to invite Christ into your heart and become his child, then refer to the Welcome Home section at the back of this book to learn how.

In God we also find the second element of a healthy self-image: a sense of worth. We are valuable to God. He placed value in us when he made us—our value is intrinsic. It does not depend on our income tax bracket or on our résumé. It does not depend on the level of influence we wield in our communities. It has nothing to do with our children's successes, our professional notoriety, or the number of our gifts and talents. The Bible tells us that we are God's "workmanship" (Ephesians 2:10). We are defined in relation to our Maker, and our value comes from him. If he made us, then we must have value. He doesn't make junk.

Our value is so great that God presented us as gifts to his beloved Son. In John 17, Jesus refers to his followers in all the ages as those "whom Thou [God, the Father] hast given Me" (verse 24). Four times Jesus describes us, his followers, in such terms—as having been *given* to him by God (verses 6, 9, 24). Consider the most special gift you have ever given to someone. Maybe you made it. Maybe you saved the money to buy it. You might have done research to make sure it was just what your friend or loved one wanted—the right size and color. Perhaps you personalized your gift. You planned for it. You invested time, thought, and energy into its preparation. Why? Because the gift reflected your love for its recipient. Because along with the gift, you were giving a part of yourself.

Now imagine God's delight when he gave you as a gift to Jesus. Planning went into your presentation. You were just what Jesus wanted, the right size and color. You were handcrafted from the finest materials with great care and attention to detail. You are one-of-a-kind, unique. God made you especially to reflect his love for his Son—think about that! You are an expression of God's perfect, boundless love. And God gave part of himself when he gave you. The next time you belittle yourself for a failure or shortcoming, remember who made you and for whom you were made. God says in Isaiah, "you are precious in My sight, . . . you are honored and I love you" (Isaiah 43:4). If God calls you precious, then you are precious. You have worth—God himself has declared it.

Finally, we go to God for a sense of competence—the third element of a healthy self-image. We cannot effectively manage life's ups and downs on our own. Life is too unwieldy. God never intended for us to shoulder the burdens of life by using our own strength. God wants us to receive strength and competence from him. It is no wonder we lose our bearings so easily. Our ability runs out; only God's ability endures. The writers of Scripture understood this. Paul explained to the Philippians that a reliance on God for capability in all circumstances, in fact, was the key to contentment. He wrote, "I have learned the secret of being filled and going hungry, both of having abundance and suffering need. I can do all things *through Him who strengthens me*" (Philippians 4:12–13, emphasis mine).

Consider again God's analogy of the potter and the clay. God is the potter; we are the clay pots on his wheel. What are some attributes of clay? Clay is common, ordinary, and functional. As clay pots, we are fragile. We are easily bumped and knocked around as we travel along with other clay pots. We get cracked and nicked. Even broken. We are fallible, imperfect.

But whom does God use to accomplish his plans and purposes? The last time I read the Bible, God did not use perfect people. Aside from Jesus, not one perfect person appears in all of Scripture. God worked with common, ordinary people. He worked with those who had blown it—those who could not cope or manage their lives on their own, those who depended totally on him for the competence and wherewithal to survive, those who were weak and looking to God for strength. God did not use self-righteous religious leaders. He used the broken, the hurting, and the humble. He raised them up and gave them all they needed to succeed. And he is doing the same thing with us today.

AUTHENTICITY IN ACTION

Working faithfully with my counselor to root out past hurts, examine flawed emotional patterns, and develop new ways of looking at life was one way I began to take care of myself after my experience in Florida. I also renewed old friendships and reenrolled at Mary Baldwin College for the fall semester. I found that, as I allowed God to repair the foundation of my self-image, he slowly began to build things on top of that foundation. He added to my life. He built my relationships. He gave me work for my hands. He awakened my interests. Brick by brick, he constructed an authentic life for me out of my ruins.

In September of that year, 1994, I took a look-see trip to Kenya, Zaire, and Rwanda with Samaritan's Purse. The organization was doing relief work in Rwanda in the wake of that country's bloody civil war between the Hutus and Tutsis, and I hoped a firsthand experience of the organization's efforts to address the aftermath of genocide would help me better describe to donors what Samaritan's Purse was doing there. I saw the trip as part job, part adventure, part diversion, and part opportunity to focus on other people's needs. I had never been to the continent of Africa, and I hoped to come away from the experience with a new outlook on life and a greater sense of purpose.

Kigali, the Rwandan capital, was a city utterly in ruins and rife with the evidence of atrocity. Driving from the airport through the city, we saw burned-out cars and the remains of buildings; many structures had gaping holes for windows. The road was pocked with mortar craters and lined with mounds of dirt my traveling companions and I assumed were graves.

We toured the city's central hospital compound, which Samaritan's Purse was diligently working to reopen, and the grounds of what would soon be an orphanage. As was true of the hospital, the orphanage complex—formerly the agricultural college—had been the sight of brutal killings during the genocide, and it had not been long since body parts, entrails, and blood-soaked clothing were strewn over the property. The stench of death seemed to linger everywhere.

From Kigali, we traveled on to the town of Rutare to see another orphanage—one that was currently functioning. The orphans here soon would be transferred down the mountain to the campus in Kigali. When we arrived, we were thronged by children calling out "Bonjour!" and "Hello!" I tried to go around and touch each child, knowing how desperately they needed a loving, human touch. Some smiled and wanted to shake hands or "give me five"; others were distant and quiet. I was drawn particularly to a young girl, said to have AIDS, who sat alone on her bed in the makeshift clinic. She was sixteen years old—Windsor's age—but looked no more than eight. Her hair was short and fuzzy. She had long fingers and beautiful, almond-shaped eyes. One of her legs was swollen and cracked.

I sat beside the girl, patted her hand, and, using my broken high school French, told her how pretty she was. Knowing that music often transcends language, I sang "Jesus Loves Me," hoping she would recognize the tune and, thus, the message. She kept her eyes on the ground, offering little response. I learned she had been discovered living and hiding out in a cornfield. Who could fathom what she had experienced or seen? All she would tell the staff was that she wanted to go to Kigali to die. I left in tears, my heart breaking. Days later I was told she had died.

By now, it was nearing time for my look-see to end, and I was scheduled to travel on to Kenya, where my companions and I would go on safari. But I began to think twice about leaving Rwanda. We had gotten word that the timetable for relocating the orphans from Rutare to the agricultural school in Kigali had been moved up, and I felt impressed to offer the staff my energy and elbow grease. I asked the appropriate people if I could stay behind, and they welcomed my offer. I even congratulated myself for making the sacrifice!

The day my traveling companions left for Nairobi, however, any sense of self-satisfaction quickly evaporated. I became apprehensive, half hoping I could change my plan. Of course, I could not. It was too late. And I wondered if the Samaritan's Purse staff might be just as apprehensive about my joining them. I was the boss's sister. I was Billy Graham's daughter. Rolling up my sleeves, I determined to fit in. I borrowed some work clothes, climbed into the back of a Land Rover, and headed to the agricultural school grounds.

As it turned out, the staff incorporated me quickly into their efforts to prepare the campus, which was still in gruesome condition. We cleaned up blood and body parts. We washed away years of filth. I cleaned kitchens and toilets. I swept away dirt, and hoped that in doing so I was sweeping away some of the horror. Trying to make the place fit for lost and frightened children, we placed a stuffed animal on each bed and put bright pictures on the walls. We did all that we could.

After supper at night, some of us would wander off to find a quiet spot, or we would gather in the living room of our house to talk of the day's work. Someone would play the guitar; others would start a game of Ping-Pong. Laughter and teasing helped offset the grim experiences of the day. We also held times of prayer and Bible reading. I so appreciated these staffers, who worked hard and played hard. They came from different walks of life. Many were gifted medical workers. At home they would have been making large salaries. Here they were confronting death, fear, terror, and evil at its worst. They were doing manual labor because God had called them to do it. No glory. No vacation. No recognition.

The horrors that had taken place on the agricultural school site were beyond my imagination, and I tried to put such thoughts out of my mind. But at night, without electricity, our house became pitch-black, and I would begin to imagine the atrocities. In my room—for our house also had been full of rotting bodies—there lingered the faint smell of death that had not been quelled by a coat of fresh paint. Lying there, I often became anxious and fearful. A Bible verse I learned as a child would come back to me: "I will lie down and sleep in peace, for you alone, O Lord, make me dwell in safety" (Psalm 4:8 NIV). I repeated it over and over every night just so I could sleep.

What was God teaching me through my experience in Rwanda? I had left my job at a desk for a short trip of adventure. Oh, I knew when I left home that I would be moved by what I saw—and I was. The reality that confronted me was harsh and brutal. I will never forget it. But I was also confronted with areas in my own life that needed to change. Yes, the events of the past year had broken me—I had suffered; but I now felt that God was exposing in me a superficiality of perspective. My look-see trip made me consider what I was doing with my life, what choices I had made and the reasons I had made them, and what was important to me.

Gradually, I began to think beyond the confines of the life I had known. Working to clean up the gore, I realized I no longer felt useless; my homemaking skills could serve a good purpose after all. Perhaps my life's work as a wife and mother had prepared me to be effective in some capacity. I even wondered if I could relocate to a developing country and take a position as a housemother to a team of Samaritan's Purse workers. I was starting to see myself as someone who could stand alone, carry her own weight, and trust her own instincts. This was a slow process, but I was catching an important glimpse of what being whole—and living authentically—seemed to mean.

Leaving Rwanda, I determined to search out God's purpose for my life with greater resolve. In a more profound way than ever before, I was struck by the fact that my life was not about me—I was made to be part of something bigger than myself. I wondered, in fact, if this realization could be the key to authentic living. I would not discover my true identity by turning inward but by emptying my life into the lives of others. Isn't that what Jesus did? The Bible says he "emptied Himself, taking the form of a bond-servant" (Philippians 2:7). I realized that taking my eyes off myself, stepping out of my comfort zone, and serving those who could not necessarily give back were activities vital not just to my recovery from past events; in these pursuits I would also find the answer to the question "Who am I?"

So what was I to do when I returned to Virginia? My own plans for my life had been wrecked many times over, but it was not too late to join in on what God was doing. I knew I could serve others with compassion if only God would show me what to do. I was willing to touch hurting and broken people with the same grace God had shown me when I was hurting and broken. But where was I to go? To whom could I minister? How was I to serve? In fact, it wasn't long before I discovered the answers to these questions. The answers were writ large—and as it turned out, I did not have to go far to find them.

Reminders for Painful Times

↪ How do you answer the question "Who are you?"

↪ Consider your labels of identity. Do they really give you a sense of significance? Do you long for something more? Ask God to help you understand what living an authentic life means for you.

↪ Do you feel that your identity is comprised only of failures, shortcomings, and mistakes? Let God show you the way *he* sees you. He loves you and does not condemn you.

↪ Would you like to trade your life for someone else's? Are you coveting? If so, ask God to forgive you. Ask him to help you be content where you are in life right now.

↪ Are you uncertain about whether you are a child of God and part of his family? If you would like to become God's child, turn to the Welcome Home section at the back of this book to learn how.

Tips for Those Who Care

↪ Are you also uncertain about whether you are a child of God? If so, turn to the Welcome Home section at the back of this book to learn more about becoming part of God's family.

↪ Does someone you love struggle with a poor self-image? Remember that God is ultimately responsible for your friend's healing. Acknowledge your own insufficiency before God—you are only an instrument.

↪ Spend time in prayer before you spend time with your friend. Pray that your friend will be open to God's healing work. Ask God to show you how to encourage your friend. Listen for God's instructions.

↪ Pray that God will prepare your friend's heart to receive your encouragement. Ask God to open your friend's understanding to the truth of Scripture.

↪ Recognize that the key to effectively giving help and love is to lean on the Creator.

⌒◞

MEMORY VERSE

Colossians 2:10

. . . in Him you have been made complete.

⌒◞

Principles for Reflection

*A healthy self-image consists
of at least three elements —
a sense of belonging,
a sense of worth,
and a sense of competence.
All three are found in Christ.
We have everything we need
in Christ to be authentic.*

MORE TRIALS? WHEN WILL LIFE GET EASIER?

Trusting God in the Dark

Windsor and I were sitting on my bed that afternoon. It was November. The Rwanda trip was a couple of months behind me. The glorious Blue Ridge autumn had passed, and the air had turned cold. My daughter had come to my room to talk; she and I were enjoying some precious moments of relative peace together. We had been struggling to get along since the summer. Windsor was sixteen now and dating a young man. I was concerned about their relationship and hoped it would run its course, but they seemed to be spending more time together. Windsor began coming home late after her dates. I told her to limit her time with her boyfriend, and tensions in our home escalated.

I tried everything I knew to get control of the situation. I grounded and restricted Windsor. I yelled, cried, prayed, and begged. I tried to resuscitate family habits, setting up time for prayer and Bible reading before school in an effort to add continuity to our days. We also were getting continued help through counseling. But little I did seemed to have an impact for the better on our relationship; it was messy. I did not do everything right.

Now Windsor and I were talking on my bed. I was grateful for a reprieve from conflict, but I was worried about my daughter. She seemed tired all the time, and her moods oscillated with more frequency than normal. I had my suspicions. I had confided them in a friend but had not yet taken steps to confirm what I feared. On this particular afternoon, Windsor put my speculating to rest. At a lull in our conversation, she turned to me with fear in her blue eyes. "Mom," she said, beginning to cry, "I think I'm pregnant."

These are words any parent of a teenage daughter dreads to hear. I tried to respond with love and reassurance. I embraced Windsor and told her it would be okay, though I was far from confident. I tried to maintain my composure for her sake. But I had no idea what to feel or do. Adrenaline kicked in as I began to wonder what lay ahead for us. Before anything else I wanted to protect my daughter. My mind was rife with questions and doubts. How would we get through this? What would others think? Could Windsor handle this? How would we tell her father? What would be the young man's position?

That night I crawled into bed exhausted and opened the *Daily Light*. I read: "The Lord of peace himself give you peace always by all means" (2 Thessalonians 3:16 KJV). And: "The peace of God, which passeth all understanding, shall keep your hearts and minds through Christ Jesus" (Philippians 4:7 KJV). And again: "Peace I leave with you, my peace I give unto you" (John 14:27 KJV).

How could God give me verses about peace? I wondered. I thought I needed assurances of God's help. Where were the verses about God sticking with us through fiery trials? Of course, deep down I recognized that God's peace was exactly what I needed. Only God knew what was coming. If I was going to walk successfully through this trial, I would need peace. Supernatural peace. I reminded myself that God knew Windsor and me far better than I did, and I returned yet again to my foundational truths: God loved us, he would lead us, and he would bring good out of our circumstances. He would have to do these things—I was out of my league.

Once Windsor voiced her fear, I found I drifted into a sort of dreamy state of inaction. I was not particularly stirred to rush Windsor to the doctor for a pregnancy test. It was much easier not knowing the truth. Denial is a wonderful thing! Perhaps I was hoping the issue would go away. Perhaps I was waiting for my emotions to settle down. Whatever the case, a psychologist friend snapped me out of my daze. She urged me to get Windsor to the doctor immediately. If Windsor was pregnant, she said, then we needed to face it and take action.

The following day I picked Windsor up at school and told her we had a doctor's appointment. She did not want to go. As long as we kept the secret between us, we could maintain the illusion of normalcy; enlarging the circle seemed threatening. Windsor was resistant, but she finally got into the car with me. Once at the doctor's office, the news was as we had feared: the pregnancy test came back positive. Windsor sank into my arms and wept bitterly. I held my daughter, wanting to shield her from the inevitable ramifications of her position, but I knew I could not. I knew our lives would be changed forever.

LEARNING TO TRUST GOD IN THE DARK

I was at a loss when considering my daughter's pregnancy. I did not feel prepared to face such a challenge. Hadn't I only just begun to recover from the fallout of my own mistakes? I wondered when life would get easier. Even so, I did not have time to dwell on such thoughts or go round and round with God asking why. I needed to focus on Windsor. My daughter was my primary concern. This was not about me. It very briefly crossed my mind to wonder what others might think about a teenage pregnancy in Billy Graham's family, but I never felt ashamed of Windsor. I loved her. She was my child. She had made mistakes. So had I. Less than a year earlier, I had gone home to my family, broken over sin and exposed. Now my daughter was in the same condition. I wanted to offer her the "Welcome home" God had extended to me through others. It was my turn to act the part of the father in the prodigal story.

Though I certainly was not the perfect parent throughout my daughter's ordeal, I worked hard to support Windsor and to do what I thought best for her. We did not have an easy time of things. Frequently, I felt like I was flying by the seat of my pants as I made decisions. I tried to school myself on the ins and outs of unplanned pregnancy, but most things I learned as I went along. I found I just had to do the next thing and trust God to work through me as Windsor's mother. I felt woefully inadequate at times. Often my faith seemed paper-thin.

Perhaps the most difficult aspect of my experience was realizing I could not take away my child's pain. I could stand by my daughter, but I could not carry the weight of responsibility for her situation. This was a difficult reality to accept. I loved Windsor desperately. I saw her talent, her beauty, and her potential. I wanted to take her pain. I wanted to carry her load. But at a certain point, there was nothing I could do to bring her relief. I had committed Windsor to God's care before she was born and many times since. Would I trust him now, when I truly could not see the road ahead for her? Would I trust him in the dark?

Deciding to trust God with Windsor and actually doing so, I discovered, were two different things. I did not want to hinder God's work in my child's life at this significant juncture. I realized I needed to let go of control in some areas so God could get ahold of Windsor. Trusting God, in fact, seemed one of the keys to walking in the role of the prodigal's father. Imagine the trust the father had to muster while his son was off in a foreign land living a profligate's life. In such circumstances, the father was forced to trust God with his son as never before. He had to let go—there was nothing else for him to do.

But letting go as a parent is no easy task. My mother has been a wonderful example in this area over the years. She must have looked at me during my struggles in much the same way I viewed Windsor. She saw my talent, beauty, and potential. She loved me more than life. She must have hated to watch me unravel, but she entrusted me to God's care. While she remained involved in my life and committed to my welfare, she also let me find my own way.

For me, letting go of Windsor meant demonstrating compassion while at the same time allowing my daughter to be accountable for her mistake. I had to get out of the way so God could work. I had to leave room for the work of repentance in Windsor's life, for without true repentance there would be no true healing. The father's joy over the prodigal's return home was not just about his son's physical return; it was also about the return of his son *in heart*. This is part of the meaning of repentance: it is the heart's return to God. Apart from a return, we miss out on his "Welcome home."

If I tried to take the sting out of Windsor's experience, I wondered, then where would that leave her in the long run? I thought back to the deep lessons I had learned about God's faithfulness in my own times of suffering—how I had wrestled to trust him, wrestled to forgive, wrestled to endure. I considered how much deeper my relationship with God had become as a result. My own emotional healing was coming through that closeness to him. Would I now rob Windsor of the same chance to know God closely for herself? I could not do that. Like my own mother, I loved and helped my daughter through her pain, but I knew that the consequences of sin were ultimately Windsor's to work out with the Lord.

LETTING GOD HAVE THE REINS

In my efforts to walk in balance as a parent, I inevitably made some mistakes. Again, I was trying to feel my way in the dark, and in doing so, I took some wrong turns. Once we confirmed that Windsor was pregnant, I began to schedule meetings with others, including the baby's father, trying to determine a course of action. One meeting, this one with Ted and some church leaders, proved particularly difficult for Windsor—agonizing really—and I deeply regretted having planned it. I was hoping the meeting would underscore for Windsor the concepts of repentance and spiritual accountability. But Windsor needed to come to an understanding of her actions and their consequences gradually. She was not emotionally prepared to handle confrontation of any kind. Rather than rush her through the process, I should have helped her along spiritually until she became stronger. Perhaps I was trying to do what I believed was expected of me by the church leaders. I was following my own assumptions about what others thought best—not trusting God, or my instincts.

What was worse, the young man who fathered the baby essentially abdicated his responsibility for the child at this meeting, causing Windsor further humiliation. Here she was at sixteen, having to deal with pregnancy, the death of her childhood, a painfully uncertain future, and now the grief and embarrassment of rejection. It seemed so unfair. I was heartbroken for my daughter. The whole experience seemed to crush her. I was terribly grieved about what I had put her through and feared I had caused a great deal of damage.

In the days that followed, Windsor and I clashed often. I let her behavior slide more than usual because I knew she was wounded. She already had many reasons to look for love in all the wrong places. I was not going to give her another one. We did share some light moments, though. On Christmas Eve I made the kids a big roast beef dinner, which Windsor promptly threw up. "What a waste of money!" I teased. All three kids were in stitches before the scene was over, and I captured their mirth in a photograph. I made sure to enjoy those kinds of moments when they came along—laughter was a rarity in those days.

Meanwhile, Windsor and I discussed the possibility of moving her to an unwed mothers' home for the remainder of her pregnancy. She did not want to go, but on this point I *was* trying to trust my instincts. I firmly believed Windsor needed to leave the Valley for her own emotional protection and wellbeing. In particular, I thought the farther away she was from the baby's father, the better. I told Windsor how much I loved and supported her; but I explained that I wanted to be her mom, not her jailer. I encouraged her that life was not over. The pregnancy was only a parenthesis. She would be able to come back home and, assuming she continued with her schoolwork as we had arranged, graduate with her class the next year.

My research finally led me to an unwed mothers' home in Florida. Windsor agreed to let me take her there on the condition that if she did not like the home, she would not have to stay. Once we got there, it seemed clear that the home would work, and with a great deal of pressure, Windsor consented to move in. I got her settled and then, breaking my own heart as I did so, left the premises. I actually left the state of Florida, knowing if I remained nearby to see how Windsor adjusted, she would try to find a way out, and I would give in.

Almost immediately Windsor began to contact me, pleading to come home. She was unhappy. Every conversation was the same. Ted and I talked about transferring her to some other home, but no real workable alternatives presented themselves. Reluctantly I told Windsor she would have to stay put. I was worried about her. I knew she felt abandoned and alone. But allowing her to live at home in the Valley did not seem wise or in her best interest. I was beside myself and simply did not know what to do.

Then came a totally unexpected breakthrough. In the spring, I attended a surprise birthday party in Philadelphia for two dear friends whom I had first met during the early years of my marriage to Ted. A small group of us from those years had stayed in touch and remained very close. On the day of the birthday, I drove to Philly, arriving just in time to hide upstairs for the surprise; and soon afterward, my friends and I settled into our usual mode of comfortable conversation. I took the opportunity in that safe environment to share with these friends the details of Windsor's situation and the anguish I was feeling. Most of these women had stood by me through many a crisis, and I knew they would support me now. In fact, I had no idea just how much support would be forthcoming.

The party's organizer was a woman named Sara Dormon. I had met Sara previously through my friends, but we were not much more than acquaintances, and I knew little of her background. As we talked over lunch, Sara explained that she had been taking young pregnant women into her home for about twenty years. She was a clinical psychologist who provided counseling, advocacy, and support for young women experiencing unplanned pregnancies. She asked me some good questions about Windsor and offered helpful suggestions. By the time I left for Virginia, I felt encouraged, even hopeful.

But encouragement was not all that came out of the connection with Sara. Within a week of the birthday party, she called me at home in Virginia and posed an unbelievable question: "Would you pray about sending Windsor to live with me so I can see her through the pregnancy?"

I was shocked. Overwhelmed. Grateful. Speechless. Here was someone with whom I had only a slight personal acquaintance demonstrating incredible generosity just when I needed it most. By reputation I knew Sara to be a remarkable woman, but I was stunned that she—along with her husband, Bill, and two teenage sons—would offer to give to us in this selfless way. Sara said she would homeschool Windsor to ensure that my daughter kept pace with her junior class in Virginia. Sara would teach Windsor the ropes of parenting and financial management, along with other practical skills. Most important of all, Sara would walk Windsor through the process of deciding whether, in fact, to parent or release the baby for adoption. In temperament Sara was both tough and loving. She was confrontational, no-nonsense, and a straight talker; but her heart was as big as all outdoors. She seemed a perfect match for Windsor.

After prayer and consideration—and it didn't take much—I was convinced that Sara's invitation was a gift from God. He knew I was doing my best; he also knew I could not tackle Windsor's challenge on my own. Windsor needed help. I needed help. And God was faithful to bring it. God was with me. He was sending others. I wasn't alone. Where I once had felt nearly demoralized, I found myself relieved, optimistic. Once Sara entered our lives, I began to face challenges with the expectation that God would show up, which meant I more readily gave him the reins. An expectant heart, I discovered, made life seem more manageable.

FOR THE ONE WHO CARES

Perhaps you are supporting someone through a crisis right now. How are you coping? Do you feel exhausted and alone? Discouraged? Overwhelmed? Do you feel that your efforts to help are just shots in the dark? I want to encourage you that God sees your efforts. He takes pleasure in our attempts to help those in need. Even if our actions seem to us to be ineffective, when our motives are right, God is pleased. The Bible says, "man looks at the outward appearance, but the LORD looks at the heart" (1 Samuel 16:7). For all you have done in love, receive God's approval. He sees your heart. Be encouraged!

Do you need wisdom in certain areas as you help your friend or loved one? Scripture instructs the one who needs wisdom to "ask of God, who gives to all men generously and without reproach, and it will be given to him" (James 1:5). Your prayers are not in vain. If you are growing weary of praying the same prayers for wisdom and direction, then ask God to refresh you. Our prayers are to be persistent, not because God wants us to jump through hoops before he answers our prayers, but in part because we need to be reminded constantly of our dependence on him. Dependence is a place of safety for us. It is when we become independent of God in our thinking that we set ourselves up to take a wrong turn.

The Scripture portion from James quoted above continues by urging the one who prays for wisdom to "ask in faith without any doubting" (verse 6). If your faith is ebbing due to your weariness, then ask God to increase your faith. When we become exhausted, we lose focus and forget that God can do anything. We fail to pray trusting that he can do anything. Who would have guessed that out of my friends' birthday party would come answers to my prayers for Windsor's primary needs?

In fact, through the group at that birthday party God took care of even more than I have related—as you will see, he took care of a great deal more. Meanwhile, I was going about my business without any idea that something of tremendous import was about to happen. So often God moves in such moments: when we are living our lives, fulfilling obligations, and completing tasks. We need to remind ourselves of this. For when we live in the awareness that God can do the impossible at any time—that he is at work in our situation even when we do not see him or feel him—we begin to believe God for the impossible in the lives of those we love.

Freedom in the Dark

When we help others, God moves on our behalf, not just for our sakes, but also—and ultimately—for those we are called to help. Paul assured the Corinthian church, "God is able to make all grace abound to you, that always having all sufficiency in everything, you may have an abundance *for every good deed*" (2 Corinthians 9:8, emphasis mine). When God calls us to serve, he gives us what we need to accomplish his purpose in the lives of those we touch. By sending Sara to me, God was not looking merely to encourage me personally, though I was encouraged. He was concerned about Windsor. She was the object of his provision. My awareness of God's love for my child helped me as I endeavored to trust him for help. I would encourage myself that God would help me because he cared about my daughter.

I also knew God had a purpose for Windsor's baby. Here was a second life depending on God's provision. Again, my trial was not just about me. I was privileged to learn a great deal and grow through the experience, but by faith I knew God also had something in mind for the generations of my family. I did not know what he had in mind, but I knew his purposes were good; and I knew I had to trust him for an outcome in our situation that would positively affect people beyond my lifetime. Considering my circumstances in this way proved challenging at times, but often my enlarged perspective on what God was doing brought more peace, more faith in God. I was learning to trust that he was in control of history; and as I did, I found that, even if my life did not get "easier," I could still live fully. I could experience freedom in the dark. I could move in God's strength. The Bible says, "as thy days, so shall thy strength be" (Deuteronomy 33:25 KJV). Walking with Windsor, I found this to be absolutely true.

Maybe you are in Windsor's position right now. Are you in a crisis of great magnitude? Are you angry with yourself? With God? Do you feel abandoned? Alone? Perhaps you feel you cannot pray at this time—maybe you do not want to pray. Let me encourage you to be honest with God. He cares about your feelings. You can talk to him. Ask him to reveal himself to you. Cry out to him and tell him how you feel. He is listening to you. He *wants* to reveal himself to you.

Ask God to show you his help as it comes to you in many ways—often through people. God uses people as his instruments to meet our needs. You may find it difficult at times to have to depend so much on others. We get frustrated with our inability to take care of things ourselves. But recognize that, as you practice dependence on others, you learn dependence on God. Dependence on God is a place of safety. It is good for us to learn dependence on him in any way we can. Do not miss your chance now! As you allow yourself to receive from others, understand that you ultimately are receiving from God. He is the source. Instead of giving in to frustration over your circumstances, open your heart and thank God for being your true Helper.

You can also ask God to help you know him in your situation as the God of the impossible. He can do anything at any time to satisfy the needs of your current crisis. Do you believe this? Do you believe that God wants to help you? At times we have difficulty believing he really wants to help us, especially when we have suffered for a long time. Our faith fails us. We wonder if God even desires to see us restored. We become angry, hurt, bitter. Take some time now to pray for your faith—ask God to give you more. Tell him you want to trust him. Tell him you are in the dark and cannot trust him without his help. As you talk to God about your feelings, you will grow further in dependence on him. And this is our goal: to trust God so completely, we find we can know him more intimately, even in the dark.

SEEING GOD PROVIDE

When I called Windsor to tell her about Sara's offer, she did not take long to think about it. She came home from Florida, and we then headed north to Philly. The Dormons provided Windsor a cozy little apartment—her own room and half bath in the basement; and their two sons treated Windsor like a sister. My daughter seemed to adjust quickly, and once she got settled, she began working with Sara to prepare for the baby's arrival.

Throughout her pregnancy, Windsor went back and forth over whether to release her baby for adoption, an extraordinarily difficult decision for any mother, let alone a teenager whose emotions and desires swing from day to day. I knew what I thought was best, and I wanted to make Windsor do it; but here, as with other things, I had to take my hands off and maintain my posture of letting go. The baby was Windsor's, and the decision likewise would have to be hers.

At the same time, as Windsor's mother I had to ask myself some tough questions, the answers to which would affect Windsor's decision. In particular, I had to determine what I was willing—and unwilling—to do once the baby was born. If she kept the baby, would I allow Windsor to live with me? If not, where might they go? If I did permit them to live in our home, what conditions would I need to impose? Could I manage the financial responsibility of both Windsor and her child? Would our medical insurance cover the baby? Was I willing to help rear the baby? How would I manage Windsor once she resumed her social life? What if she fell back into destructive patterns? And, if so, what would that mean for the baby?

I weighed these and other questions. I prayed. I agonized. I went to a pastor who helped me examine my motives and consider the spiritual and emotional aspects of the dilemma. My heart was torn—who wouldn't want her precious grandbaby at home? I longed to be a part of my grandchild's life. Yet the baby's future hung in the balance. I could not make a decision based on emotion alone. I had to think clearly about what was best for the child. Talk about trusting God in the dark!

In the end, I did not believe that God was asking me to take responsibility for Windsor's actions and their consequences. I knew my daughter was not mature enough to parent a child. She would not become mature simply by virtue of parenting. I desperately wanted her to stabilize, finish school, and enjoy being a teenager. My stepping in to rear the baby would not be best for Windsor, the baby, or me. I determined I could not provide a home for Windsor if she decided to parent. Considering the unique context of our lives, I believed this was the right decision. I still do, though it tore my heart in two.

Windsor was angered and frustrated by my decision, and a new level of struggle between us ensued. Tough love is painful to practice. Windsor argued and pleaded. I tried to hold firm. She did have other options. If she wanted to parent the baby, I would give her legal emancipation so she could get a job to support her child. Or she could live with her father in Texas. I knew my limitations. I assumed I knew Windsor's. Even so, my decision was hard to sustain. I questioned and second-guessed myself countless times.

Eventually, Windsor chose to release her baby for adoption. She changed her mind seemingly every hour, but Sara assured me this was normal. Windsor was making a choice about the destiny of her firstborn. I tried to imagine the grief, fear, loneliness, and turmoil she must have been experiencing. She was in a great deal of anguish and wavered on the adoption question until the very end. I found the only way to endure the ride was to stay off the roller coaster. I had to remind myself this was Windsor's decision. To keep grounded, I relied on a small circle of friends and remained in counseling.

In the meantime, Sara continued to work with Windsor, as well as with another young woman who was a bit further along in her pregnancy. This young woman had decided to release her baby for adoption and was in the process of sorting through the adoptive parent profiles Sara kept on hand. Windsor, it turned out, also looked through the profiles, and she came across one that particularly struck her. The husband was a lawyer, the wife a special education teacher. For years I had teased Windsor, saying she would make a great lawyer because she could argue the legs off a table! She also had mild learning disabilities and needed extra help in school. Considering these "connections," Windsor thought the couple might be a good fit.

What I later learned about Sara's association with this couple stunned me. Here again, God showed us his fingerprints on our lives and proved himself a faithful provider for Windsor and her baby. As it happened, the couple's paperwork had ended up in Sara's file thanks to one of the women at the birthday party I had attended in Philadelphia. This intermediary lived out of state and went to church with the couple who was seeking to adopt.

That Windsor had selected this couple's profile out of those in Sara's possession seemed unbelievable to me. I knew that only God could have arranged for so unlikely an intersection. Through my Philadelphia friends, God had provided Windsor a living situation, a mentor, and now potential adoptive parents for her baby. The connections brought me great comfort. We seemed surrounded by a group of people handpicked by God, and I stood in awe of the ways God seemed to be working behind the scenes. In fact, God now was assuring me in the strongest terms that he would carry us through to the end. I became convinced that Windsor and I would do more than just survive our ordeal.

Reminders for Painful Times

↪ Are you in a crisis of great magnitude? Cry out to God in your pain. Be honest with him about what you are feeling. Ask him to reveal himself to you.

↪ Try to see those who are helping you in your life right now as being God's own instruments. See God as the source; depend on him. He is helping you through others.

↪ Ask God to give you more faith so you can believe him for the impossible.

↪ Do you believe that God really wants to help you? Ask God to help you trust him in the dark.

Tips for Those Who Care

↪ Are you serving someone who is going through a crisis right now? Do you feel exhausted and alone? God sees your efforts. He is pleased with what you do out of love for both him and others.

↪ Do you need wisdom as you help your friend or loved one? Pray persistently for what you need. As you pray, you will cultivate your dependence on God.

↪ Is your faith failing due to your exhaustion? Pray for more faith. Ask God to help you remember that he is the God of the impossible. He can do anything at any time. Walk in this awareness.

MEMORY VERSE

2 Corinthians 9:8

And God is able to make all grace abound to you, that always having all sufficiency in everything, you may have an abundance for every good deed.

Principles for Reflection

*Dependence on God is a place
of safety and freedom.
As we learn to trust him,
we can experience joy
and move in strength,
even if life does not get easier.*

HOW DO I KEEP
ON TRUSTING GOD?
More Lessons in Letting Go

Windsor's baby came right on time at the end of July. It was late in the evening, and Sara and I stood by, coaching my daughter through labor and delivery. Holding Windsor's hand, I tried to encourage her as she worked. I reminded her to breathe, to keep pushing. I smoothed back her hair from her forehead and wiped the perspiration from her cheeks. I was so proud of my child, so overcome with emotion. From time to time the surge of emotion became so strong I felt faint and had to sit down. Sara would continue coaching; then I would stand again and tend to Windsor. *Almost there,* I would say. *It's almost over.* Finally the baby arrived, a beautiful baby girl. Hearing the baby's cry, I experienced immeasurable joy, astonishment, and gratitude. Here was a new life. My daughter's baby. My first grandchild.

By this time, we had interviewed the couple whose profile Windsor had found in Sara's files, and my daughter had decided to release the baby to them. The adoptive mother, later joined by her husband, flew to Philadelphia for the delivery and was present with us at the hospital when the baby was born. This arrangement proved to be very difficult for Windsor.

Following the birth, Windsor's emotions understandably were somewhat off-kilter, and the adoptive mother's presence caused my daughter to become very distressed. When I first suggested the woman join us for the delivery, Windsor reluctantly had conceded. I thought the adoptive mother's presence would facilitate this woman's own bonding process with the baby and be especially important for the child in coming years. But now in the delivery room, my daughter's emotions were all over the place and she became upset. She had just given birth to a baby she knew she would have to release, and, though the woman was understanding, an adoptive parent in Windsor's midst seemed a threat.

At the time, I could only imagine the storm raging in Windsor's heart. The Bible says, "Greater love has no one than this, that one lay down his life for his friends" (John 15:13). Windsor had laid down her health, figure, and reputation to carry her baby to term. She had walked through the valley of the shadow of death to give birth. She was falling desperately in love with her baby, knowing she would have to release her into the arms of others—a completely unnatural act. I realized I had never sacrificed as much as my daughter, and watching her caress her newborn child, I stood in awe of her.

Meanwhile, I tried to protect myself from becoming overly attached to the baby. Knowing the baby had been entrusted to us for a very brief time, I wanted to guard my heart as best I could. But looking on as Windsor tended to her new daughter nearly broke me. I suddenly became very tired. Though we had come a long way on our journey, I realized we still had mountains left to climb. Many mountains. Not the least of which was the baby's release to the adoptive parents. Considering the arduous emotional distance that remained, I wondered if I could locate the stamina to keep going. And what about Windsor? I had walked life's path much longer than she. I had endured heartache of my own. I thought I knew something about the well of grief around the bend. I would have given anything to shield my daughter from becoming acquainted with the permanence of loss at such a young age, but I could do nothing. I prayed for the grace to keep on trusting God. My sense of helplessness was profound.

GOD'S HELP

At four o'clock in the morning I left Windsor in the hospital room and drove back to the Dormons' house alone. The streets of Philadelphia were quiet. I was exhausted, emotionally numb, and badly in need of rest. My limbs felt heavy. The blocks of houses and commercial buildings went by in a blur. I did not seem able to hold thoughts or register impressions—only the desperate desire to lie down and close my eyes.

Then something unusual happened. I do not remember where I was exactly—I cannot recall the intersection. I only know I pulled up to a traffic light somewhere along the way and shifted the car into neutral. As I sat waiting, the words to a song written by Bill and Gloria Gaither flashed across my mind:

So be silent ye mountains, ye fields and ye fountains,
for this is the time I must sing.
It's the time to sing praises to the Rock of the Ages,
for this is the time I must sing. *

As I resumed driving through the city's lonely streets, I opened my mouth and began to sing. I wasn't thinking. I just did it. In my utter fatigue, I sang. It was the time. The song came out of my heart as praise to God. I did not sing because I was happy; I was experiencing something much more profound. What came out of my heart was joy. Joy in the sure knowledge that God was still in control. He loved us. He would lead us. He would bring good out of our circumstances. In that moment, I knew at the deepest level that God was helping us, and as I sang, I found myself quieted by an inexplicable peace.

When I consider the whole of my experience with Windsor surrounding her daughter's birth, I often revisit this late-night encounter with God on the streets of Philadelphia: How I sensed his presence as I sang; how my heart was glad; how I felt his peace. What strikes me particularly is that my praise did not seem the result of any conscious choice on my part. Praise just happened. A song came out of me. Though I was the one offering praise to God, I realized that my praise was actually his gift to me. God's Spirit, living in me, stirred my heart and gave me the ability to praise.

Moreover, God knew that praise was exactly what I needed at that moment. As the song said, it was the time to sing praises. God knew what was coming— he saw the painful days ahead. He knew I needed to experience joy right then, and the reassurance and profound peace that followed. Without those, I do not know how I would have fared as we released Windsor's baby to the adoptive parents and went home. I needed reminding that God was in control—that even in our grief he was still caring for us, still loving us, still sticking close by us. This understanding, as only God knew, was available to me through praise. And it came at the perfect time—in the silence of the Philadelphia night during perhaps the only few moments in those days when I was alone.

God used praise to help me stir my faith. He met me in my exhaustion just when I needed him. Perhaps you are in a situation that requires a level of

* "This Is the Time I Must Sing," words by William J. and Gloria Gaither; music by William J. Gaither. Copyright © 1975 William J. Gaither, Inc. All rights controlled by Gaither Copyright Management. Used by permission.

spiritual stamina you know you cannot come up with on your own. Are you wondering how in the world you are going to keep on trusting God for the long haul? Maybe you already have journeyed a long way by trusting God and now find yourself faced with the hard truth that you still have a distance to go. You are tired. You want to come to a point where you can look back at the past from a position of relative calm, but "calm" seems such a long way away. Seeing this, maybe you want to quit. Or lie down and rest. Maybe you no longer even care about finishing the race. All you know is that you have run out of steam.

Let us remember what Jeremiah wrote when he felt the kind of exhaustion and discouragement you may be feeling. He wrote, "It is of the LORD's mercies that we are not consumed, because his compassions fail not. They are new every morning: great is thy faithfulness" (Lamentations 3:22–23 KJV). Find comfort in this Scripture. For right now, precisely when you feel you are about to be consumed by weariness, fatigue, irritability, and frustration—right now— is when the Lord's mercies take over. He will help you stir your faith. You can ask him to do that. When Jesus told the father of a possessed boy that all things were possible to those who believe, the father, desperately wanting Jesus to deliver his son, cried out, "I do believe; help my unbelief" (Mark 9:24). This father recognized he needed help maintaining his faith. Take a moment and tell God how you feel. Tell him how exhausted you are, how thin your faith seems, how badly you want to trust him, and how inadequate you feel. Ask him to build your faith for what lies ahead. Pray as the father of the possessed boy prayed: "Help my unbelief." God will meet you in his own way.

RELEASE

Windsor had decided in advance that she would keep her daughter for four days before letting the adoptive couple take her home. I was concerned that this plan would make the release all the more heart-wrenching, but Windsor was the birth mother. She had thought of little but the baby every day for nine months. The baby was literally the heart of her heart. I, on the other hand, had spent nine months thinking about the baby *and* Windsor. My heart was divided. I was looking down the road toward the self-doubt, agony, and pain my daughter would face. I wanted to protect her, but again, I realized it was not my role at that time. I had to let go, and she had to make her own choices.

In fact, those four days with the baby were both wonderful and nearly unbearable. I watched as my daughter did things like change the baby's diapers and give her bottles. I saw the tenderness in Windsor's eyes as she rocked the new little life in her arms. The baby captivated all of us and claimed a piece of our hearts. Graham carefully held the baby as if she were made of glass and kept commenting on what a beautiful little girl she was, how perfect she was, and what a good job Windsor had done. I cherished seeing my daughter so happy. She could take comfort in knowing she had made something lovely and perfect—her first child.

Much too soon the time came for Windsor to sign the adoption papers. Our lawyer brought the documents to the Dormons' house, and Windsor and I sat with the paperwork at the dining room table for a long time. Signing the papers was incredibly difficult for Windsor. I cannot imagine having to do such a thing. She was preparing to sign away her parental authority and go against all of her maternal instincts. The documents' legal language was brutally cut-and-dried.

Again and again, I tried to call Windsor back to her original reasoning. She would look at me, tears streaming down her cheeks, and say, "Mom, please let me keep my baby." It was a horrible experience. I knew with one word I could bring great, if temporary, relief to my child. But I too had to call myself back to the reasons I had made my decisions. In this kind of situation, there is no easy way out of pain. Whether Windsor parented or released the baby, the repercussions were going to be serious and life altering. I continued to hold firm to my decisions; and in the end, Windsor reluctantly signed the papers.

On the day of the actual release, Windsor and I went for a spa treatment while the adoptive couple staying with us at the Dormons' home kept the baby. I had a massage. Windsor got her hair done. We tried our best to relax with some much-needed pampering, but the distraction did not help. Windsor was restless. I carried a feeling of enormous dread. Waiting for the baby's release was like waiting for certain doom. I could put it out of my mind for a short while, but then I would remember and be jerked back to the cruel reality. I counted down the hours. *We have twelve hours. We have six hours. We have one hour.* I felt like I was waiting for an execution.

We had planned a special service for the baby's release at the home of my dear friend Martha Ayers. The focus of the service was to be a baptism ceremony. Windsor had been dedicated to God as a baby but never baptized. I wanted my children to choose baptism at a time they deemed appropriate in their own spiritual walks. When Windsor was planning for the baby's release, I suggested she consider holding a joint baptism ceremony with her child. She liked the idea, and we arranged for the Presbyterian minister who was my pastor at the time of Windsor's birth to conduct the service.

After our morning at the spa, Windsor and I drove out to the Ayerses' home. Sitting in the backseat of the car, Windsor held the baby in her arms. Now and then I would turn around and quietly watch my daughter gazing at her child. Windsor looked beautiful. Dressed in a pretty pink outfit, her soft blond hair framing her face, she had a Madonna-like air about her. But though she smiled, in her eyes was fathomless grief. I remember having to look away, with tears streaming down my cheeks and my heart close to bursting. I was not sure I could go through with the ceremony. How on earth does one survive the release of one's own flesh and blood? How would Windsor survive it, this ultimate letting go? God would have to give us the strength. Otherwise the next couple of hours would break us.

A small crowd gathered at the home for the event. The pastor baptized Windsor and the baby in the living room; it was a sweet, very meaningful ceremony. Afterward we took dozens of photographs, and one of Sara and Bill's sons videotaped the gathering. Each of us took a turn holding the baby and saying our good-byes to her. Once we had finished, Windsor asked all but a few of us to leave.

My daughter sat quietly in a wingback chair, weeping and cooing over her child. One last hug, one last kiss, one last photo. We were all crying and wondering what to do next. We could not take the baby from Windsor. She would have to give the baby to the adoptive parents when she was ready, but we knew it had to happen soon. I looked to Sara for guidance. Then, after some minutes, I said, "Windsor, it's time." Windsor continued to weep, holding the baby closer.

"Windsor," I said again gently, "it's time." She looked at me with unspeakable sorrow, trying to be brave.

"Please, Mom," she pleaded. I fought to hold myself together.

Finally, she posed for one more photograph, tenderly kissed her daughter, and carefully placed her in the adoptive mother's arms.

"I love you," Windsor whispered.

The adoptive couple wept as they said their good-byes. Then they placed the baby in their car, got in, and drove away.

FAITH AND PAIN

As the adoptive couple departed, Windsor wailed and sobbed with unbelievable passion. Hers was pure grief. Pure despair. She was in agony. I was in agony. My heart broke doubly—first for the loss of my grandchild, then for my own child as I watched her heart disintegrate in front of my eyes. I could do nothing to comfort Windsor, nothing to help her. I could not make the pain go away. There was now a permanent hole in my daughter's heart, a hole I could not fill. Her grief was deeper than what many people experience in a lifetime, yet she was only seventeen. Most of her friends had just learned to drive.

Rather quickly, we got Windsor outside, helped her into the car, and got on the road for Virginia—home. I longed for the comfort of our mountains and believed that Windsor needed to get into her own bed as soon as possible. Thankfully, she soon fell asleep in the backseat. I quietly wept mile after mile. Now I was totally spent. I knew we had done the best thing for the baby, but the pain was tremendous. Had we really made it? Had our faith held? I did not know. When Windsor awoke, we tried to encourage ourselves by talking about the future; but the ache remained. And it remained long after the letting go.

Are you suffering pain that seems unbearable? Has the pain been with you a long time? Do not fear. Allow yourself to grieve. Let your heart break if necessary. Do not feel condemned. Your grief does not indicate a lack of faith on your part. Faith and pain are not mutually exclusive. You can have faith *and* experience pain. Jesus did. Consider the gospel story of Jesus and Lazarus. When Jesus' friends Mary and Martha sent word that their brother, Lazarus, was sick, Jesus first responded in faith: "This sickness is not unto death, but for the glory of God, that the Son of God may be glorified by it" (John 11:4). So great, in fact, was the faith of Jesus that he delayed two days before even setting out for Bethany, where his sick friend lay (verse 6).

By the time Jesus and his disciples got to town, Lazarus had been in the tomb for four days (John 11:17). Jesus already was aware of this. Before traveling to Bethany, he had told his disciples that his friend's death would be good for their faith (verse 15). Of course, Jesus knew what he was going to do: he planned to raise his friend from the dead. He had delayed his trip from the outset for this very reason. He knew that Lazarus's death would create an opportunity for a miracle that would build faith.

Nevertheless, when Jesus saw the group of people mourning his friend, he felt pain. The Bible reads, "When Jesus therefore saw [Mary] weeping, and the

Jews who came with her, also weeping, He was deeply moved in spirit, and was troubled. . . . Jesus wept" (John 11:33, 35). What was Jesus doing? He was hurting. Did his grief diminish his faith? No. Faith and pain coexisted in Jesus. And they can coexist in us. To live fully is to live in a double reality—to know our pain and loss, but also to know God's love. Continue to build yourself up with the truth of Scripture concerning God's faithfulness, and do not let grief cause you to be afraid that you have lost your faith or failed in some way.

FOR THE ONE WHO CARES

Maybe you are watching a friend or loved one come apart emotionally at this time. Be patient. Do not assume that your friend's emotions signify a loss of faith. Love your friend. Feel with your friend as Jesus did with the mourners in the gospel story. Jesus understood at the core what it meant to be human, what it was like to feel what we feel. If we hope to be like Christ to others—which is our calling, our purpose, as Christian believers—then we must be unafraid to enter into the pain of others when necessary. Though you are not responsible for your hurting friend, ask God to give you the strength and courage to feel with your friend in his or her situation.

Though your friend's pain does not negate his or her faith, nonetheless continue to pray that your friend's faith will hold up under the pressure of pain. Let us not forget we have an adversary. Jesus said to Peter, "Simon, Simon, behold, Satan has demanded permission to sift you like wheat; but I have prayed for you, that your faith may not fail" (Luke 22:31–32). Even as I had to pray for my daughter—that she would endure the grief, that her faith would not crumble—so you pray for your suffering loved one. It is a short distance from grief to bitterness, from sorrow to doubt and then to despair. Pray for your friend, understanding that your prayers will help protect his or her heart. Pray like Jesus prayed: that your friend's faith will not fail.

Pray for your own faith as well. Be aware that when you watch a loved one experience the kind of devastation I saw my daughter suffer, your faith may be shaken. You may find yourself wondering, as I did at times, whether God really can meet your need. Like your broken friend or loved one, you need God to build your faith. Ask God to help your unbelief. Ask him to help you trust him for new compassions every morning. Pray for the faith to stand by your suffering friend as you continue believing in God's faithfulness—which is great.

GREAT IS THY FAITHFULNESS

Windsor seemed to do well after we got back to the Valley. We prioritized leisure and took a trip to the beach. We drove up to the mountains. Windsor lounged around the house a good bit and seemed able to relax. She was pleasant, cooperative, and loving. I had my Windsor back home, and it felt wonderful.

Of course, she continued to grieve. She mourned her baby in much the same way one mourns the death of a loved one. At times I wondered if she truly would be able to let the baby go; and in fact, more than once during the grace period permitted her by law, Windsor called the adoptive parents and told them she wanted the baby back. All of us were on the edges of our seats while the baby's destiny seemed to hang in the balance; but in the end, Windsor let the deadline pass, and the adoption became final.

Soon afterward, my daughter's life took a turn for the worse. She entered her senior year at the public high school that fall and almost immediately began a downward spiral that ran its course for the next several months. I believed Windsor was trying to bury the pain of releasing the baby: she had an empty womb, empty arms, and an empty heart. She connected with kids who seemed directionless. She was listless and lax about her studies. She skipped school and behaved intolerably. I finally told her she could not live at home unless she abided by the rules. In a heartbreaking scene, she chose to walk out.

During the months that followed, I learned many more lessons about letting go. Things got very bad for Windsor, and I feared for her. I could not get through to her and realized I had to let my daughter go with an entirely different measure of abandon. I was confident that God loved her and could look out for her far better than I could; she would never be able to outrun his love and care. Though I desperately loved my daughter and wanted to rescue her, all over again I had to learn to let God carry my burden.

To my great relief, Windsor came back home early the next year. Perhaps I was not as gracious as my father was to me when I came home to Montreat from Florida. I felt I needed to hold back a little and see what happened. At the same time, I did not want my daughter to fear I was going to exact retribution or make her pay for all of the heartache. I loved her and wanted her to rest. I rejoiced at having her under my roof again. I knew her actions had not been malicious; she had been broken and running from the pain.

I did ask my daughter to sign a behavior contract as a condition for moving back home. She agreed to do so, and she abided by the contract. She also prepared for her high school graduation and worked with an educational counselor to get ready for college. As time passed, things began to look up, and we settled back into life together.

Then the road took another unexpected turn. In May, Windsor traveled with us to Washington, D.C., to attend a ceremony for my parents, who were being awarded the Congressional Gold Medal. On this trip, I began to sense that something was wrong with Windsor. For the first time, she talked of perhaps abandoning her plans for college. I became suspicious and very concerned. We had worked so hard together on developing her future plans. What was causing her to pull back now? Shortly afterward, I learned the reason. She was pregnant once again.

These were long roads with Windsor. And painful times. Very painful times. I was not able to process my own emotions for months, even years—to this day I likely still have some grieving left to do. Yet through our challenges I learned the practice of surrender on a more profound level than ever before. Caught in the rapid-fire sequence of events, I was helpless to control anyone or anything. I could only respond to one emergency and then get ready for the next one. God had to handle everything else; I no longer had time to think. Though I often felt frazzled and ineffective in these years, my complete helplessness seemed to suit God. If I had been given much time to consider my course, I might not have thrown myself into his arms. As it was, I had to remain totally dependent on him for help at every moment.

During Thanksgiving week of 1996, I stood alongside Windsor's hospital bed, squeezing her hand tightly while she gave birth to her second child, a little boy named Wyatt. Windsor decided to parent him, and I am so glad. He is an extraordinary, well-behaved little man, and I love him more than I ever thought it possible to love one's grandchild. No life is a mistake. Wyatt may have arrived out of the proper sequence, but he is my "premature blessing" and great joy.

For her part, Windsor has done a remarkable job as a mother and provider. She went on to finish college with honors, and she and Wyatt eventually settled near Sara Dormon in Philadelphia. She passed both the real estate and insurance licensing exams on her first try and is a very competent businesswoman, taking after her dad. I have consulted with Windsor concerning some of my own business affairs, and she continues to be a valuable adviser to me during times of transition.

Over the years, Windsor also has involved herself with young women experiencing unplanned pregnancies. At one point, following Sara's example, she took a pregnant teenager into her home. Windsor advised the young woman through the decision to parent or release her baby, coached her through labor and delivery, and supported her through a volatile release ceremony. While the experience stirred many difficult memories for Windsor, she handled herself with grace and real maturity. God was redeeming her ruins, even as he continued to redeem mine. I am proud of her.

Looking back, I distinctly remember the day Windsor told me she was going to parent Wyatt. I was sitting in my home office, studying for one of my classes at Mary Baldwin College—I was still trying to finish my undergraduate degree! When my daughter came into the office and told me of her plans for the baby, I remember feeling relieved. I was thinking back to Windsor's vacillation over whether to parent her first baby—how painful the uncertainty was for her and for the rest of us. Now she was at a different place in her life. She was a little older. She had attended college in another Virginia town. She was holding her own, and I was pleased. She was an adult. Whatever she decided to do, I sensed that everything would be okay. The peace I had learned to recognize was calming my heart.

When Windsor left the room, I picked up my *Daily Light,* and my eyes fell on the verse: "The earth is the LORD's, and the fulness thereof" (Psalm 24:1 KJV). Through this simple verse, God gently reminded me of what he had been telling me all along—that Windsor and Wyatt were his. They belonged to him, and he would see them through. I was free: Free to surrender. Free to let go. As I sat quietly over my *Daily Light,* I relaxed before God and thanked him. Thanked him for Windsor. Thanked him for Wyatt. And thanked him for his faithfulness to us on our journey. From the depth of my own heart—from a place of authenticity—I could emphatically say with Jeremiah: Great is thy faithfulness!

Reminders for Painful Times

↪ Are you are in a situation that requires a level of spiritual stamina you do not believe you have? Mediate on the words of Jeremiah in Lamentations 3:22–23. Pray for God's new compassions every morning.

↪ God will help you stir your faith. You can ask for his help. Like the father of the possessed boy in the gospel story, you can pray, "Help my unbelief." Ask God to do this, and trust him to respond in his own way.

↪ Are you suffering pain that seems unbearable? Continue to remind yourself of God's faithfulness, and stay in the Scriptures; do not allow your grief to make you think you have lost faith or have failed in some way.

Tips for Those Who Care

↪ Are you watching a friend or loved one come apart emotionally at this time? Be patient. Do not assume that your friend's emotions reflect a failure of faith.

↪ Feel with your friend as Jesus did with the mourners at Lazarus's tomb in John 11.

↪ Continue to pray that your friend's faith will hold up under the pressure of pain. Understand that your prayers are protection for your friend or loved one's heart.

↪ Pray for your own faith to be strengthened. Ask God to help your unbelief, so you can stand by your suffering friend as you trust in God's ability to come through.

⌒

MEMORY VERSE

Mark 9:24

Immediately the boy's father cried out and began saying,
"I do believe; help my unbelief."

Principles for Reflection

When life seems too difficult to manage,
God steps in and meets us where we are.
He will help us stir our faith
so we can keep on trusting him.

GREAT IS THY FAITHFULNESS
Learning the Language of Heaven

It was early when I awoke. I got out of bed quietly and went to the window. Sea and sand lay beyond the walls of the rented beach house, and I could faintly hear the roar of the waves. Anxious to get started with my day, I thought I would go outside and take a walk; but as I parted the blinds, I saw it was still dark. My walk would have to wait.

Unable to go back to sleep, I went out to the screened porch and sat down. There I waited for what seemed like a long time. I watched the sky for the first traces of light. Minutes ticked by. But the darkness did not yield. To pass the time I went to the kitchen and made coffee, but I had to wait for the coffee too. With little else to do at that early hour, I resumed my position on the dark porch and tried to relax. All was quiet and still.

Gradually, night began to give way. First I noticed the morning star and the very faintest hint of light in the sky. A lonely gull called, and through the gray mist the world began to take shape. I could make out the walkway railings on the beach, the sea oats on the dunes, and a gull flying low while combing for food. Then I began to see color in the sky—touches of gold and orange. Finally, sea and land took on shades of color as well. The water now looked blue and the grass green. The dawn was revealing what the darkness had covered. My eyes were adjusting slowly, and I found myself appreciating each new stage of clarity.

As I sat there on the porch, I considered God's wisdom in setting the dawn at a measured pace. If the sun had come when I wanted it to come, the glare and heat would have been too harsh for me. I would not have been ready. I would not have been able to handle the strain. As it was, I entered the day with ease. I had time to adapt. The experience was pleasant. My mind was at peace.

199

God, I realized, worked in my life in much the same way—he worked gradually. How often I had tried to rush into life with my own schedules and plans! I was impatient with darkness, impatient with God's leisure. I wanted to have things settled and to know what I could count on. I wanted a plan. But someone has said it is out of mercy that God does not reveal the future all at once; rather, he graciously unfolds it for us over time. I fully agree. There are so many things in my life I now am thankful I did not foresee. They would have overwhelmed me. I needed a gradual awakening.

My life has not turned out as I imagined it when I was a young woman. I expected happy endings of a fairy-tale sort; but God did not fit into that box, and I am glad. If I had had my way, life would have been easy and I would have needed God for little, if anything. Consequently, I would have missed opportunities to know him better. I would have lived perhaps unable to recognize his faithfulness. I would have remained at arm's length from the richness and depth of life, with all of its jagged edges, unexpected twists, and dramatic reversals. Of course, I certainly could do without some of my mistakes, but even those God continues to fit together with the rest of my life's broken pieces to create something for himself. As we have seen, that is God's way: to construct from ruins. If life were perfect, who would need an Architect? Who would need a Builder?

My story is still being written in its ever-unpredictable way. After Windsor had Wyatt, my children and I continued to experience ups and downs. Graham in particular went through a difficult time. On the Easter morning following my grandson's birth, Graham called me from the road and told me he was sick. En route to a technical school where he had enrolled, Graham said he had pulled over because he couldn't keep driving. I urged him to find the nearest hospital and seek help, but then he explained. He told me he was on drugs and could not go any farther. This was heartbreaking news—not to mention that Graham was out of reach on a highway somewhere. But we managed to get through the ordeal. Fortunately, while Graham had been experimenting with drugs, he was not yet addicted. Ted flew out to retrieve our son, and soon afterward, we sent Graham to a Christian youth home, where he responded well to the program.

Then came another challenge, this one of great magnitude. Graham was still at the youth home in the fall of 1997 when the kids suffered a devastating loss. In September of that year, Ted collapsed after exercising in the extreme

Dallas heat and did not recover; he died of heart failure before paramedics could get him to the hospital. Thankfully, all three of the kids had spoken with their father by telephone the day before he passed away. Windsor and Wyatt by then had spent some time living with Ted in Dallas. But while the kids could take some comfort in these final connections, the loss of a father is an incomparable one. The children suffered greatly.

Ted's death impacted me in a way that is difficult to describe. I had grieved the loss of my husband long and hard when our marriage collapsed. Death, however, is startlingly final, and Ted's passing brought with it an emotional ache that still comes and goes. We shared so much history. We married young and grew up together. We experienced life's "firsts"—first home, first child. Those memories were already tinged with sadness because of the divorce. Now the sadness took on a different hue. I had known Ted so well and for so long, it was difficult for me to believe he was gone. I still experience intermittent sorrow over his loss and am sad Ted has not lived to see our family grow. I imagine the sorrow in some measure will always be with me. And that is okay.

After his dad's death, Graham worked for a while at a variety of jobs. He had difficulty finding his niche, but I was not worried about him. Graham had become a man. I trusted he would make his way in time, and he did. He has wonderful people skills and business savvy, much like his dad. He is very independent and until recently, as I have written, owned a health and fitness gymnasium—a business he built from the ground up—in Asheville, North Carolina. He attends a church he likes, and one year he helped lead a mission trip to Nicaragua, where he chose to be baptized. Graham has turned out to be an impressive leader, and he continues to make me very proud.

Exactly a year after Ted died, Noelle married a wonderful man named Maury Davis, whom she met in Atlanta, Georgia. After she graduated from college, Noelle had taken a job as a medical assistant apprenticing with a cardiologist in Atlanta. She and Maury seemed to fall in love very quickly, and I was not keen on their relationship at first. I believed that Noelle was vulnerable, just having lost her dad and living in a new city. When Maury decided to ask Noelle to marry him, he called each member of her immediate family. I was very frank with my prospective son-in-law about my concerns, but his maturity and total acceptance of and love for Noelle reassured me of his integrity and goodness. Long before the wedding, I fully believed God had orchestrated the marriage.

Today Noelle and Maury live near Charlottesville, Virginia, where they relocated so Noelle could attend nursing school. She graduated with honors and works part-time at a local hospital. She and Maury now have a baby girl they named Virginia Ruth. They serve in a good church. Maury is a professional services director for a software, sales, and consulting company; he is easy to be with and stable, a real gift to our family.

My children are terrific people, and I am proud to be their mother. They have had to navigate rough waters early in life. They have suffered things no parent ever wants his or her children to suffer. But God is redeeming my kids' hurt and adding depth to their lives. He is working out the kinks, and I have the wonderful privilege of being able to watch the process unfold. It is one thing to experience God's faithfulness in your own life; it is quite another to look on as the Lord comes through in the lives of those you love. Seeing my prayers for my children answered does more than bring comfort; it inspires me to keep expecting more from God. It builds my faith as I continue to wait for the further restoration of my ruins.

LEARNING TO CLING

Eventually, I completed my undergraduate degree in religion and communications at Mary Baldwin College. My desire was to finish before I turned fifty at the millennium—and I did it! My father graciously offered the benediction at my commencement in May 2000, and I was awarded the Outstanding Adult Graduate Award! Mother, escorted by Gigi, flew in at great cost to her physical comfort to attend a special luncheon after the ceremony. Unable to be there, my sister Anne noted my achievement on *Larry King Live*. Friends and family cheered and feted me, and my father presented me with a life-size, glazed ceramic sculpture of a boxer dog. After all, he remarked, I had "worked like a dog" over the nine years it took me to finish my studies!

In the meantime, new opportunities in public speaking had opened up for me. What became the first in an ongoing series of speaking engagements took place at Samford University in the spring of 1997, the year Noelle graduated. I was invited to address a group of women, and, though nervous, I believed that due to the struggles I had faced in recent years, I had something of value to say. Culled together from my Bible study notes and life experiences, the message I gave was simple. I called it, "What Good Is Faith?" and the women seemed moved by it. They even stood to applaud me when I finished.

I was both surprised and embarrassed by the women's response at Samford, but I later found myself so very appreciative of what their support seemed to indicate. I thought God had put me on a shelf in the area of public ministry. I expected I might speak at the occasional event—like the one in Owen Sound, Ontario—if that. But after Samford, things changed. Opportunities to speak started to present themselves, and I began to wonder if God did have plans for me in this area. I came to understand that God had put me on a shelf, not in order to leave me there, but in order to let me heal. Again, he was moving in my life gradually. I had to wait for healing—in some areas I am still waiting—even as I had to wait for the dawn that dark morning at the beach.

While perusing a newspaper article a few years ago, I read that one of the scriptural words for "to wait" could also mean "to cling." I could not verify this definition, but I liked the idea and the mental image. Clinging is a physical act. I pictured wrapping myself around God and refusing to let go, much like Jacob did when he wrestled all night with the Lord at Peniel (Genesis 32:24–32). Wasn't this the kind of waiting God had taught me to do through all the ups and downs in my life? Hadn't he shown me that the only way to wait in darkness was to hang on to him—to trust him completely, to believe in his desire and ability to redeem what was lost or ruined?

In fact, I am learning profound lessons at this time about waiting by clinging to God. It grieves me to confess I am in the midst of another very difficult chapter in my personal life. During Windsor's first pregnancy, I entered into a third marriage, which now has taken a heartbreaking turn—as of this writing, my husband and I are going through the painful process of a divorce. I have placed the matter in God's hands. I want to grow through the experience and learn all that God desires to teach me. Meanwhile, I cling to God. I constantly return to my foundational truths and rehearse them for myself: God loves me, he will lead me, and he will bring good out of my circumstances. I have placed my trust in God, and now I must look to him daily for help so I can keep trusting him through this painful and stressful time.

What does clinging look like in the day-to-day? How do we do it? As I explained, I am learning the answer to this question on a new level now, and I am finding that I can cling to God as I wait by making a practice of praising him. Remember my "Praise" list from chapter 2? I made that list so I could better see how God had prepared me for Ted's admission of infidelity. I needed the list to encourage me in my pain and to build my hope for the future. As praise becomes an ever more consistent, ongoing practice in my life, I notice I frequently make "Praise" lists—and for the same reasons. This book, in fact, is a "Praise" list of sorts. In writing it, I have seen the clearer picture of just how God has carried me through shock and devastation, doubt, depression, isolation, unforgiveness, anger, transition, my own sin, complete brokenness, insecurity, the suffering of my children, and a great deal more. During the various trials of my life, I often felt I was grasping for God's arm, only to catch hold of nothing. Now I have come to see that God was there all along. He never moved. His arm was sure. His arms are everlasting!

Perhaps now I better understand the faith of those whom I have always admired—my parents and grandparents, the retired missionaries in Montreat, Darlene Deibler Rose. While I would never compare myself to these heroes and loved ones, I think I am beginning to see why they did not seem plagued by the dilemma of suffering. They must have understood the truth about God's arms: that his arms would not fail. They must have believed that, whatever circumstances they were required to endure, God's arms would hold, comfort, and protect them. They must have believed this with deep conviction, for though I am sure they struggled at times, these individuals never seemed to waver in their confidence in God.

As I learn to praise God in times of both pain and peace, I find that I too become more confident in the sureness of his arms. And even if I do not recognize or "feel" his arms all the time, it is not as hard for me now to believe that his arms are there, wrapped around me—and that I am secure in his embrace. Praise helps me see where God is, and where I am. That is the beauty, the power, of praise.

Praise opens our eyes to the understanding that we are in God's arms— that's what it did for me the night I sang those lines from the Gaithers' song while driving through the streets of Philadelphia after the birth of Windsor's first baby. With my praise came the awareness that my loved ones and I were safe in God's care. But the gift of that late-night experience was not only the confidence I gained about God's closeness to me and his sovereignty in my situation; it was also the encounter I had with God praising him in those moments.

As I praised, I was fully present with God. I was enjoying him. He had my undivided attention. He was the focus of my emotions. As I praised, I realized I was doing what I was made to do. We were made to praise God—in all situations. The psalmist wrote, "All thy works shall praise thee, O LORD; and thy saints shall bless thee" (Psalm 145:10 KJV). In praise we experience the deep fulfillment that comes in doing what we were made to do: Loving God. Enjoying him. Being with him. Living in the awareness of his embrace. Great joy comes with praise, for praise is what we will be doing in heaven.

THE LANGUAGE OF HEAVEN

Traveling in a foreign country without knowing the language can be a frustrating experience. When we travel abroad without the ability to communicate, we only vaguely understand what is going on around us. We lack insight into the culture of the country we are visiting. We misinterpret others' gestures or tone of voice. We fail to pick up on the nuances of human interaction. Often we feel too foolish to jump into conversation, so we hang back and just let life happen. We are at a disadvantage. A barrier stands between us and a full experience of life where we are.

When I traveled to Switzerland one summer with my sister Gigi, we went out to dinner with a French-speaking friend. Armed with only the vestiges of my high school French, I had difficulty understanding much of anything. I used all of my energy trying to concentrate but picked up little of the meaning, and I came down with a terrible headache. Traveling to China in 1989 with Mother, Anne, and Gigi was an even more disheartening experience in communication. I had no clue what was being said to us or, much of the time, what was going on. I was totally lost. Once I got home to the States, I found I was thankful just to be able to carry on dialogue with strangers in the grocery store.

One day I will go to heaven. Heaven is my ultimate destination. Heaven is my home. Jesus awaits me there. Friends and loved ones await me. When I get to heaven, I don't want to miss out on anything. I want to understand the nuances, events, and exchanges of heaven. I want to be able to comprehend everything being communicated. And even more important than that, I want to participate in the activities of heaven. I want to contribute. I want to have something to offer the Lord. What can I do now to get ready? How can I prepare for eternity? For starters, I must learn the language. And I must learn it well.

The language of heaven is praise. We've learned about praise as we've walked through the lessons of this book together—we've practiced some forms of praise. But how can we define it? What is praise? In simplest terms, praise is adoration. It is more than expressing thanks to God, although thanksgiving is an important part of our worship. While we thank God for what he has done, we praise God for who he is. We ascribe worthiness to God when we praise him. We admire God. We love him. We esteem his attributes. We glorify him.

When we praise, we use our hearts, our imaginations, our words, and our bodies. The writer of Hebrews calls praise "a sacrifice" (Hebrews 13:15). When we sacrifice something, we give it up. In praise we give up ourselves. We hold nothing back from God. We override our contrary feelings and make the decision to praise. As we praise, we tell God he is worthy of all that we are, all that we have, all of our plans and dreams. We take our minds off of those plans— off of ourselves—and we turn our attention to God.

Let's look at the way they do it in heaven. The apostle John, writing in Revelation, gives us a glimpse of praise in eternity. He sets the scene by describing God on his throne:

> Immediately I was in the Spirit; and behold, a throne was standing in heaven, and One sitting on the throne.
> And He who was sitting was like a jasper stone and a sardius in appearance; and there was a rainbow around the throne, like an emerald in appearance.
>
> REVELATION 4:2–3

Also positioned around the throne, we learn, are twenty-four thrones for twenty-four elders who are all dressed in white and wearing golden crowns. Thunder and lightning proceed from the throne of God, and seven lamps of fire burn there. Before the throne is a crystalline sea; and surrounding the throne are four winged creatures, whose job it is to cry out night and day, "HOLY, HOLY, HOLY IS THE LORD GOD, THE ALMIGHTY, who was and who is and who is to come" (4:8).

During the creatures' ongoing chorus, the twenty-four elders fall down before God, cast down their crowns, and worship. They say, "Worthy art Thou, our Lord and our God, to receive glory and honor and power; for Thou didst create all things, and because of Thy will they existed, and were created" (4:11). Praise continues in this manner without interruption.

Consider the content of heaven's praise. The four creatures start by saying, "HOLY, HOLY, HOLY." Before anything else, they esteem God's purity. Who would want to praise a God who was less than pure—whose motives were mixed, whose heart was misguided? Next the creatures call God "ALMIGHTY." They praise his power. If God had no power, why would anyone bother praising him? These worshipers call God the one "who was and who is and who is to come." Here they praise his eternal nature. If God were not eternal, then the world would live wondering when his goodness and mercy were going to run out—we would have no security. At last, when the twenty-four elders of heaven join in the praise, they tell God he is "worthy." They honor his infinite value. They acclaim him as deserving of glory, honor, and power. Why? Because he created all things. God is the Creator and Sustainer of life. He is responsible for us. He is worthy of our praise.

Notice that the beings of heaven praise God for his nature, his character, and his essence. Their praise is God-focused. Their acclamations have to do with God's attributes. The praise of heaven zeroes in on God himself. Here we see how praise can differ from thanksgiving. While thanksgiving and praise are often intertwined, when we thank God for what he has done for us, our own wants and desires may vie for a bit of our attention. The context in which we live remains in view, and there is nothing wrong with that. But when we praise God simply for who he is—for his very heart—our focus shifts wholly to the One who sits on the throne. This is how we will live in heaven. We will remain fixed on the beauty and majesty of the Creator. We will cast down our crowns and worship. We will love him with our whole heart. He will be our center.

BECOMING FLUENT

Are you walking through a hard time? Are you helping someone walk through a hard time? Do you know the language of heaven? Do you want to gain proficiency in it? I do. If I never make it out of certain trials in my life, if I never see the changes for which I hope, I want to be fluent in heaven's language. I want to become an expert at praise. I want to be able to elaborate on my feelings for God in the language of his choosing—not just so I will be ready for heaven, but also so I can experience my relationship with God fully here on earth. David wrote, "In Thy presence is fulness of joy; In Thy right hand there are pleasures forever" (Psalm 16:11). I don't want to miss out on the joy and pleasure God has for me right now.

Throughout this book we have prayed by using the Scriptures, and we have meditated on Bible verses. Not long ago, I heard a sermon in which the preacher suggested I try a scriptural exercise that is now revolutionizing my praise and devotional life, and I would like to share it with you here. So often we go to the Scriptures and ask, "What's in it for me?" It is just fine to do that. We need to understand how God's Word relates to our lives.

But there is another way to read the Scriptures—through the lens of praise. This approach brings balance to our experience of the Bible. I'll start with a Scripture verse from 1 Thessalonians:

> Now may the God of peace Himself sanctify you entirely; and may your spirit and soul and body be preserved complete, without blame at the coming of our Lord Jesus Christ.
>
> 1 THESSALONIANS 5:23

In considering this verse, let's begin the usual way—by asking what's in it for us. The verse conveys God's desire to sanctify, or purify, us. Paul prays, *May God sanctify you.* Our sanctification is God's desire, and even now he is at work fulfilling it. We need him to do that work. We need him to clean us up and make us better. We want to become more like Christ—that is God's ultimate purpose for us. Pause and thank God for his work of sanctification in your life. You can make it a simple "Thank you, Lord, for sanctifying me!"

Now let's go deeper into the verse. Ask, "What does this Scripture verse tell me about God?" It tells me that God does the work of sanctification in my life himself: He *personally* sanctifies me. I also see that God is thorough in the work of sanctification. He does his work in my life "entirely." He completes my sanctification—he does not abandon me partway through the process. He sticks with me. He doesn't give up on me. He is patient. He is faithful. Further, the verse describes God as a "God of peace." God is not harsh with me. He is tender and loving while he does his work. He is calm, peaceful, and gentle. He isn't going to harm me. Having read the verse in this second way, I now understand God more fully. I see him as a God of love and peace, a tenacious, loyal, personal God—and that brings praise from my heart!

Do you see the difference in the two ways we approached the verse—asking "What's in it for me?" versus "What does it tell me about God?" Reading the Bible in this second way, we learn to praise God in greater detail for his attributes because we become better acquainted with his attributes. We focus on him, not so much on our own needs; and as we do, our hearts fill with praise.

Wherever you are in life—if you are in a valley or helping someone walk through a valley—I encourage you to practice this dual approach to Scripture as you do your daily Bible reading. Your heart for God will expand and your relationship with him will deepen. You will become less self-centered and more in tune with God's perspective. Your praise will become more thorough and creative. You may find yourself praising God in the mundane activities of life, not just during your devotional times, not just when you are feeling good. Waiting on God—clinging to him—will become more natural, less forced. You will find that you are becoming fluent in the language of heaven.

PRACTICING PRAISE

To become fluent in heaven's language, we must practice here on earth. I encourage you to pause now and practice the above exercise, using one of the memory verses in this book or any verse that speaks to you. Once you have chosen a verse, take a moment and ask God to give you understanding as you read it. Now read the verse and ask yourself the first question: "What's in it for me?" You may want to write down your answers. Thank God for his specific promises in the verse. Use your own words. Try saying aloud what you are feeling.

Now reread the verse with the second question in mind: "What does it tell me about God?" Write down your answers if it helps you to do so. As you make your list—and it doesn't have to be long—praise God for the attributes you see highlighted in the verse. Again, try praising God with your voice, your words.

Looking back to the verse from 1 Thessalonians, I might praise God by saying, "Lord, you are such a personal God. You see me. You care about me. You sanctify me with your own hand—the same hand that created the world! How amazing that you are so majestic yet you care about me. All of your creation is important to you. You who are worthy of all praise and honor and glory stoop to sanctify me. You love me so much! Your love is great—and I praise you for your love!" Ask God to remind you throughout the day of the attributes revealed in your devotional time so you can continue to praise him.

Let your praise carry you in different directions. You might start out praising God for one thing and end up having praised him for several unexpected things. The key is to give your imagination freedom in praise. Just open your heart and speak your praise to God. Or write your praise as a prayer or love letter to God. You can keep a praise journal. Try singing your praise—use a hymn or a song. Let praise and thanksgiving mingle naturally.

As you praise this way—freely—God will lead you. You will find he is giving you words and drawing out praise that will speak specifically to your need. When we praise, God comes on the scene. Praise is never a monologue; it is a dialogue. As we offer praise, God speaks to our hearts. Scripture says that God inhabits or is enthroned on the praises of his people (Psalm 22:3). I want to be where he is!

There are many ways to approach praise. You can try going through the letters of the alphabet and naming God's attributes accordingly in a spirit of praise: A is for awesome, B is for beautiful, C is for compassionate, and so on. Some of the letters are tricky. Someone once suggested xenophile for the letter X—God loves the stranger!

No matter what way you choose to praise, the important thing is to be creative. Vary your praise. Don't let it become stale or boring; then it will be a rote religious exercise and not a God-honoring or life-changing act. Remember, God the Creator—the most creative, exciting Being who exists, the one on whose existence everything else depends—gave us praise to use as a language! This means praise is dynamic; practicing it should change us. If you are struggling to praise God, do not give up or become discouraged. Begin to pray. Ask God to help you persevere so you can grow in becoming fluent in the language of heaven.

THE EVERLASTING ARMS

As long as we live on this side of heaven, we will never be perfect. We will fall short. We will fail to give God adequate praise. We will grow tired in our clinging. We will come to a point in the darkness when we feel we cannot hold on any longer, and we will grow faint of heart. During such times we do not need to fear. God is a loving, merciful God. He sees our struggles, our striving. While we do our best to obey God in this life, our salvation, our position at the foot of God's throne, our place in God's family—these we cannot earn or maintain by our own efforts. Our ability to endure in the dark ultimately is not up to us. God is our Creator and Sustainer. He is responsible for us. When I am too worn out to hang on to him, when the strength of my own arms gives way, I have the assurance that "underneath are the everlasting arms" (Deuteronomy 33:27).

God is a God of grace. Remember the love of the father in the story of the prodigal son. Recall again the father's heart when he saw his bedraggled son in the road and began to run to him. He did not see his son's shortcomings and wrecked endeavors. He was not weighing his son's mistakes or judging his performance. The father simply saw that his beloved son had come home. And what did the father do? He extended grace. He extended welcome; he opened his arms and said, *Welcome home. You belong. You are loved. I will honor and restore you.*

Marvel at the incredible, transforming power of God's love. You who are broken, you who are weak and tired, you who are mourning, you who are lonely and without hope: Take heart! The father is at hand. He sees you in the road. Open your eyes and look, for he is running to you with arms open and a heart breaking with joy. Rejoice in his embrace! This is where you belong. Be transformed in the arms of *Abba,* Daddy. Be renewed. Be the person he made you to be. Open your heart and praise him. Now is the time! He has looked with compassion on all your ruins. He is making your deserts like Eden. Let joy and gladness, thanksgiving and singing, be found in your heart again. Praise the Lord. For he is good. His mercy endures forever. And his faithfulness is very, very great!

Reminders for All Times

- Do you know the language of heaven? Read Revelation 4 and consider the way the residents of heaven give praise to God.
- Practice using the Scriptures as a springboard for praise. Find a verse you like and ask God to give you understanding as you read it.
- Consider the verse and ask first, "What's in it for me?" Thank God for the specific promises in the verse. Next ask, "What does the verse tell me about God?" Praise God for the attributes of his character you see described. Use your own words.
- Ask God to remind you of these attributes so you can continue praising him throughout the day.
- Give your imagination freedom in praise. Try writing your praise as a love letter or prayer to God. Keep a praise journal. Try singing your praise. Go through the letters of the alphabet and name God's attributes accordingly in a spirit of praise.
- Vary your praise—don't let it become boring! If you are struggling in praise, ask God to help you persevere.

⌒

Revelation 4:8, 11

HOLY, HOLY, HOLY IS THE LORD GOD, THE ALMIGHTY, *who was and who is and who is to come.*

Worthy art Thou, our Lord and our God, to receive glory and honor and power; for Thou didst create all things, and because of Thy will they existed, and were created.

⌒

Principles for Reflection

Praise opens our eyes to the understanding that we are secure in God's arms. Praise also enables us to experience God's embrace. As we praise, we are doing what God created us to do. We will spend eternity giving God praise.

WELCOME HOME

I am so grateful God accepts me as I am—hurting, wounded, broken. I am glad he chooses me to be part of his family, regardless of my past mistakes and sins. He wants me. He cares about me. His arms are open to me at all times. Even when I am in the ruins, God stands watching the road, anxious for me to come to him. He does not hold in his hand a list of my failures. He is not waiting to judge me. He is waiting to be with me. He is waiting to embrace me and welcome me home.

God is waiting for you as well. Now that you have read this book, I encourage you to quiet yourself for a few minutes and listen. What is God saying to you? Is there an area of your life he is asking you to entrust to him? Your marriage? Emotions? Children? Finances? An addiction? Whatever the issue is, will you take it to God? The Bible says we can cast all our care upon him because he cares for us (1 Peter 5:7). Do you believe this? Do you believe that God cares about you?

Perhaps you are full of regret and plagued by guilt because of your own sins and mistakes. Will you let God pick up the pieces and make something beautiful out of your ruins? Scripture teaches, "If we confess our sins, He is faithful and righteous to forgive us our sins and to cleanse us from all unrighteousness" (1 John 1:9). God is not condemning you. He is watching the road and waiting for you. Will you go to him and let him renew you in his embrace?

Maybe you are angry, confused, or bitter about something that has happened in your life. Will you give your emotions to God? Will you let him set you free from your anger, bitterness, wounds, and disappointments? In John's gospel we read, "If therefore the Son shall make you free, you shall be free

213

indeed" (John 8:36). Do you want to be free? God is waiting to take your burden and unbind you. Will you let him do that?

You may be one who just feels empty, discontent. Life does not seem to have any meaning for you. Will you ask God to show you who you were made to be? He knew your name before the beginning of the world. He made you for a purpose—a purpose only you can fulfill. Remember what he told Jeremiah: "Before I formed you in the womb I knew you, And before you were born I consecrated you; I have appointed you . . ." (Jeremiah 1:5). Will you let God assure you of your significance?

Perhaps as you have been reading, you have paid attention to my relationship with God and noticed how personal it is—how involved God seems to be in my life. You realize that you do not know God in a personal way, and you would like to. Or maybe you read about the difference between being God's creation and being his child, and you recognize that you have never chosen to follow Christ and be part of God's family. You can do that now! You don't have to get yourself together first. The prodigal son simply got up from where he was and went home to his father. So can you. You can go to God as you are. He is not looking for perfection. He just wants you!

Would you like to become part of God's family and know that you belong? Do you want to know God personally? Do you want to walk with him daily? Do you want to spend eternity with him? It is very simple. All you have to do is ask. God stands eager and ready to respond.

Right now you can open your heart and tell God that you want to belong to his family, that you need him, that you are sorry for your sins and want to start fresh. You can tell him that you believe Jesus died on the cross and rose from the dead for you. You can ask Jesus to take up residence in your heart and life as Savior and Lord. The moment you ask, God is right there welcoming you—he accepts you totally and completely. You don't have to understand it all. You can take the first step now. If you would like, you can pray the prayer below. The words you use are not as important as the sincerity of your heart.

God, I read in this book that you are my heavenly Father and want to welcome me into your family. I want that. I have struggled for so long. I am disappointed with some things in my life and broken by the choices I have made. I want to change. I need your help. I believe that Jesus died and rose again for me. Please forgive my sins, and come and take up residence in my heart and life. I receive you as Lord and Savior. I turn it all over to you. Help me to trust you more and more. I rest in your embrace. Thank you. In Jesus' name. Amen.

If you prayed, asking God to welcome you into his family, then he has done it! You have given your life to him, and he accepts you. You are his child. You have turned a page and started a new life with Christ. I'm so glad for you! Now I would like to encourage you in some practices that will help you grow in your relationship with God.

- Tell someone about your decision. Doing so will help confirm it in your own mind.
- Get a Bible. Set aside time every day to read and study it. John's gospel is a good place to begin. Read until you think God has spoken to you. Ask God to help you understand what you read.
- Pray each day—talk to God as you would to your best friend. Tell God everything, and ask for his help throughout the day.
- Find a church that teaches and practices what the Bible says, and go there regularly. It is important to be around others who can encourage us in our faith. We need people!

If you would like more information about living your new life with Christ, or if you are thinking about following Christ and would like to learn more about what this means, you can visit www.billygraham.org and click on the "Believe" tab. If you do not have access to a computer, you can call toll-free at 1-877-247-2426 or write to the following address:

Billy Graham Evangelistic Association
1 Billy Graham Parkway
Charlotte, NC 28201

In the meantime, may God continue to lead you on your journey.

God bless you,
Ruth

ACKNOWLEDGMENTS

I have been told that acknowledgments are made in ascending order—the closer to the end one's name appears, the more significant one's contribution. Or is it the other way around? I have decided to jumble everyone up! Each of you is a very important thread in the fabric of my life. Some of you are shorter threads than others, but without you my fabric would not have the color, texture, pattern, or resilience it does now. All of you are significant to my life and heart. Therefore, you all are stirred together with love and gratitude.

To Mother and Daddy, who have loved me unconditionally and prayed for me consistently through it all: By your example of faith and loving nurture you have shown me more of my heavenly Father.

To those who have always believed in me: my Philadelphia ladies—Martha Ayers, Carloyn Blish, Jean Livingston, and Flossie Merritt; and special lifetime friends Wynn and Bonnie Lembright, Cindy McCrory, Maya Paul, Clare Davis, and my "guardian angel" Millie Zimmer. Encouragers all.

To the Oates family members, who make me feel as if I am one of them: Yours is a friendship that has spanned generations, and it is very precious.

To those who listened to me and were unafraid to speak the truth cushioned by grace: Kathy and Lanier Burns.

To friends along the way: the Nelsons, who got me out of my comfort zone; my Bible study group, which encouraged my heart; and Rolly and Pam Laing, who accompanied me to Africa and opened their hearts to me.

To Stacy Mattingly, whose insights, sensitivity, joy, and hard labor transformed this book; and to Cindy Hays Lambert, senior acquisitions editor at Zondervan, who made sure this book got written. *In Every Pew Sits a Broken Heart* would not have come to fruition without them. No one could have better co-laborers.

To others at Zondervan for their creativity, hard work, and commitment: senior marketing director Sue Brower, senior editor Dirk Buursma, art director Curt Diepenhorst, and interior designer Beth Shagene.

To my three children, who have endured my dysfunction with grace, humor, and faithfulness, supporting me, loving me, and encouraging me: Noelle, Graham, and Windsor—and to my wonderful son-in-law, who is also my friend, Maury Davis.

To Mary Baldwin College, for giving me the opportunity to fulfill a thirty-year-old promise to my parents and empowering me to do it!

To others who walked along the way with me: Mary T. O'Brien and Lee Hersch.

To the loving memory of my maternal grandparents, Nelson and Virginia Bell; my uncle Clayton Bell; and my family's long-time pastor, Calvin Thielman. They gave me sound wisdom and unconditional love, and they demonstrated grace—even now I can hear them cheering me on!

And in memory of Darlene Deibler Rose, whose impact on my life is still being felt.

To my friend extraordinaire, Sara Dormon, who is fiercely loyal, a sister, counselor, sounding board, adviser, and protector. You have made such a difference in my life. Thank you.

To Anne Frank, who has gotten me organized and brings a ray of sunshine into my life.

To my agent, Wes Yoder; his executive assistant and speaker representative, Gloria Leyda; and all of the staff at Ambassador Agency. I have come to depend on their integrity and wisdom.

To my siblings: Gigi, Anne, Franklin, and Ned, who have shared this journey as only they could.

To those I know from Bible Study Fellowship, for the training and community you provided me—and a special thanks to my BSF friends in Texas.

To all who have encouraged, comforted, counseled, and challenged my broken heart and to all who have been channels of God's grace, please accept my profound thanks for what you have added to my life.

And to the difficult people in my life. You have taught me about myself—and about grace!

Thank you all from a truly grateful and humbled heart.

We want to hear from you. Please send your comments about this book to us in care of zreview@zondervan.com. Thank you.

ZONDERVAN™

GRAND RAPIDS, MICHIGAN 49530 USA

W W W . Z O N D E R V A N . C O M